WITHDRAWAL

A Teaching Assistant's Guide to Completing NVQ Level 3

A Teaching Assistant's Guide to Completing NVQ Level 3 is a must-have for all teaching assistants embarking on this course, as well as invaluable reading for tutors and assessors.

This textbook addresses both the performance and knowledge requirements of the course. A key element of your NVQ Teaching Assistant course is to show *evidence* that you can apply your knowledge to everyday classroom activities, and students often find this is their biggest challenge. This book provides a range of tried-and-tested materials and practical advice on how to gather evidence that covers key performance indicators, to ensure that you complete your course successfully. This essential guide:

- Gives detailed guidance on how to collect evidence from a variety of sources to match performance indicators
- Provides photocopiable templates for teacher/teaching assistant discussions on roles and responsibilities, appraisals and self-appraisals
- Gives examples of IEPs and Behaviour Plans
- Provides the necessary underpinning knowledge in a clear and reader-friendly manner
- Provides summaries of relevant legislation and national documents.

Following the new and updated occupational standards (2007) for Supporting Teaching and Learning in Schools, this textbook offers truly invaluable advice for NVQ Level 3 students. Including extracts of imaginary evidence, the book follows the experiences of imaginary candidates, showing how they successfully put forward their portfolios of evidence to complete the course.

Highly practical, rooted in everyday classroom practice and very closely tied to NVQ course requirements, this accessible book is an essential comprehensive guide for all students, as well as tutors, assessors and teachers supporting candidates for this course.

Susan Bentham is a Senior Lecturer at the University of Chichester.

Roger Hutchins is the Inclusion Manager at two primary schools in Portsmouth.

A Teaching Assistant's Complete Guide to Achieving NVQ Level 2

How to meet your performance indicators

Susan Bentham & Roger Hutchins

'This book is good preparation for TAs who may wish to continue their professional development – that is, it teaches them how to make links between theory and practice.'
– *Sue Woodhouse, Belfry Associates (Adult Learning Unit)*

Are you a Teaching Assistant?

Are you enrolled, or thinking of enrolling on an NVQ training course?

Or are you a tutor or assessor on such a course?

Then *A Teaching Assistant's Complete Guide to Achieving NVQ Level 2* is the book you cannot afford to be without . . .

A key element of your NVQ Teaching Assistant course is that you have to show *evidence* that you can apply your knowledge to everyday classroom activities, and students often find this is their biggest challenge. This book provides a range of tried-and-tested materials and practical advice on how to gather evidence that covers key performance indicators, to ensure that you complete your course successfully. The essential course companion will:
Give detailed guidance on how to collect evidence to match performance indicators from a variety of sources
Provide photocopiable resources to include templates for personal accounts, appraisals and self-appraisals

- Give examples of IEPs, Behaviour Plans and teaching planning sheets
- Provide the necessary underpinning knowledge
- Provide summaries of relevant legislation that TAs need to know
- Detail how the knowledge outlined in the text can be mapped onto the mandatory units for VQs in Support Work in Schools (SWiS) Level 2

Highly practical, rooted in everyday classroom practice and very closely tied to NVQ course requirements, this reader-friendly book will be an essential comprehensive guide for all students, as well as tutors, assessors and teachers supporting candidates for this course.

ISBN: 978–0–415–40341–2

Available at all good bookshops
For ordering and further information please visit
www.routledge.com

A Teaching Assistant's Guide to Completing NVQ Level 3

Supporting teaching and learning in schools

Susan Bentham and Roger Hutchins

Routledge
Taylor & Francis Group

LONDON AND NEW YORK

First published 2009
by Routledge
2 Park Square, Milton Park, Abingdon, Oxon OX14 4RN

Simultaneously published in the USA and Canada
by Routledge
270 Madison Ave, New York, NY 10016

Routledge is an imprint of the Taylor & Francis Group, an informa business

© 2009 Susan Bentham and Roger Hutchins

Typeset in Sabon and Gill Sans by
Florence Production Ltd, Stoodleigh, Devon
Printed and bound in Great Britain by
The Cromwell Press, Trowbridge, Wiltshire

British Library Cataloguing in Publication Data
A catalogue record for this book is available from the British Library

Library of Congress Cataloging in Publication Data
Bentham, Susan, 1958–.
   A teaching assistant's guide to completing NVQ level 3: how to meet your
   performance indicators/Susan Bentham & Roger Hutchins.
      p. cm.
   Includes bibliographical references and index.
   1. Teachers' assistants – Vocational guidance – Great Britain.   2. National
Vocational Qualifications (Great Britain).   I. Hutchins, Roger, 1953–.
   II. Title.
   LB2844.1.A8B4553 2008
   371.14′124023 – dc22   2008009459

ISBN10: 0–415–43244–8 (pbk)

ISBN13: 978–0–415–43244–3 (pbk)

Contents

Illustrations

Figures

Tables

Acknowledgements

Susan Bentham says: 'Thank you' to Michael, colleagues, especially Jackie and to my many students for their support and a very special thank you to my son, Matthew – for his great artwork.

Roger Hutchins says: 'Thank you' to Anne and to the staff at both schools for their continuing support, hard work and dedication.

Glossary

Active learning/active learners The process when learners take responsibility for their learning and are given the opportunity to participate and be actively engaged in their own learning.

Active listening Communicating to the person we are talking with that we have indeed heard and understood them, accomplished by techniques such as rewording and reflecting.

Annual reviews Legal reviews to be held at least once a year for pupils who have a statement of special educational need.

Attainment levels/targets – see National Curriculum

Attention Deficit Hyperactivity Disorder (ADHD) A medical diagnosis that describes a range of emotional and/or behavioural difficulties such as extreme impulsivity, inattentiveness and continuous activity.

Auditory learners – see Learning Styles

Autism/Autistic Spectrum Conditions (ASC) A disability severely impairing a person's ability to maintain normal contact with the world; appears before the age of three.

Behaviour plans/behaviour support plans A tool to plan intervention to modify pupil behaviour – sets out what is expected from the pupil and states how the school and home will support the pupil in reaching these targets.

Board of governors A body of volunteers who have the legal responsibility of ensuring that the school is following correct national and local procedures; governors act as 'critical friends' to schools.

Children in care (looked after children) All children and young people who are on Care Orders or who are accommodated under The Children Act (1989) or who are remanded into the care of the Local Authority.

Designated Officer for Safeguarding Children (DOSC) The designated member of staff who is responsible for overseeing and administering issues relating to child protection.

Differentiation A means by which teachers offer a common curriculum to all pupils in their classes, but tailored to meet the needs of individuals.

Disability A condition that is substantial and long-term, i.e. lasting longer that 12 months, which impairs learning and normal living.

Dyscalculia A specific learning difficulty relating to problems in developing an understanding of mathematics.

Dyslexia Primarily a specific difficulty with learning to read, write and/or spell, often accompanied by poor organisational skills.

Dyspraxia (Developmental Coordination Disorder) Impairment of the organisation of movement that is often accompanied by problems with language, perception and thought; symptoms are evident from an early age, often from birth.

Educational Psychologists (EPs) Qualified teachers who have trained further in psychology; support pupils and adults working with pupils who are experiencing sustained difficulties in learning or behaviour; not to be confused with medical psychiatrists.

Education Welfare Service (EWS) Local authority staff working with students and families who have social difficulties with school such as poor attendance.

Ethnic minority A pupil who is identified by parents/carers as belonging to any ethnic group other than 'white British'; parents/carers have the right not to state an ethnic identity.

Every Child Matters A government initiative seeking to ensure that every organisation involved with providing services for children works together, shares information and develops networks so that every child, whatever their background or their circumstances, benefits from the stated 'five outcomes':

- Be healthy.
- Stay safe.
- Enjoy and achieve.
- Make a positive contribution.
- Achieve economic well-being.

Formative assessment Ongoing, continuous assessment that measures progress in small stages and informs planning for future teaching.

Foundation Stage Pre-National Curriculum schooling – the Reception and Early Years of infant or primary schools.

Gifted and Talented pupils Those pupils identified in school as being the most able in academic subjects or the most talented in areas such as art, sport or music.

Higher Level Teaching Assistant (HLTA) A status given to TAs who reach certain standards of education and performance that enables them to be given greater spheres of responsibility in schools.

Ideal self How an individual would like to be.

Inclusion The process whereby, so far as possible and in compliance with parental preference, all pupils regardless of ability or disability are educated in their local mainstream schools.

Individual Education Plan (IEP) A tool to plan intervention for pupils with special educational needs – sets out what should be taught that is *additional to* or *different from* what would normally be delivered in the class, focusing on three or four short-term targets that are SMART (Specific, Measurable, Attainable, Relevant and Timed).

Interactive whiteboard An ICT tool that enables programs to be displayed in front of the whole class and which enables pupils and teachers to write their own comments and notations.

Kinaesthetic learners – see Learning Styles

Learning objectives The focus of any one particular lesson that should be understood by all pupils and their work assessed in relation to that learning objective.

Learning styles An individual's unconscious preference in regard to how they process and learn new information: some learn better through hearing (**auditory learners**), others through what they see (**visual learners**) and others through what they touch or handle (**kinaesthetic learners**). Most employ a combination of all three learning styles, which is why schools seek to teach using 'VAK' techniques (Visual, Auditory and Kinaesthetic).

Local authority The body comprised of elected members (councillors) and employed officers who, together, are responsible for a range of services in a given local area, including all services for children. There are 150 local authorities in England and Wales.

Medical protocol A simple text setting out the nature of a pupil's medical condition, the likely symptoms, the response required and people to contact.

Multi-sensory Materials that seek to employ as many senses as possible in the learning process.

National Curriculum (Curriculum 2000) The National Curriculum sets out the minimum that has to be taught in schools, and a framework against which attainment can be measured. For each subject there are *programmes of study* that set out what pupils should be taught, and *attainment targets* that set the level of performance pupils are expected to achieve.

National Literacy Strategy (NLS) Introduced in 1998 to provide teaching plans for literacy to put the National Curriculum into practice in primary schools, it gave teaching objectives for each term.

National Numeracy Strategy (NNS) Introduced in 1999, it illustrated how maths can be taught from Reception to Year 6. 'Key objectives' were set out for each year group.

Pastoral Support Programme This is similar to an individual behaviour plan but is more detailed and is put into place when a pupil is at risk of being excluded from school.

Personal Education Plans (PEPs) Plans drawn up by social services in conjunction with other services such as education for children who are being looked after by the local authority.

Personalised learning A government agenda seeking to ensure that learning is adapted to the needs of each individual pupil.

Phonics The 'building blocks' of written language allowing the 'decoding' of written words into sounds or the construction of written sounds into words.

Phonological awareness/phonology Awareness of sounds within words – e.g. ability to generate rhyme and alliteration, or to segment and blend sounds.

Programmes of study – see National Curriculum

QCAs National tests published by the Qualification and Curriculum Authority (QCA) used voluntarily by schools at the end of Years 3, 4 and 5.

Renewed Primary Framework The renewed Framework for Literacy and Mathematics was introduced to primary schools during 2007. It is an electronic resource, building on and replacing the National Literacy and Numeracy Strategies.

Rose Report (2006) A government-commissioned report into the early development of reading skills chaired by Jim Rose; this report informed the renewed Primary Framework for Literacy.

SATs (Standard Attainment Tasks) National tests published by QCA that schools must use at the end of Key Stages 1, 2 and 3 to measure pupil progress and the effectiveness of teaching.

Scheme of work What schools decide to teach in a particular subject or topic taken from the National Curriculum within a limited timeframe.

Self-image How an individual describes themselves.

Special Educational Needs (SEN) '*A child has special educational needs if he or she has a learning difficulty which may be the result of a physical or sensory disability, an emotional or behavioural problem or developmental delay*' (Education Act 1981). Children have special educational needs if they have a *learning difficulty* which calls for *special educational provision* to be made for them' (Education Act, 1996, Section 312).

Special Educational Needs Co-ordinator (SENCO) The person or persons in school responsible for overseeing the day-to-day operation of special needs provision.

Statements of special educational need Documents regulated by law setting out the educational and non-educational needs of individuals and the provision to be put in place to meet those needs.

Summative assessment Testing (either formal or informal) that assesses how much pupils have learnt in a particular subject or over a specific time period.

Teaching styles The way in which a teacher approaches the teaching process: often an individual's teaching style is based on their own preferred learning styles and their experience of being taught themselves.

Visual learners – see Learning Styles

Introduction

Overview of NVQ course – what you need to know before you begin

Getting started

Congratulations! Starting an NVQ (National Vocational Qualification) course for teaching assistants is both challenging and exciting. NVQs are designed to provide valid and relevant vocational qualifications that are valued by the workforce. Gaining an NVQ can provide progression routes to further training and career opportunities. Whatever level you wish to aspire to, enrolling on an NVQ course will give you the opportunity to study and discover more about supporting the students you are working with. An NVQ gives you the opportunity to reflect or think about what you are doing in the classroom and to think about how you can improve on your practice.

NVQs in Supporting Teaching and Learning are worthwhile but they are also hard work. This book aims to help you through the process.

One of the first questions TAs enrolling on an NVQ course ask is: What does an NVQ involve and what do I have to do?

NVQs are about demonstrating that you are competent at a particular task or skill, for example, being able to give feedback to the teacher on the pupil's response to a certain activity. **Competence** is about demonstrating that you are able to do a task and demonstrating that you understand why that task is important.

Therefore, an NVQ requires you to:

- Show that you are able to do the task. This requires you to provide evidence of **performance**.
- Show that you understand why that task is important. This requires you to provide evidence of underpinning **knowledge**.

To complete an NVQ you will need to provide evidence of **performance and knowledge**.

Let's look at an example of giving feedback:

> Samantha has been asked to work with a group of Year 6 pupils reviewing their answers on a practice test. In regards to feedback, Samantha will be involved in feedback to the pupils involved in the session and to the teacher after the session.

In regard to providing evidence of **performance in regard to feedback** Samantha will need to give real examples of how she has provided the teacher and pupils with feedback. Perhaps Samantha has been required to fill in evaluation records regarding the session. Perhaps Samantha has noted down what she has said to the pupils. Perhaps Samantha has been observed conducting this session.

In regard to providing evidence of **knowledge** Samantha will need to show that she understands why it is important to give feedback in a constructive manner and how feedback relates to the planning and evaluation of learning activities.

Structure of the course

The NVQ 3 Teaching Assistants course is divided into units of competence. To achieve the NVQ 3 a teaching assistant needs to complete ten units of competence.

There are six **mandatory units** of competence. You must complete these units:

- Help to keep children safe.
- Support pupils' learning activities.
- Promote positive behaviour.
- Develop and promote positive relationships.
- Support the development and effectiveness of work teams.
- Reflect on and develop practice.

In addition an NVQ3 candidate will be required to achieve four optional units with no more than two units taken from Group E. There are now 50 optional units. The sheer volume and diversity of optional units recognises the varied role that teaching assistants and support workers carry out in their respective schools. The optional units covered in this textbook are:

- Use information and communication technology to support pupils' learning.
- Support literacy development.
- Support numeracy development.
- Contribute to assessment for learning.
- Support bilingual/multilingual pupils.
- Support pupils with cognition and learning needs.

The general index at the back will help candidates find further information in regard to optional units. In addition, there is a chapter on common themes to cover issues that are featured in many units.

Which units you choose to complete very much depends on your role within the school. For example, teaching assistants supporting students in Reception and Year 1 might choose to select:

- Supporting the development of literacy and numeracy.
- Supporting the use of information and communication technology.
- Contributing to assessment for learning, as ongoing formative assessment is essential!

However, another TA working for the science department in a secondary school might choose the options of:

- The use of information and communication technology, as their department seeks to use technology as an integral part of most lessons.
- Contributing to assessment for learning.
- Supporting bilingual/multilingual pupils, as the school has a large intake of pupils with English as a second language.
- Supporting pupils with cognition and learning needs, as they support pupils who are either on school action plus or who have statements.

So we see that what you choose to cover for an optional unit really depends on what you do on a day-to-day level.

Let's get complicated

Once you have settled on what units you are going to cover you will need to start the lengthy process of collecting evidence. Each unit is subdivided into elements or smaller units and each of these requires you to demonstrate evidence regarding both performance and knowledge.

Individuals who choose to do this course are often referred to as candidates. Teaching assistants who enrol on this course will come from a variety of backgrounds. Teaching assistants could be working in primary, secondary or special schools. TAs come in all shapes and sizes.

Some TAs who enrol on this course will do so through colleges while others might be working towards the qualification within their school as a form of in-house training. Regardless of how you are doing the course, all candidates will have an assessor. An assessor will guide candidates through the process, help them collect the required evidence and give feedback on evidence.

Figure 1.1 TAs come in all shapes and sizes

Once you have enrolled on this course you will receive a copy of all the standards; that is performance indicators and knowledge-base criteria that you will need to provide evidence for. Do not panic. Your assessor is there to guide you.

What is evidence?

In NVQ-speak, for evidence to be accepted as evidence it needs to be:

Valid   To be valid, the way assessment is carried out and the nature of the evidence collected must be appropriate, that is, it really must demonstrate the competence of a candidate. For example, to demonstrate competence in giving teachers feedback on pupil performance it is not enough for the candidate to write a statement saying that they do this on a day-to-day basis. The candidate will need to present evidence in regard to how they do this, for example, the candidate may:

- include reading and spelling records that they have filled in;
- have the teacher write a statement regarding how they report on pupil performance;
- write a personal account of how they give feedback that is countersigned by the teacher.

Reliable   Reliability refers to consistency. On the one hand, does the candidate provide evidence of performing this behaviour on more than one occasion and in a variety of situations? On the other hand, reliability refers to consistency between assessors. If the evidence is reliable then all assessors should judge it as valid evidence.

Sufficient   Sufficient means that the evidence presented by the candidate is enough to prove competence. If the evidence is not sufficient it may mean that the candidate needs to write or say more. For example, a photocopy of the school's behaviour policy is not sufficient evidence that the candidate understands the school's behaviour policy. A candidate may be required to write a short summary of the behaviour policy focusing on their role and others' roles within this policy. A candidate may be questioned by an assessor on their understanding of the behaviour policy.

Authentic   This relates to whether the evidence produced is genuine and has been produced by the candidate. It is important that all personal accounts are countersigned by a witness to say that this event did happen as described. It is important that the witness is familiar with and knowledgeable of the standards relating to the work of teaching assistants.

Current   The evidence produced must reflect current understanding and practices.

All evidence that is presented must be valid, reliable, sufficient, authentic and current to count as appropriate evidence. All the above points may seem complicated but they are essential to ensure the integrity and quality of the qualification. When you present your evidence, an assessor will be judging your evidence on the above points and give you any necessary advice.

Ways of gathering evidence

Personal accounts

A personal account can be compared to a diary in which you describe 'what you did' during a particular period of time at school. What you write will need to be matched to performance indicators, that is, the type of behaviour you need to demonstrate that you can do. Personal accounts, in order to be considered as appropriate and authentic, will need to be countersigned by someone who has observed what you have done, usually this will be the teacher.

There is a real art in writing personal accounts. Examples of writing personal accounts will be given in this book. Templates for writing various forms of personal accounts can be found in the appendix. In addition to help you get started a 'writing personal accounts and matching' can be found on pp. 281–2.

Case studies

This involves a short account of one individual student and your interaction with them. Again the case study will need to be signed by a witness to ensure that it is genuine.

Products of performance

These will often support your personal accounts. These could be individual or session plans, feedback forms, reading records or copies of **IEPs** (**Individual Education Plans**). Confidentiality is important. It is essential that when writing personal accounts or case studies you do not use the full names of pupils with whom you are working. Some candidates will refer to the pupils by their initials. If including copies of IEPs as supporting evidence it is important to block out names.

Expert witness statements

Colleagues in the workplace can write a short statement describing your practice. Their statement can provide evidence of your performance. Again, witnesses need to be familiar with the work of teaching assistants. Your assessor will give you more details in regard to who can be a witness and the relevant forms that witnesses will need to sign.

Observation

Direct assessment in the workplace can be carried out by a classroom teacher, **Higher Level Teaching Assistant (HLTA)**, **SENCO (Special Educational Needs Coordinator)** or college assessor. These individuals will write up their observations and this can be used as evidence.

Questioning

Your assessor may ask for more details regarding what they have observed, what you have written in a personal account or on issues relating to underpinning knowledge.

Professional discussion

This will involve having a discussion with your assessor on aspects of your role. This conversation will be taped and used as evidence. A professional discussion is more than just answering a set of questions, but allows the candidate to demonstrate their understanding of their role.

Accreditation of prior learning

Your past experience relating to courses attended and qualifications gained may provide evidence. You will need to talk to your assessor regarding this, as evidence to be considered valid will need to be judged as current.

Written knowledge

Certain elements require you to demonstrate knowledge and understanding, this can be shown by writing answers to various questions.

What you need to do

As a candidate enrolling on an NVQ 3 course for teaching assistants your responsibilities are to:

*   identify and collect evidence to meet the required indicators for knowledge and performance;
*   present the evidence in a structured format called a portfolio.

This might seem overwhelming to begin with but there are many people you will meet who will help you in this process.

Figure 1.2 Where to start

Who will help you

The Course Tutor   If you enrol for a course run through a college the course tutor will be responsible in part for delivering the course. They will give you valuable advice regarding how to collect evidence and set up your portfolio as well as discussing issues relating to underpinning knowledge.

The Assessor   The role of an assessor is to look at the evidence you present and to make judgements regarding whether the evidence meets the required indicators or not. They are there to help you collect the necessary evidence.

The Mentor   Candidates may have a special person within the school to whom they can go to ask for help and advice.

Internal Verifier   An internal verifier may be based in a college. They are responsible for ensuring that the quality and the integrity of the course are maintained. In particular they need to ensure that all assessors are marking to the same standard.

External Verifier   All NVQ 3 courses for teaching assistants are accredited through exam boards. An external verifier is employed by the exam board to visit various colleges and centres who are offering the course to ensure that all centres are maintaining the appropriate standards.

This book aims to help you complete the process of an NVQ by:

- providing you with examples of how to collect the required evidence through personal accounts, case studies and products of performance;
- covering relevant underpinning knowledge;
- giving examples of how to use feedback from assessors to improve your work;
- providing photocopiable resources;
- outlining summaries of important government documents plus website references;
- presenting a Glossary of important terms.

Who are Miranda, Nicola, Sadie, Nazreen and friends?

One request often heard by candidates just starting an NVQ 3 is to have a look at someone else's completed portfolio – just to get an idea about what is expected. In this book we have presented examples of ongoing work submitted by imaginary candidates. Miranda works in a primary school, Nicola works in a secondary school and Nazreen and Sadie work in a junior school. In a sense this book tells the story of their struggles to put forward a portfolio of evidence. As you will see some of their evidence is better presented than others. At all points both their teacher and assessor will give comments about their work. The assessor will explain terminology and give ideas about how to collect further evidence. It is hoped that through this ongoing dialogue between the assessor and the candidates you will acquire a real sense of what is needed to gain this qualification.

Confidentiality is important. At some points first names may be used in writing personal accounts and at other points initials may be used. When you write your personal accounts check with your assessor to agree procedures regarding confidentiality.

All names of characters used in this book are fictitious and any relationship to real persons is purely coincidental.

Advice on starting out from an assessor

Be organised! Remember evidence needs to be detailed and relevant. Collect evidence from a range of sources to include observations, expert witness statements, work products, professional discussions, personal accounts and case-studies. Remember that evidence regarding knowledge can be inferred from evidence relating to performance. But most of all remember assessors are looking for quality of evidence not quantity.

Tips on writing personal accounts

- It is always helpful to read the standards (indicators that you are required to cover) carefully before beginning to write a personal account. If you have already provided several pieces of evidence for a standard it isn't worth your time writing up another personal account showing that you have met the standard again!
- Use appropriate terminology to enable you to match the standard. Sometimes you can incorporate the words from the standard into what you write.
- Do not waffle. Keep the personal account concise and to the point.
- Always look out for opportunities to cross-reference your evidence to other units. This will cut down on the work you have to do.
- Remember it is not necessary to provide a personal account for every single performance indicator. It is better practice to collect evidence from a variety of sources. For example:
  - copies of students' work;
  - copies of memos you have written;
  - copies of reading records/student records;
  - a record of a conversation you may have had, however brief, with a member of staff regarding a student;
  - a note received from a parent or guardian;
  - copies of differentiated work you have provided;
  - minutes of meetings you have attended.

However, all these sources of evidence will need to be **ANNOTATED.** Annotation requires that you write a few lines explaining what the evidence means and how it meets the standard.

Have fun!

Chapter 1

Help to keep children safe

> **In this chapter we will look at three elements:**
> 1   Preparing and maintaining a safe environment.
> 2   Dealing with accidents, emergencies and illness.
> 3   Supporting the safeguarding of children from abuse.

KNOWLEDGE AND UNDERSTANDING

Prepare and maintain a safe environment

Every member of staff employed in a school has, as a primary duty, to give consideration to the health, safety and security of both pupils and adults. It is everyone's responsibility to ensure that the school environment is both safe and secure for all the community.

School procedures

Health and Safety Policy

Every school must have a Health and Safety Policy that should:

- outline the responsibilities of staff;
- state how a healthy and safe environment will be established and maintained;
- stipulate procedures for recording and reporting accidents, injuries and emergencies;
- outline fire safety procedures;
- state how First Aid is to be administered and how pupils' medical needs are to be met.

Staff responsibilities

Class and subject teachers are responsible both for the safety of their learning environment and for the children in their care. This begins with the responsibility to take registers at the start of each morning and each afternoon. It is a legal requirement of every school to know which pupils are present on site.

The school is required to ensure that all facilities, including washrooms and toilets, are regularly cleaned and inspected for health and safety.

Recording and reporting procedures

Every member of staff in a school must act like a 'prudent parent' in the event of an accident, injury or emergency. As soon as possible after any incident the illness, injury or accident must be fully reported and accurately written up in the appropriate logbook. You will need to be familiar with the school's Health and Safety Policy to make sure you follow appropriate procedures. It is vital that the correct person or persons are informed at the earliest opportunity if any such health problem arises.

Specific duties of care

There are also specific duties required of you if you are responsible for pupils:

Don't strain yourself or your children

You are not required to try to move objects beyond your strength. Where you have children under your direct supervision, it is your responsibility to instruct them in how to safely move equipment, should that be needed. They should never be allowed to move awkward objects such as pianos or televisions.

Don't clutter the doors or corridors

You are required to ensure all exits and access points to the learning environment within which you are working are clear and free from obstruction.

Figure 1.1 Don't strain yourself

Don't drop rubbish

All waste products must be disposed of safely in line with school procedures. If you are cooking, for instance, you are responsible for the disposal of food waste and for cleaning the equipment both before and after use.

School visits and trips

If your duties include that of accompanying teachers and pupils on off-site visits and activities you should be clear as to what your responsibilities are. If you drive a minibus you will have received appropriate training and gained a recognised qualification. You may be asked to keep a register of small groups of children, collect pocket money, medicines, and so on.

In the event of an emergency

As a teaching assistant you may be asked to perform specific functions in respect to emergency procedures, for instance, checking the toilets or other non-teaching areas in the event of evacuation of the building.

National legislation and regulations

Acts and regulations

Various Acts of Parliament and government regulations relate to health and safety in schools. Some of the most significant are:

- The Health and Safety at Work Act, 1974
- Health and Safety (First Aid) Regulations, 1981
- The Manual Handling Operations Regulations, 1992
- The Health and Safety of Pupils on Educational Visits Act, 1998
- Health and Safety at Work Regulations, 1999.

Probably the most familiar government publication is *Every Child Matters (ECM)*. Two of the five ECM outcomes relate to health and safety – Be Healthy and Stay Safe.

Manual handling of pupils

Employers have to take steps to avoid manual handling involving the risk of injury so far as is reasonably practicable. Where manual handling cannot be avoided, risk assessments must be undertaken and, consequently, risks must be reduced to the lowest level.

Training and an Intimate Care Policy

Full training must be given to all staff involved in this procedure, which will include correct handling and lifting procedures with particular emphasis on back care. When pupils require manual handling, the school must have an Intimate Care Policy in place.

Risks associated with the manual handling of children

There are a number of risks associated with manually handling or lifting pupils, perhaps the most obvious of which is the physical risk of injury to either the pupil or the person lifting. Improper lifting can seriously injure either pupil or adult, or both, which is why proper training is essential.

Safety and security

Responsibilities

Although ultimate responsibility for safety and security rests with the employers, all employees have a responsibility to maintain a safe and secure environment. Nobody can say it is somebody else's job.

Each class teacher and teaching assistant working with them needs to be aware of and observe standards of health and safety as they apply to their learning environment. This includes cables safely secured; exits free from obstruction; tables and chairs safe to sit on and use; as well as potentially dangerous equipment and materials safely and securely stored when not in use and adequately supervised when they are in use.

School environment

Inside the school building you may work in classrooms, halls, general working areas, ICT suites, science laboratories, gymnasiums, cooking areas, workshops and many others. Each of these will present different issues of health and safety that must be considered and responded to carefully.

You may also work outside of school buildings with children – the school playground, during sports activities, on educational visits, joining residential trips and so on. These, too, pose issues of health and safety that must be responded to appropriately.

Safety and security also relates to pupils arriving at and departing from the school. Care needs to be taken that younger children are met by appropriate adults whereas older students must be protected from dangerous traffic or from undesirable activities outside the school gates.

The context of the school

Issues of safety and security are likely to be different for village schools than for those situated in busy and crowded inner cities. Where schools are located on main roads, safety will relate to road crossing patrols, whereas village schools may face issues of pupils needing to be escorted along narrow roads without pavements, possibly with poor street lighting in the winter.

Security

Each school will have its own system of external and internal security. You need to be familiar with this and maintain the relevant procedures. Most schools operate some

Figure 1.2 Security is important

system of identifying visitors. Every member of staff has a responsibility to challenge anyone on the premises they do not recognise and who is not showing appropriate identification.

Road safety

Although travel to and from the school is the responsibility of parents and carers rather than school staff, the school has a duty to teach and train the pupils in road safety. The school may have a policy on using bicycles, skateboards or roller blades to come to school. You must be familiar with this and reinforce school procedures whenever the occasion arises.

Off-site activities

The level of pupil–teacher ratio required by law varies according to the age of the pupils and the type of activity engaged in. The younger the pupils, the higher ratio of adults to children will be required.

Risk assessments

A school's risk assessment will take into account the size and nature of the school buildings. There may, for instance, be more than one building on site, which will have implications for health, safety and security.

Safe supervision including the balance between challenge and protection

Health, safety and security education

The younger the children, the more need there will be to enforce consistent, explicit and firm rules for safe behaviour. Safety procedures and rules will need to be continually reinforced, particularly those relating to personal hygiene and to interacting with strangers ('stranger-danger').

As children get older they need instruction on how to play and explore safely, for example riding bicycles, swimming, road safety, going to and from school on their own. Although all children need to learn to take responsibility for their own safety and well-being, this is going to be especially developed during their junior school careers. They must be allowed to participate more and more in decisions regarding their safety and their health.

Adolescents need to be given increasing responsibility and more flexible boundaries while maintaining limits. They need to be instructed and encouraged to discuss and respond to many dangers – abuse, use of weapons, criminal activity, gang culture, drugs, alcohol, and irresponsible sexual activity. New levels of road safety are needed when they begin to ride motor cycles and drive cars.

Self-assessment questions

1   Name at least three pieces of information that should be found in a Health and Safety Policy.
2   What do you think acting as a 'prudent parent' means?
3   What responsibilities do you have for safety and security in your school?

Deal with accidents, emergencies and illness

Responding to and reporting accidents and emergencies

First Aid

Legislation requires that all schools have adequate First Aid available – both in the form of appropriate equipment and in trained personnel. This applies whether on site or off-site on school activities. There are minimum requirements for the contents of First Aid boxes and guidance is given regarding the numbers of trained First Aiders who should be in place relative to the size of the school population.

Only those trained by agencies recognised by the Health and Safety Executive (HSE) should give First Aid to pupils or staff, and these should not go beyond what their training allows. At all times care should be taken for personal safety and to the prevention of cross infection. Disposable gloves must be worn when treating pupils, especially if there is the presence of blood or other body fluids. Only those members of staff with appropriate qualifications, training and recognition are to administer medication.

Legislation requires that schools must have an 'appointed person' to take charge of First Aid arrangements. This person is *not* necessarily a First-Aider.

First Aid boxes

First Aid boxes should contain, at the very least, a guidance card, scissors, safety pins, disposable gloves, sterile coverings, individual sterile dressings, a cloth triangular bandage, medium dressings, large dressings and eye pads. Any use of materials from the First Aid box must be reported to the appropriate person.

Storage and administration of medicines

Every school's Health and Safety Policy should address the type of medicines allowed in school, the measures taken to ensure their appropriate use and safe-keeping, the members of staff available to administer medicines and so on. National policy states that, although no member of staff has to administer medicines if they choose not to, schools must have someone on site trained to do so should the need arise.

Accidents and emergencies

Emergency procedures

All schools must have emergency procedures in place as part of their preparation to respond to incidents such as a fire or bomb scare. Training in these procedures must be given to all staff and they must be practised. For instance, evacuation drills must take place at least once a year, preferably once a term.

Responding to common illnesses and conditions

- **Colds and flu** – runny nose, coughing, temperature, difficulty breathing
  Rest at home; infectious; medicines available from a pharmacy; see GP if symptoms persist.

- **Chickenpox** – itchy red spots with white centres on parts of the body
  Infectious; keep at home for five days after the rash begins; calamine lotion to ease itching; can be very serious in adults.

- **German measles (rubella)** – pink rash on head, torso, arms and legs, slight fever, sore throat
  Infectious particularly before diagnosis is possible; keep indoors for five days from onset of rash; keep away from pregnant women.

- **Impetigo** – small red pimples on skin that weep
  Infectious – stay at home until all weeping has stopped; treat with antibiotics from GP.

- **Ringworm** – infection of the skin, flaky circles under the skin
  Contagious; see GP for antibiotics.

- **Diarrhoea and sickness**

  Keep taking fluids; keep at home until 24 hours after sickness and diarrhoea has stopped; see GP if persists.

- **Conjunctivitis** – redness and sore eyelids and around the eyes, irritant

  Infectious; swab with warm water; visit GP if persists; school may have a policy on length of time to stay at home.

- **Measles** – fever, runny eyes, sore throat and cough, red rash over the body

  Rest; lots of fluid; visit GP if symptoms persist; some form of junior painkiller to reduce fever.

- **Tonsillitis** – very sore throat, tonsils enlarged, fever, earache

  See GP and treat with antibiotics; frequent and/or severe cases may require surgery.

- **Meningitis** – severe headache, fever, stiff neck, rash on skin that does not go when pressed with a glass

  See GP immediately or call ambulance urgently – can be fatal.

Signs and symptoms of emergency conditions

- **Severe bleeding** – Minor grazes would not count as a health emergency, but bleeding that is severe and continuous would – either the initial amount of blood loss or the continuing loss of blood would constitute an emergency – both may result in the patient feeling faint.

- **Cardiac arrest** – Vice-like chest pain, spreading to one or both arms; difficulty breathing; discomfort in the upper abdomen region; fainting; collapse; pale skin and blue lips; pulse gains in speed, then weakens; sweating.

- **Shock** – Rapid pulse; pale, cold clammy skin; sweating; grey-blue skin later; weakness and giddiness; nausea or thirst; rapid, shallow breathing; weak pulse.

Figure 1.3 'Miss, I don't feel well'

- **Anaphylactic shock** – Anxiety; red, blotchy skin; tongue and throat swells; eyes become puffy; breathing becomes laboured, possibly with wheezing and gasping for air; signs of shock.

- **Faints or loss of consciousness** – Body slumps; pulse rate immediately slows but should pick up soon; skin becomes pale; sweating.

- **Epileptic seizure** – Suddenly loses consciousness; goes rigid and back arches; convulsive movements as muscles seize; muscles relax; there may be fever, twitching of the face, holding of the breath, drooling at the mouth.

- **Choking and difficulty with breathing** – Difficulty in breathing; coughing; distress; flushed face and neck; uttering strange noises or making no sound at all; blue-grey skin later – could lose consciousness.

- **Asthma attack** – Difficulty in breathing; may be wheezing; difficulty in speaking; grey-blue skin; exhaustion and possible loss of consciousness.

- **Falls** – Potential and actual fractures – distortion, swelling and bruising at the site of the injury; pain; difficulty in moving the injured part; there may be bending, twisting or shortening of a limb, there may even be a wound with a bone sticking out.

- **Burns and scalds** – Red skin; pain in the area of the burn of scald; skin swells and blisters.

- **Poisoning** – Vomiting that may have traces of blood in it; consciousness impaired; pain or burning sensation in the gut.

- **Electrocution** – Collapse; loss of consciousness; breathing becomes difficult or even stops; heartbeat may stop; there may be burns where the electricity enters the body and where it exits the body to go to 'earth'; there may be muscular spasms indicating the person is electrically 'charged'.

- **Substance abuse** – Similar to poison; hallucinations; loss of memory or rational thought; random or slurred speech; extreme lethargy or excessive activity.

Responding to accidents, injuries and emergency conditions

If you are not a trained First Aider, the actions you should take are restricted to summoning help and providing reassurance to the person concerned unless it is absolutely necessary. You should avoid moving the person unless it is essential. The following suggestions about how to respond to specific emergencies are only outlines and *should not be regarded as full instructions*.

- **Severe bleeding** – The flow of blood needs to be stemmed as soon as possible. This is best achieved by applying pressure to the wound for ten minutes if there is nothing within it. By then the appropriate person should have arrived and they will take over. If there is a foreign body in the wound, this should not be removed but pressure should be placed around it without putting pressure on the object itself.

- **Cardiac arrest** – If the patient is unconscious, place in the recovery position; if he or she is conscious have them half sit up, supporting them with cushions. Do not give them anything to eat or drink.

- **Shock/Anaphylactic shock** – The victim should be lain down and any tight clothing loosened, particularly at the neck to help with breathing. If possible, raise the legs higher than the head and keep the victim warm. Do not give them anything to eat or drink.

- **Faints or loss of consciousness** – If someone complains of feeling faint, sit them down and put their head between their knees. If they do faint, lay them on their back and raise their legs so the blood flow is increased to the brain. Tight clothing must be loosened to help with breathing.

- **Epileptic seizure** – The patient must not be moved or restrained; any furniture or other people near them must be moved out of the way to prevent injury. Something soft should be placed under the patient's head if that is possible.

- **Choking and difficulty with breathing** – If there is something actually choking the patient, encourage them to cough. If that does not work, bend them over with their head lower than the chest and slap them five times between the shoulder blades with the flat of your hand.

- **Asthma attack** – Provide reassurance and administer medication (inhaler); possibly giving two doses. Encourage the casualty to breathe slowly. Call for an ambulance if the inhaler has not taken effect after five minutes.

- **Falls** – All suspected fractures must be treated as actual fractures. The casualty must not be moved but a qualified First Aider called for immediately. The casualty must be made as comfortable as possible without moving the limb injured.

- **Burns and scalds** – The affected area needs to be cooled with cold water; any clothes attached to the wound must not be removed.

- **Poisoning** – If possible, find out what the victim has swallowed and inform the medical team when they arrive. You should provide reassurance to the patient and watch for them becoming unconscious. Do not try to make them sick.

- **Electrocution** – The source of electricity needs to be cut off, preferably by removing the plug from the socket. You should not touch the victim unless it is absolutely necessary. If you have to move them in order to remove them from the electrical source, stand on dry insulating material, such as paper or wood, and push the person away using an insulated item such as a stick or a chair. Once the person has been disconnected from the electricity source, place them in the recovery position.

- **Substance abuse** – If you can, find out what they have taken and inform the medical team when they arrive. Do not try and make the patient sick. Provide verbal reassurance and comfort to the patient. Place them in the recovery position if they become unconscious.

Do no more than you have been trained to do. Never take matters into your own hands. Always call for those with the training and the responsibility.

Children who have witnessed the emergency may be distressed and even traumatised; so might members of staff, including you. Once the initial danger is passed it is important *not* to carry on as if nothing had happened. The responsible members of staff should ensure that all involved, pupils and staff alike, have the opportunity to talk about the situation and have space to be quiet and respond as they want to.

All accidents, injuries and emergencies must be recorded in accordance with national legislation, local practice and school procedures. Records will include the time and date of the incident, details of how and where it happened and what response was given.

Prevention

Good hygiene

At all times you are to have concern for your own health and safety so, for instance, you need to wear protective clothing such as disposable gloves when touching or potentially touching any bodily fluid. After any incident you should make sure that all involved wash their hands.

Figure 1.4 TAs should wear protective clothing

Information sharing

Schools should communicate to all staff information about the appointed person and the First Aiders – who they are and how they can be reached at any moment in the day. You need to know who to go to and how to reach them if an emergency were to happen.

Where individual pupils have medical conditions requiring specific responses, information needs to be shared with all adults coming into contact with those pupils. The relevant information will normally be in the form of a **medical protocol** that sets out the nature of the condition, the likely symptoms, the response required and people to contact.

Diet and allergic reactions

Included in the records kept on every pupil in school is medical information given by parents or carers. This information will relate to specific dietary requirements and allergies where appropriate. Any pupil who has an allergy should be in receipt of a medical protocol drawn up by the parents/carers, school nurse and appropriate school staff. This protocol should be prominently displayed in the school office, the staffroom and all places where the pupil works.

You need to be familiar with pupils in the classes where you work who have allergies and, consequently, specific dietary requirements such as not eating nuts or not being in the vicinity of eggs. This information should be given to class and subject teachers via the school's procedures and should be passed on to you as a matter of routine.

Support the safeguarding of children from abuse

Legislation

A large number of Acts of Parliament and government publications relate to child protection. Among these are:

- The Children Act 1989
- The Education Act 2002
- The Children Act 2004
- Safeguarding Vulnerable Groups Act 2006
- *Every Child Matters: Change for Children* (DfES 2004a)
- *What To Do if You Are Worried a Child is Being Abused* (DfES 2006d)
- *Working Together to Safeguard Children* (HMSO 1999, revised 2006e).

Although you do not need to be familiar with the details of all these, you do need to know how they impact on schools.

Safe working practices

A number of procedures are mandatory for all schools and local authorities:

- A Child Protection Policy must be in place.
- CRB (Criminal Record Bureau) checks for all staff, governors and regular volunteers must be made.
- Information must be shared within and between agencies.
- The school **governors** must ensure that a **Designated Officer for Safeguarding Children (DOSC)** is in place with responsibility for child protection and that that person has received appropriate and up-to-date training.
- The DOSC needs to make sure that all school staff receive training every three years to inform them of up-to-date issues and procedures.
- Local Safeguarding Children Boards (LSCB) must be established in every region with core members coming from local authorities, health bodies and police.
- Each **local authority** must have a senior officer responsible for coordinating policy and action on child protection.

Concepts such as 'significant harm', 'joint working' and 'abuse of trust' must be understood within all schools. The overarching principle is that the welfare of the child is paramount.

Significant harm – an official term used to indicate when compulsory intervention in family life will take place, which can be as a result of children witnessing domestic violence even though they may not have experienced this themselves.

Abuse of trust – it is illegal for an adult in a position of trust (which includes all school staff, governors and volunteers) to engage in sexual activity with any person less than 18 years of age with whom they have a 'relationship of trust'. This is the case whether or not there was consent from the young person.

Joint working – all agencies need to work together, including sharing information, in order to safeguard children and young people.

Physical contact with pupils

It is illegal to use any form of physical punishment, although pupils can be physically restrained in certain circumstances – dealt with in your school's Physical Restraint Policy. However, young children and even older ones who are distressed may look for physical contact with adults for comfort. In such cases there are no concrete legal requirements; staff need to use their own discretion, taking into account the following principles:

Physical contact:

- must be normal and natural, not unnecessary or unjustified;
- should not persist for long;
- should not be with the same pupil over a period of time.

Adults:

- should be aware that physical contact could be misinterpreted;
- must never touch pupils in ways that might be considered indecent;
- should avoid being alone with a pupil in confined or secluded areas.

Signs and impact of possible abuse

Duty of care

Every adult regularly involved in a school has a duty to ensure that children are safe and secure. All such adults will therefore need to be alert to signs of abuse and must report any suspicions in line with the procedures of the school and local authority.

Categories of abuse

Working Together to Safeguard Children (DfES 2006e) identifies four categories of abuse – neglect, sexual abuse, physical abuse and emotional abuse. Certain aspects of bullying can also be abuse. Children can be considered to be at risk of abuse if their basic needs are not being met or if those needs are in some way being violated.

Possible signs of abuse

Signs of abuse and/or neglect include:

- physical marks (cuts, bruises, etc.) beyond what would normally be expected for children;
- sudden or prolonged change in behaviour, e.g. aggression or withdrawal, which is out of character for the child;
- personal hygiene issues, e.g. persistent dirty clothes, children unwashed, regular incidents of soiling;
- language, terminology and subject matter used by the child in conversation, e.g. overtly sexual at a level of understanding beyond what is normal;
- actual disclosure by the child to an adult (or to other children and reported to an adult).

Children and young people who are the subject of abuse may show signs of challenging behaviour or emotional difficulties.

Responding to disclosure

There are important guiding principles that must be recognised and adhered to when responding to children who disclose abuse:

- The prime consideration at all times must be the child's welfare.
- Children who are at risk of abuse have the right to be protected.

- Children who may have been abused will be treated with sensitivity, dignity and respect.
- Any person who feels that a child may be at risk has a duty to refer that child promptly to the appropriate person or agencies. It is not their responsibility to make a value judgement about what the child has told them.

A child making an actual disclosure of abuse is likely to do so because they trust that particular member of staff. Alternatively, children, particularly younger ones, may simply be talking with a member of staff about what is happening to them without being aware that it actually is abuse. Either way, the adult will need to respond very carefully. At one and the same time they must not destroy the trust shown in them but they must take action.

There are a number of procedures to follow when responding to disclosure:

- Listen carefully to the child, staying calm and dispassionate.
- Let the child recall events without interruption or comment.
- Any questions you ask must be to clarify what is being said. Do not ask leading questions.
- Do not offer alternative explanations for what happened.
- Explain to the child that you are there to help them and this involves telling others in the school who need to know. Assure them their information will not become common knowledge.
- Record the discussion using the actual words spoken by the child. Note when and where it happened and who was present. Make sure your name is on the record and that you have signed and dated it.
- Written reports should be based on evidence and be objective. They should distinguish between fact, observation, allegation and opinion.
- Report to the designated person in school as soon as possible, but certainly within the day.
- Be available for any follow-up investigation.

If a child makes a disclosure of sexual abuse, or sexual abuse is suspected, social care agencies must be informed and they will decide upon medical examination. To arrange a medical examination of the child is beyond the responsibility of the school.

Investigating disclosures

Schools are not investigative bodies. Any investigation of possible abuse is the responsibility of social care and/or the police. Every member of staff, however, has a duty to report any concerns they may have regarding a particular child. Often it is only as information from several sources is pieced together by social care or the police that incidents of child abuse come to light. The piece of information you hold could be significant in building up a picture of a particular child's situation.

Case study

Sadie Molapo is a TA working in a junior school. She provides general support for pupils in Year 3. From the records provided by the infant school, Sadie and the class teacher (Katie Russell) were aware that concern had been expressed in the past about one of the pupils, Eric.

By the middle of the first term, Sadie and Katie had both noticed changes in Eric's behaviour. They had observed marks on his arms that could not easily be accounted for and had overheard some of his conversations with other children where he had been using vocabulary and language not expected from a seven-year-old. On one occasion he had grown very angry with another pupil, which was unusual in itself, but then he shouted, 'I'm going to kill you. I'll strangle you until you're dead and it'll really hurt.'

Sadie completed a Safeguarding Children Report and a Skin Map each time the concerns were observed and gave these to the Designated Officer for Safeguarding Children (DOSC). The DOSC logged these in the appropriate file and asked Sadie and Katie to closely monitor the situation.

One week, Eric was absent for the first three days. This was the first time he had been absent from school. When he returned to school on the Thursday, Sadie and Katie knew right away something was wrong. He was not only withdrawn, he also seemed frightened. Sadie took Eric for a walk by himself in the playground and asked him if everything was all right. He immediately burst into tears and told her about the abuse he had been experiencing on and off over the past weeks and months. It turned out that his father, who he sees at weekends, is violent towards him and hurts him badly. His father has told him that he must not tell anyone; if he does he will kill him. His father, according to Eric, drinks a lot and is violent when he gets drunk. His mum did not want anyone to see what had been happening and so kept him off school until the bruising had died down.

Sadie listened to all this without comment or showing shock and knew that she must not ask any leading questions. When Eric finished talking Sadie reassured him of her concern for him and told him that she needed to write down what he had told her and that she needed to tell the head teacher. Eric silently nodded.

She completed another Safeguarding Children Report, as accurately as she could, using the actual words Eric had himself used. She handed this report to the DOSC, verbally telling him what happened as well and he immediately referred the matter to the duty officer at social care.

Policies and procedures

Confidentiality

Confidentiality is a crucial issue, but you must never allow yourself to be placed in a situation where a child tells you something on the condition that you keep it to yourself. Where there is a risk of abuse you have a legal duty to follow your school's procedures and report it to the appropriate person in the designated manner. It is vital that you follow correct procedures in all aspects of child protection.

Child Protection Policy

Every school must have a Child Protection Policy that reflects current legislation. This policy is to be reviewed annually and must be made available to parents. Other policies that have a bearing on child protection may be those relating to anti-bullying, equal opportunities and physical restraint.

Procedures

All schools will have similar procedures in place:

- A senior member of staff who has responsibility for overseeing all aspects of child protection – the Designated Officer for Safeguarding Children.
- Education to understand and prevent abuse will be given within the curriculum via PSHCE (Personal, Social, Health and Citizenship Education).
- All records relating to child protection will be stored in a secure location with access restricted to only those with genuine reason to see them.
- Child protection records can be kept on computer and are exempt from the disclosure provisions of the Data Protection Act 1984.
- At times of transfer or transition any such records will be securely sent to the new school.
- Allegations of abuse made against a member of staff must be treated following Local Safeguarding Children Board procedures.

Schools differ in detail as to how procedures are carried out. You will need to become familiar with how your particular school operates. This information should be given to you as part of your induction. You certainly need to know who your Designated Officer for Safeguarding Children is and how they can be contacted. You should also be invited to take part in whole-school training on child protection.

Recording concern

Schools will have identified means of recording concern – a form to fill in and, in the case of physical marks or injury, a skin map to complete. Examples of these are given on pp. 27–8. You need to know where these forms are kept and what the procedures are for completing them. Forms need to be completed on the same day that a disclosure is made. Reasons for any delay must be recorded. Form completion must take place away from the child to ensure confidentiality.

Once you have raised the matter with the DOSC, they will take the decision as to whether or not to inform social care. This decision will be made on the same working day as the initial reporting unless there is a clear reason for the delay. Any reason for delay will be documented. Over the following days or weeks there may be continued involvement with social care and/or the police. Children may be placed on the Child Protection Register of social care or the police may become involved in a criminal investigation. It is vital that any information you provide accurately conveys what was said or observed rather than opinions expressed as this may form part of an official or legal process.

Vulnerable groups

Different groups of children within schools may be more vulnerable to abuse than others. These include:

- **children in care**;
- refugees and asylum seekers;
- children where domestic violence is experienced, including those staying at a women's refuge;
- children from socially disadvantaged home environments where there may be a higher risk of substance or alcohol misuse;
- children with **special educational needs (SEN)**;
- children with **disabilities**, particularly where there may be difficulties with communication;
- young carers.

For children who are learning English as an additional language, the provision of a bilingual interpreter may be an important part of the process, bringing extra security to the child. Cultural norms, however, must never be a 'cover' for abusive situations or activities.

Checklist

✔ I am familiar with my school's Health and Safety Policy and understand its implications for my role and responsibility.

✔ I understand my school's procedures for ensuring the safety and security of the pupils.

✔ I know how to respond to accidents and emergencies, keeping within the boundaries of my role and responsibilities.

✔ I am familiar with school policies and procedures with regards to safeguarding children.

✔ I know what signs to be aware of in children regarding possible abuse.

ANYWHERE SCHOOL
SAFEGUARDING CHILDREN REPORT

NAME OF ADULT REFERRING:

NAME OF PUPIL:

DATE OF BIRTH OF PUPIL:

DATE: LOCATION:

NATURE OF CONCERN:

REASONS FOR CONCERN (give details of why you are referring to the DOSC, where possible use the actual words spoken by the pupil):

RECORDS COMPLETED (date and time):

SKIN MAP COMPLETED: Y/N

REPORTED TO DESIGNATED SENIOR PERSON (date and time):

REASON FOR ANY DELAY:

Signed: _____

SKIN MAP

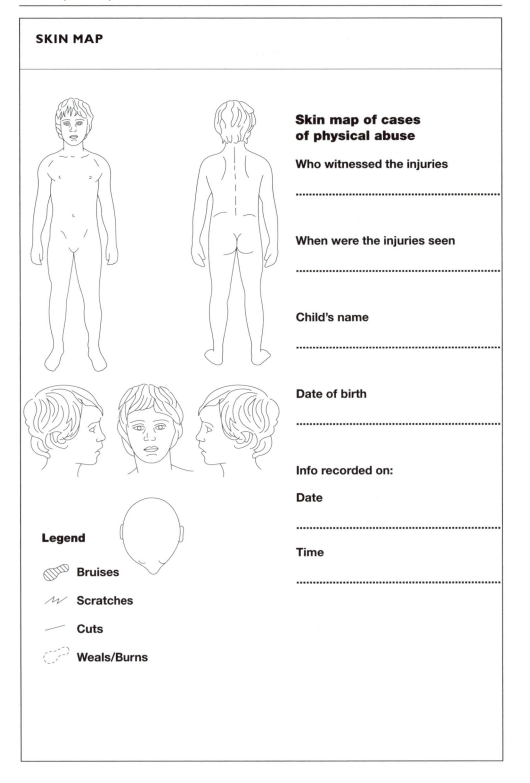

Skin map of cases of physical abuse

Who witnessed the injuries

....

When were the injuries seen

....

Child's name

....

Date of birth

....

Info recorded on:

Date

....

Time

....

Legend

- Bruises
- Scratches
- Cuts
- Weals/Burns

GATHERING EVIDENCE

 ### Setting the scene

Miranda is supporting a Year 4 teacher in a Design and Technology (DT) lesson. The pupils are to make a wooden maze using a 10 cm-square hardboard base, balsa wood spars for the sides and walls of the maze, a small ball bearing to place within the maze and a clear plastic covering. They need to plan their maze, draw it onto the base, cut the appropriate lengths of spars, glue them on to the base using a glue gun, place the ball bearing in the maze and finally tack the plastic covering over the whole piece using drawing pins.

Writing personal accounts: collecting evidence

PERSONAL ACCOUNT

Name: **Miranda Appleton**
Date: **8 May**

Prepare and maintain a safe environment

Y4 Design and Technology lesson

- *Use equipment, furniture and materials safely, conforming to the manufacturers' instructions and setting requirements*

During lunch I went to the DT cupboard and took out four glue guns and several packs of glue. As I had never used them before I practised with them without any children present. Mr Canning (the teacher) showed me how to use them safely and I followed his instructions. He was with me while I read the manufacturer's instructions, plugged one in, switched it on and laid it down safely on a piece of wood rather than directly onto the surface of the cupboards, which may burn. Once it was hot I used it to stick spare pieces of wood together so I knew how it was supposed to be done. Then I felt more ready for the lesson.

- *Check the environment, materials and equipment to ensure hygiene and safety at the start of, during and at the end of the session, reporting faults promptly*

My specific area of responsibility for this lesson was the row of low cupboards along one wall of the classroom. The lesson took place in an afternoon. During the preceding lunchtime I cleared the top of the cupboards of everything else, making sure that the only things out in that part of the learning environment were the glue guns. I placed spare tubes of glue in a tray at one end of the cupboard surface. I also covered the surface of the cupboards with a long cloth so that any glue spilled would go onto that. During the activity I made sure that this cloth remained flat.

Throughout the lesson I kept checking the guns were working properly, that they had enough glue in them to operate safely and they were not overheating.

After the activity I unplugged the glue guns and waited until they had cooled down before returning them to their boxes and replacing them on the top shelf of the cupboard in the resources room, which is only used by teachers. I stored unused sticks of glue in their boxes and placed them alongside the guns. I also helped Mr Canning put away the saws and unused pieces of wood and ball bearings in the same cupboard. None of the guns had developed faults, but we were running low on supplies of glue, so I informed the school office as per school procedures and the Admin Officer placed an order for some more.

- *Recognise potential hazards in the setting and deal with these promptly, according to procedures*

In line with the school's Health and Safety Policy, Mr Canning and I undertook a risk assessment several days before the lesson was due to take place. We discussed the areas of hazard that were likely to be encountered by the pupils – the use of small saws that have sharp blades, the use of glue guns that require attachment to electric sockets and that grow hot, small ball bearings that could be thrown, slipped on or even swallowed.

Mr Canning said that, in his experience, as pupils varied in the length of time they took to make their mazes, we only needed four glue guns. These will all be placed on top of the low cupboards at the side of the classroom so they can be plugged into sockets without their leads trailing on the floor. Pupils will bring their mazes to the glue guns as and when they are needed. My role will be to supervise the use of these glue guns. This means that I need to ensure the safety of all the pupils using the guns and to ensure my own safety – it is just as easy for me to get burnt as the children.

- *Deal with waste safely, according to the procedures of the setting*

After all the equipment had been put away I gathered up the cloth, which had a fair amount of glue stuck to it, and disposed of this in the big bins in the school playground. I watched over a few pupils as they were asked to collect up all the bits of wood and plastic that were left over as waste. I made sure that everything was placed in a large black bin liner, which I took to the bins along with the cloth.

- *Supervise children/young people's safety appropriately and consistently, according to their age, needs and abilities*

Neither Mr Canning nor I wanted children queuing up at the cupboards waiting to use the glue guns as this would have created a risk. When explaining the activity to the class, therefore, Mr Canning had told the pupils that only four pairs of pupils at a time were allowed to come to the glue gun area. He explained carefully how to use the guns and pointed out the dangers.

During the activity I made sure that only the required number of pupils used the guns, I sent others back to their seats to wait their turn. I watched over the pupils as they used the glue guns, making sure they were using them properly. I made sure that no one messed about and they all followed the procedures they had been shown.

- *Encourage children/young people to be aware of personal safety and the safety of others*

All through the lesson I reminded pupils to take care when using the gun. One or two began to mess around and I asked them very clearly to explain how they should use the guns safely. I also asked them to tell me what dangers they were placing both themselves and others near them in by not treating them properly. Both pupils realised they had been silly and behaved properly after that. They realised that they could have easily burnt themselves or someone else if they continued to wave the guns about, pretending to use them as swords, light sabres or wands.

- *Encourage children/young people to develop good hygiene practices*

Once the gluing had been completed, I asked the pupils to go a group at a time to wash their hands. I told them they needed to use warm water and soap to make sure that any glue was removed from their hands. Several pupils told me they did not need to do this as their hands were not dirty. Although I agreed with them that they did not look dirty, I encouraged them to wash their hands nevertheless as prevention against germs.

- *Implement safety and security procedures at the start of the day/session and when children/young people leave*

At the end of the day I stood at the door to the playground making sure that all the pupils left the room sensibly. By this age they do not need to be collected by parents and many go home independently, but five of them are collected by staff from a local after-school club. It is part of my responsibility to make sure that these five pupils wait in the appropriate place for their escort, which I did again this afternoon.

TEACHER'S COMMENT

Miranda is very knowledgeable about aspects of health and safety and worked within the school's guidelines in this situation.

I certify that this is a true statement of what occurred.

Staff signature   Name (printed and role)

J. Canning   Jacob Canning, Class Teacher

ASSESSOR'S COMMENTS

Miranda, your personal account is clearly structured into sections that refer to the performance indicators you should be covering. I am sure this helped you to write such an account. In this personal account you demonstrate knowledge regarding health and safety matters. We will follow this up in class next time we meet. I will ask you questions relating to health and safety matters. I will record your answers and then we will be able to sign off some of your knowledge-base indicators. Remember to include the risk assessment form as this is good evidence.

Signed: **Terrie Cole**, NVQ Assessor

GATHERING EVIDENCE

 Setting the scene

Miranda is on duty in the Key Stage 1 playground during morning break. She is informed that a pupil has fallen over and appears to be seriously hurt; she is crying, her ankle is twisted under her and she is unable to get up from the ground. A large group of children are beginning to gather around her.

Writing personal accounts: collecting evidence

PERSONAL ACCOUNT

Name: **Miranda Appleton**
Date: **28 April**

STL3.2 Deal with accidents, emergencies and illness

* *Remain calm and follow your organisation's procedures for accidents and emergencies, according to your role and responsibility*

When I went over to Pamela I saw that she was very distressed, crying and in a lot of pain. Her leg was in an awkward position under her body and she was complaining that her ankle hurt. I had been told to treat any possible fracture as an actual fracture, so took this very seriously. My immediate reaction was to become as upset as Pamela and those pupils around her, but I took myself in check, took a few deep breaths and reminded myself of what I needed to do.

- *Call for qualified assistance as appropriate to the incident*

As I was not trained in First Aid, I did not touch her myself but sent two pupils I knew to be sensible to run to the school office to ask the school Administration Officer (who is one of the trained First Aiders) and the head teacher (the Designated Officer for Safeguarding Children) to come as quickly as possible.

- *Maintain the safety of the people involved*

While we were waiting for the other members of staff to come I asked the other pupils to move away from Pamela. Two of her close friends stayed with her, but the others spread out around the playground. Some began playing again, but most stood still watching from a distance. The playground was unusually quiet, but this benefited Pamela who was not distressed by shouting and movement around her.

- *Provide reassurance and comfort to the people involved*

After the pupils had gone to the office I continued speaking with Pamela, reassuring her that help was on its way. I took off my jacket, placing it under Pamela's head to make her more comfortable. I held her hand to give her comfort and gently wiped her forehead with my other hand.

- *Recognise that children/young people are ill and follow procedures*

Within two minutes the Administration Officer and the head teacher both arrived. They, too, agreed that Pamela could have potentially fractured her ankle and that she should not be moved. I was asked to go to the office as quickly as possible to ask the school secretary to summon an ambulance and contact Pamela's parents in line with school procedures. This I did. The ambulance came within fifteen minutes, and by then Pamela's mother had arrived as well. The ambulance crew agreed that Pamela had probably suffered a fracture and took her to hospital.

- *Follow reporting and recording procedures*

I complied with legal and school requirements in this incident by responding immediately and by not going beyond my own training and qualifications. After the incident had been dealt with I went to the school office and wrote my account in the school accident log. The school secretary had already noted the incident and logged the time of calling the ambulance and the parents.

TEACHER'S COMMENTS

This was clearly a difficult situation that Miranda handled well.

I certify that this is a true statement of what occurred.

Staff signature   *Name (printed and role)*

M. Biggins   Mabel Biggins, School Administration Officer

ASSESSOR'S COMMENTS

I agree with the Administration Officer's comments. Well done. Can you let me have a copy of the accident log as further evidence?

Signed: **Terrie Cole**, NVQ Assessor

Chapter 2

Support pupils' learning activities

In this chapter we will look at two elements:

1   Support learning activities.
2   Promote independent learning.

KNOWLEDGE AND UNDERSTANDING

Introduction

This unit focuses on providing effective support to both teachers and pupils. Effective support involves supporting learning activities, promoting independent learning and giving feedback.

Curriculum matters

The relevant school curriculum and age-related expectations of pupils in the subject/curriculum area and age range of the pupils with whom you are working

The National Curriculum is applied to all pupils of compulsory school age. The aim of the National Curriculum is to set out clearly what is to be taught and to describe attainment targets for learning.

The National Curriculum covers all subject areas. Subject areas include: English, Mathematics, Science, Design and Technology, Information and Communication Technology, History, Geography, Modern foreign languages, Art and design, Music, Physical Education and Citizenship. Further, what is taught is divided into Key Stages and **attainment levels**. Attainment levels that pupils should be working towards are set for each Key Stage. The levels of attainment for each Key Stage are described in Table 2.1.

So far we have talked about Key Stages and attainment levels – now we need to discuss **attainment targets** within subject areas.

Table 2.1 Key Stages and attainment levels

	Key Stage 1	*Key Stage 2*	*Key Stage 3*	*Key Stage 4*
Age	5–7	7–11	11–14	14–16
Year groups	1–2	3–6	7–9	10–11
Range of attainment levels within which majority of pupils will be working	1–3	2–5	3–7	4–8 + exceptional performance
Expected attainment levels for majority of pupils by end of Key Stage	2b	4b	5/6	5 GCSEs (C – A*)

(National Curriculum website 2008)

Table 2.2 Science – attainment target: life processes and living things

Attainment level	Level descriptions
1	Pupils can recognise and name external parts of the body and of plants
2	Pupils use their knowledge about living things to describe the basic conditions that animals and plants need in order to survive
3	Pupils use their knowledge and understanding of basic life processes when they describe differences between living and non-living things

(National Curriculum in Action website 2008)

QUIZ

The National Curriculum aims to _____

There are _____ key stages.

Within each key stage there is a range of attainment _____ which the majority of pupils will be working at.

The government sets expected attainment levels for the majority of pupils to achieve at the end of each _____.

Each subject area has a designated number of _____targets.

Level _____ explain in detail what is expected at each attainment level.

Within each subject and each attainment target the level _____ explains the type and range of performance that pupils should demonstrate.

Level descriptions guide the teacher in _____.

Let's consider the attainment targets within the subject area of science.

Table 2.2 does not give a complete description of what pupils need to learn within each level and there are more levels – but the aim is to give readers a flavour of the detail involved in the National Curriculum. These 'level descriptions', that is, descriptions of what a pupil needs to learn at a certain level of attainment, guides the teacher in planning, reporting progress and target setting. As a TA you will be expected to know the age-related expectations of the pupils with whom you work. Of course nothing stands still. With the introduction of the Primary Framework for literacy and mathematics the structure of learning for these areas has been divided into strands and objectives aligned to these strands.

The teaching and learning objectives of the learning activity and the place of these in the teacher's overall teaching programme

Pupils attend school to learn. The staff of schools put much thought and planning into creating appropriate learning opportunities. To achieve this, plans are made and desired learning outcomes are specified.

Plans will follow a **scheme of work** as detailed in the National Curriculum. From the scheme of work the teacher will write up plans that would cover what the class will do during a term or half term. From these long-term plans, weekly and daily plans are drawn up.

An important part of the plan will be to specify the learning objectives, learning intentions or desired learning outcomes. Schools will vary in regard to what term (learning objectives, intentions, outcomes) they prefer to use. **Learning objectives** define what the teacher hopes the pupils will achieve by the end of a session. For example, a learning objective may state that a pupil will be able to correctly identify verbs in a sentence, or, correctly answer questions on differential equations. An example of a daily plan, with comments from a teaching assistant on how they use this plan, can be found on p. 40.

Knowing the learning objective allows the teacher and the teaching assistant to measure the progress of a pupil or group of pupils.

Some pupils will need to have their work **differentiated**, that is adapted to their ability level.

Teachers and TAs working together will plan and deliver the lesson. The next step is to feedback and evaluate. Evaluation is an important part of what teachers and TAs do and will be covered in Chapter 11, Contribute to Assessment for Learning.

Policies, expectations, roles and responsibilities

The nature, extent and boundaries of your role in supporting teaching and learning activities, and its relationship to the role of the teacher and others in the school

Table 2.3 illustrates how closely linked the roles of teachers and teaching assistants are in regards to the planning and delivery of lessons. The most useful advice for a teaching assistant starting out or starting to work with a new teacher or new group of teachers is to make time to talk to the teacher regarding mutual expectations. What

Table 2.3 Teachers and TAs working together

Responsibility	Role of the teacher	Role of the TA	Examples
PLANNING	The teacher will set out the plans (daily plans, weekly plans and long-term plans).	TAs can offer suggestions as to the type of support they can provide to the planned activities.	'I attend an adult education class in cake decoration. I volunteered to take responsibility for helping pupils to decorate and design their Christmas Cakes.'
		TAs can point out any difficulties they see in the proposed plans.	'Though my teacher is relatively new to the school we are on the same wavelength – we work as a team – the teacher takes time to show me the weekly plans in advance. In that way I can offer comments on whether I think a particular pupil could cope with a set piece of work, or what other resources we could use in delivering the lesson.'
		TAs can make sure that they are prepared for their contribution to the lesson.	'I work in a secondary school where I am assigned to support specific students within a year group – as I work with many specialist teachers I always make a point of trying to get to the class before the pupils so I can have a quick word with the teacher before the class starts.' 'I always make sure I have a supply of pens and pencils in case any of the pupils have forgotten their material.'
DELIVERY Implementing the lesson plan and checking for understanding.	An important part of planning is to specify how a session will be delivered. For example, what teaching techniques will be used, what resources are needed, who is to work with whom and how much time will be allotted to the session.	TAs will need to follow the teacher's plan for delivery. It is always important that as you deliver a session you check for pupil understanding as you go along.	'The pupils in the group that I was working with had been given a maths worksheet to complete. After 5 minutes all the students were still struggling on the first question. There were 15 questions on the sheet that needed to be completed in 15 minutes. Though the teacher had explained how to do such questions – as a group they had not really understood.' If pupils seem not to be able to cope with the work set – then there is a need to adapt and modify your interactions to suit pupils needs and interests.

Table 2.3 continued

Responsibility	Role of the teacher	Role of the TA	Examples
DELIVERY Adapting and modifying		Adapting the work that has been set. *Change the work*	'As it was clear that the maths sheet was not appropriate for the ability level of the group – I had a quick word with the teacher. She suggested that we might like to use the worksheet that had been set for the lower ability group. She stated that she had been over-ambitious in terms of what she thought the group could do.' In this case the learning objectives were altered. It is important at all times that pupils are set work that they can do.
		Adapting the work that has been set. *Change or modify your approach*	'Though the pupils were clearly struggling with the maths worksheet – I thought that they could do the work, but that I needed to take another approach. I quickly gathered some mult-link to help them to do the sums.' 'I was working in a chemistry lesson supporting a group of students who were trying to learn the periodic table. They were quickly getting bored and disruptive. I suggested that we create our own rap version. We needed to go out of the class to a more quiet area, but the pupils attitudes changed dramatically.' In these examples the TAs used their knowledge and understanding of the group's abilities and interests to modify the approach so that the learning objectives were achieved.

ANYWHERE PRIMARY

Literacy planning

Date: Tues 28 Nov.   Class year 2

> *By looking at this plan I know what the learning objectives are for my group – as well as the class*

Learning Objectives:

Collect words and phrases to write poems – ponds

Design simple poems or patterns of words – swamps

Express their views about a story or poem – rivers and puddles

Identify words or ideas to support or back up their view – rivers and puddles

Whole class work	Individual/group tasks	Plenary session
Model how to collect words and lines from different poems. Read several poems with the children first. Talk about writing down some of the words and ideas that we liked.	**Rivers and Puddles** – with Mrs Goldbottom **Swamps** – with Miss Moss **Ponds** – with Miranda Appleton Higher ability groups will have already selected an idea for a poem. They need to be encouraged to collect words and phrases related to that idea from a range of books. Lower ability groups to read books on their table and to write down some words and sentences that they like. TAs will need to assist with spelling and handwriting skills.	Ask pupils to read out the poems they liked best. Ask pupils what it was that they liked about these poems. Ask pupils what words and sentences they have collected for their poem.

> *I am working with a lower ability group, **Ponds**. I have two students with IEPs. I need to be familiar with their targets as I will be giving additional feedback to the teacher regarding their progress in meeting their targets.*

> *The teacher discussed the books/resources needed.*

> *Knowing the learning objectives allows me to focus my feedback to the teacher on the extent to which the pupils have met their learning objectives.*

many teaching assistants say is that different teachers have different expectations and that time taken at the beginning of working relationship can prevent unnecessary misunderstandings.

Consider the following:

> *Samantha, a secondary TA, describes how she works supporting pupils working in French.*

> 'I am fluent in French and German and enjoy working with pupils in language lessons. With most of the pupils I support, I will sit next to them and if necessary quietly talk to them about what the teacher is saying. Of course this does mean that sometimes I may be talking at the same time as the teacher – but I do this very quietly. We had a new teacher starting in the department this term and everything seemed to be going fine. Then one session there happened to be many pupils talking over the teacher and the teacher lost her temper and told the pupils off. Then she had a go at me – in front of the class – for setting a bad example by talking when she was talking. I just didn't know what to say. I was furious. I talked to the SENCO and of course everything is now sorted. The teacher in question apologised. But it was all down to different expectations. I thought I was doing what I should be doing and the teacher thought I was deliberately undermining her authority.'

Teaching assistants will have a close working relationship with the teacher, but they will also be involved with other members of staff. See Chapter 5, Support the Development and Effectiveness of Work Teams, for further details on what constitutes good working relationships. On p. 263 there is an example of a structured template for a discussion between teachers and TAs relating to roles and responsibilities is given.

The importance of working within your own sphere of competence and when you should refer to others

Part of behaving professionally is to know what you can do (working within your own sphere of competence) and when you need to refer situations or seek advice from others. Though mutual roles and responsibilities have been established there may be times when you feel you are struggling.

In terms of supporting learning there may be times when you feel you are not getting through to a pupil:

> 'No matter how I have tried to explain multiplication – he is just not getting it.'

> 'I know that part of my role is to support this pupil – but she has made it clear that she does not want me to help her.'

In terms of supporting the curriculum there might be areas that you as a TA feel the need for further input.

'I used to work on the **interactive whiteboards** – but in the last year I have been working one-to-one with a pupil. However, now that I have been assigned to a new class I will be expected to use the interactive whiteboards. Help!!!'

Being professional requires a TA to recognise when further support is needed, to know how to access the necessary support and to take responsibility for seeking support.

School policies for inclusion and equality of opportunity and the implication of these for how you support teaching and learning activities

School policies for inclusion and equal opportunity affect every aspect of school life. See p. 169.

FACTORS TO CONSIDER WHEN SUPPORTING LEARNING

The key factors affecting the way pupils learn, including age, gender, and physical, intellectual, linguistic, social, cultural and emotional development

- **Age** – When are pupils ready to learn?
- **Gender** – Do males and females approach the learning situation in different ways?
- **Physical** – Do physical changes, such as puberty, influence learning?
- **Intellectual** – Does the ability to think change with age?
- **Linguistic** – How does the ability to understand and communicate influence learning?
- **Social** – How do others (pupils, teachers, TAs) influence the learning process?
- **Cultural** – How does cultural background influence the learning process?
- **Emotional development** – How does the ability to deal effectively with emotions influence the ability to learn?

Age makes a difference – thinking changes with time

Theorists, such as Jean Piaget (1970), state that children's thinking changes with time. Piaget states that children go through stages reflecting their thinking abilities or cognitive development. The precise age when a child will go onto the next stage will vary from child to child. However, all children will go through all stages in the same order:

Stage	Age
Sensori-motor	0–2
Pre-operational	2–7
Concrete operational	7–11
Formal operational	11+

Figure 2.1 The 'Three Mountains Test'

Pre-operational stage

When a child first starts school Piaget would describe children as pre-operational thinkers. This stage lasts from two years to seven years. Children within this age group are learning at an incredible rate. However, Piaget states that their learning is limited by egocentrism and the failure to conserve.

Children between the ages of two and seven are egocentric

Egocentrism refers to the difficulty in seeing the world from another's point of view. The classic test for egocentrism is known as 'The Three Mountains Test'. Here a child is presented with a model of three mountains, one with snow on the top, one with a cross on the top and one with a cabin on the top. The child is then shown a range of pictures of this model. The child has to choose the picture showing the view that they see. This the child can do.

Then the test gets more complicated. The child is shown a doll and the doll is placed at a point around the model of the three mountains. Then the child is asked to select the picture that the doll sees from where the doll is sitting. Often the child will select the picture that they can see.

From this test Piaget concluded that a young child tends to think that others see the world as they do. It is not till a child is eight or nine that they will realise that others will have their own viewpoint on the world and correctly select the picture that the doll can see.

Tips for classroom use

Although this three mountains test seems obscure, the fact that a child has difficulties appreciating another's viewpoint has implications for those working with children in this age group. The ability to see the world from another's viewpoint is related to the ability of empathy, where a child can imagine what another child would be feeling.

Teaching assistants can encourage children to think about how other children think and feel.

Children between the ages of two and seven have difficulties conserving

Piaget also said that this pre-operational stage was dominated by the inability to conserve. Conservation or to conserve requires an individual to hold two apparently conflicting ideas in their mind at the same time. Again this idea seems complex. Let's take the example of conservation of number:

> One child, aged four, is shown two identical lines of chocolate buttons.
> As a teaching assistant you ask the child if the lines have the same amount of chocolate buttons. The child says yes.
> You then re-arrange the lines so that in one line the chocolate buttons are spread out more than the other line.
> You then ask the child whether the lines have the same amount of chocolate buttons.
> The child says the line that has the chocolate buttons spread out more, has more chocolate buttons.

One TA commented: 'I tried this task. The child had great difficulties with this. I kept moving the lines back and forth and counting the buttons each time but still the child was confused.'

From the child's perspective if the lines looked different they were different! However, an older child would be able to reason that though the lines looked different, what changes is the space between the buttons and not the amount of buttons.

This skill of logic, involving holding two apparently conflicting views in your mind is the ability to conserve.

Figure 2.2 Same, More and No More

Tips for classroom practice

What is interesting about the example in regard to conservation of number is that the TA tried to point out to the child the correct way of thinking by having the child count and re-count the lines. However, the child was confused. Central to Piaget's view of learning is that children need to be active in their learning and that confusion is an important part of the learning process. Piaget would call confusion in this case cognitive dis-equilibrium. We will come back to this point (pp. 46–7).

Concrete operational stage

Children of seven to eleven are concrete thinkers

Children can do more complex operations such as multiplication and division and fractions but can only do these calculations on objects that actually exist, hence the word concrete. For example three-quarters of 12 can be calculated but, '3/4 of x' does not make sense.

Formal operational stage

Children of 11-plus move into the stage of formal operations

Piaget felt that children do not gain the ability to think abstractly until they reach the final stage of formal operations. This stage applies to children of the ages of 11 and over. It is for this reason that algebra is not taught to children until they are this age.

Tips for classroom practice

TAs can help pupils develop skills in logic by encouraging pupils to experiment and discover things for themselves. Pupils learn new information more easily if you can give them specific examples of real-life experiences to which they can relate the new information. Pupils benefit from using real apparatus.

If we remember, Piaget said that although children will go through all the stages in the same order, the age with which they can enter the next stage will vary from child to child.

Therefore, though the curriculum in secondary school assumes that older children can think more abstractly, some pupils who are struggling will not have this skill and will benefit from being given specific examples related to real-life objects. Though the pupils are older, Piaget might say that they are still thinking at a less advanced level.

To learn, children need to be actively involved

Piaget felt that a child's thinking ability was influenced by the age of the child and the interaction the child has with its environment.

Certain topics cannot be taught to a child until the child is biologically or mentally ready to understand these concepts. Piaget talks about maturational readiness. If a child in Reception is having difficulties learning to read perhaps it is because they are just not ready and that when they are ready they will learn.

Figure 2.3 The perils of discovery learning

However, to learn a child needs to be actively involved in the learning process. Piaget sees children as little scientists and that they need to discover knowledge for themselves.

Piaget believed that when we learn information we store this information in the form of schemas. Schemas are units of mental thought. Schemas are developed through the process of assimilation and accommodation.

Assimilation involves taking in new information and filing this information into an existing schema.

Accommodation is involved in the creation of new schemas or new ways of thinking. Accommodation is complex. To create a new schema or unit of new knowledge the individual first has to realise that:

- there is a gap in their understanding;
- others are seeing things differently;
- they are wrong and that they need to think in a different way.

Piaget called the state of being aware that there was a gap in understanding, cognitive dis-equilibrium. Piaget said that being in a state of cognitive dis-equilibrium was unpleasant but that it was a motivating force to learn new information.

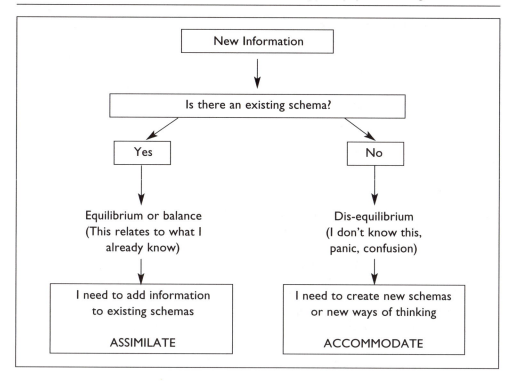

In a sense, what Piaget is saying is that to learn new information you first have to realise that there is something you don't understand.

Tips for class practice

TAs can help pupils to realise that getting stuck and not understanding is an important part of the learning process.

Remember, pupils need to discover things for themselves. TAs can create situations or asks questions so that children can realise for themselves there are things that they don't understand.

Social influences: a more experienced learner can help to guide a less experienced learner

While Piaget stated that children learn new information through the process of discovery, Vygotsky (1986), another theorist, argued that children learn by being guided by a more experienced learner. This experienced learner could be the teacher, the TA or a more able pupil. One of Vygotsky's key ideas was the *Zone of Proximal Development*.

The Zone of Proximal Development sets out what the pupil can do by themselves and what they can do with assistance. It is believed that what pupils can do today with help, in time they will be able to do by themselves. To learn, pupils need guidance. Successful guidance involves:

- *Communicating knowledge to the pupil in a language that they can understand.* Central to Vygotsky's theory is the idea of *intersubjectivity*. Simply put, intersubjectivity involves coming to a shared understanding. As a TA you might ask a pupil to summarise the notes on page 24 of a textbook. The pupil in turn copies word for word all the information presented on page 24. Here, what you understand by summarising is not what the pupil understands of the term.
- *The considered use of questions.* For further information on questions see pp. 119–22.
- *Scaffolding.* That is, giving the pupils more support when needed and withdrawing support when the pupil is succeeding.

Gender influences learning

Some teachers will comment that in mixed-sex classes boys demand and receive more attention. This raises questions as to whether female students are receiving adequate attention.

In your experience as a TA, who demands more attention, boys or girls and why?

Analyses of national test results reveal that girls are outperforming boys in regard to GCSE achievement results. It is important to realise that such analyses are dealing with averages and that there are always exceptions. However, some commentators blame male underachievement on a 'laddish culture' that dismisses the value of education. Other commentators focus on the difficulty of providing age-appropriate material for struggling readers, especially boys, in secondary schools.

Emotional factors influence learning

Some pupils are identified as having emotional difficulties. For these pupils, emotional disturbances can interfere with their ability to learn and their ability to form relationships with teaching staff and other pupils. Much recent attention has focused on emotional intelligence. Emotional intelligence involves recognising, understanding, managing and expressing our emotions in a positive manner. Individuals who have emotional intelligence are said to be emotionally literate. As a TA working with pupils you need to encourage pupils to become emotionally literate, but in order to do this you need to respond to them in an emotionally literate manner. For further information relating to emotional aspects of learning see pp. 78–85.

Culture influences learning

Research on ethnicity and education (DfES 2006b: 5–7) reveals that:

- 21 per cent of primary school pupils and 17 per cent of secondary school pupils are classified as belonging to an **ethnic minority**;
- minority ethnic pupils are more likely to experience deprivation than white British pupils;
- Asian pupils appear to have the most positive attitudes to school, work and lessons whereas mixed heritage pupils appear to have the least positive attitudes;
- Gypsy/Roma, Travellers of Irish heritage, black Caribbean, white and black Caribbean and other black pupils are much more likely to be excluded.

Again, while this document provides evidence in regard to trends and identifies certain groups that are at risk, there will always be exceptions. Teachers and teaching assistants need to challenge negative stereotypes and to have high expectations for all pupils.

In addition to cultural background the environmental circumstances that children find themselves in will influence their ability to learn. For example, children from families who are suffering economic hardship may need extra attention, reassurance and help. Children of families who are living in bed and breakfast or hostel accommodation may lack proper food, clothing and the time and space to do their homework.

Linguistic factors

Language is central to learning. More in-depth information on this aspect is presented in Chapter 12 (Support Bilingual/Multilingual Pupils) and Chapter 13 (Support Pupils with Cognition and Learning Needs).

How social organisation and relationships, such as pupil grouping and the way adults interact and respond to pupils, may affect learning

Types of groups

As a TA you will be involved in supporting all sorts of groups:

- single-sex groups, for example, some schools will have separate sport activities for girls and boys;
- friendship groups;
- ability groups;
- groups targeted for special support;
- activity groups or extra-curricula groups; choirs, football teams, drama club;
- discussion groups set within a class session.

Some of these groups will last longer than others. For example, a group of pupils might only come into existence to produce the Christmas pantomime. Some groups that are put together for special support might be scheduled to run for a fixed time only. Some groups focused on project work might only be together until the completion of the project. On the other hand, friendship groups within a class might last for years. Table 2.4 illustrates possible advantages and disadvantages of various group structures.

Opportunities for collaborative learning

Collaborative learning is a broad term that describes teaching and learning situations where pupils come together in groups to learn. A classroom discussion could be an example of collaborative learning. Co-operative learning refers to a specific kind of collaborative learning where pupils are required to work together in small groups on a common project. Obviously techniques to facilitate discussion and encourage pupils to work effectively together are of interest to teaching professionals.

Table 2.4 Advantages and disadvantages of group structures

Type	Advantages	Disadvantages
Single sex	Some pupils find this more comfortable Some research indicates that some boys and girls benefit from single-sex lessons	Can lead to competition Can lead to gender stereotypes
Ability group	Work set can be tailored to ability of group	Division in regard to who goes into which group can be difficult to determine Can lead to self-fulfilling prophecies, for example: 'we are bottom group – so not much is expected of us'
Mixed ability group or activity groups	A wide range of views, experiences and opinions can be presented	More effort is needed to design a suitable task in which all group members can equally participate If group members cannot equally participate, those who are left out may feel isolated, less valued and less able
Friendship groups	Pupils will often feel secure working with friends	Might not be suitably challenging Might be tempted to discuss other topics What do you do with pupils who are loners and do not fit into existing friendship groups? What do you do when friends fall out?

The function of groups: encouraging exploratory talk

Often, groups are put together to discuss ideas. What teachers hope to see are good examples of 'exploratory talk'. Exploratory talk happens when pupils engage critically but constructively with each other's ideas and suggestions (DfES 2001). However, pupils need to be shown how to do this.

Exploratory talk happens when pupils are encouraged:

- to come up with new ideas or suggestions;
- to respond to others' suggestions by adding, clarifying, altering or modifying;
- to constructively challenge ideas;
- to evaluate ideas, both their own and others, in terms of strengths and weaknesses;
- to use reasoning to explain or justify their ideas;
- to ask questions that require other pupils to explain, expand or clarify their ideas;
- to summarise what everyone in the group has said in order to move the discussion forward.

Wow – this sounds complex!

Ways of encouraging groups to work together

A TA can make sure that:

- clear and specific goals are given to groups;
- rules about working together and listening to each other are established;
- in mixed-ability groups achievable tasks are given to individual group members;
- defined roles and responsibilities are established. Sometimes it is helpful to assign roles such as chairperson, timekeeper, spokesperson and secretary;
- every group member has a say. One strategy is to give every group member the same amount of tokens. Each time a pupil speaks they use one token.

Ways of encouraging groups to talk or feedback to each other

Here you need to think about how you want the groups to feedback to the class. There are some clear strategies that you can use to do this. One strategy involves selecting one group to give feedback and have subsequent groups offer suggestions only if they have not already been mentioned. Another strategy involves asking each group in turn for one point. Alternatively you could ask each group to display their findings on A3 paper and then present this to the class.

Stages in the development of groups and how these affect group dynamics

Tuckman and Jensen (1977) outlined five stages of group development that can be applied to groups.

Forming

At this stage the group has just met or has just been put together and ground rules need to be established. These rules can be set by the teacher or teaching assistant or the group can be encouraged to set these rules for themselves.

Storming

This is the stage where there may be conflicts as the group negotiates ways of working together.

Norming

At this point the group has established ways of working together and can get down to the task at hand.

Performing

This is the stage where the group works together to complete the set task or goal. At any point if conflicts emerge and get out of hand, work might stop and the group could return to the storming stage. The role of the teacher or TA is to monitor the dynamics of the group and provide information, advice and encouragement that enables the group to work effectively together.

Figure 2.4 Some pupils find it hard to wait their turn

Adjourning

The task is complete and the time has come for the group to disband. At this stage there can be a certain amount of reflection and evaluation of how things have gone. The role of the TA is to help in the process of evaluation and reflection.

The importance of balancing individual and group calls on your attention and how to achieve this

One of the hardest tasks for a TA working with a group is to divide their attention between individual group members. For a TA it is the question of who do you go to first.

Perhaps from the outset it is important to tell the group that you will help everyone – but that they must be patient. However, as TAs have often pointed out, this is easier said than done:

> 'I will always say to the group that I will try to give everyone the same amount of time. But, let me tell you about a group I work with supporting literacy skills. Amy needs and demands constant reassurance and is constantly asking me whether she is right. Graham is much less demanding but actually he needs just as much guidance as Amy. Jimmy needs help but sees my help as interfering. To make matters more difficult, when I praise Graham and Jimmy for their work, Amy feels that I am ignoring her though in actual fact I spend most of my time with her. Let me tell you – being aware of all their needs and balancing my attention is hard work.'

So what can a TA do?

- Get all pupils started and then prioritise. Help those most in need and then move on to those needing less attention.
- Remind pupils of group rules, taking turns, being polite.
- Encourage pupils to work together.
- Keep calm.

STRATEGIES – TO SUPPORT LEARNING

The importance of having high expectations of all pupils with whom you work

In a discussion of high expectations it is important to understand the meaning of 'self-fulfilling prophecies' and to understand how 'self-fulfilling prophecies' work. Simply, self-fulfilling prophecy can be defined as the tendency for things to turn out as expected. For example, a teacher or TA who expects a pupil to fail might treat the pupil in a manner that increases the likelihood that they will fail. A teacher who has low expectations for a pupil may not set them challenging work, may not ask them searching or difficult questions and be satisfied with minimal progress. The pupil in turn picks up how others perceive their ability and can internalise these beliefs or incorporate them into how they define themselves.

However, the good news about self-fulfilling prophecies is that they can work both ways. For example, a teacher or TA who expects a pupil to succeed might treat the pupil in a manner that increases the likelihood that they will succeed. A teacher or TA

Figure 2.5 Learning-styles super heroes

may set pupils suitably challenging work, may ask questions that pupils can answer and therefore encourage pupils to achieve more.

How to use and adapt learning support strategies to accommodate different learning needs and learning styles

Matching teaching style to learning styles

Learning styles refers to the preferred manner in which an individual would choose to learn. There are many measures of learning styles. Table 2.5 (see pp. 56–7) illustrates just a few learning styles; as you go through this chart tick those learning styles that apply to you.

Self-assessment questions

1   What learning styles do you have?

2   What choices in learning style preferences can you give to the pupils you work with?

3   Does the educational system favour certain learning styles over others?

Tips for classroom use

What Table 2.5 shows is just how complex learning styles are.

How can a teaching assistant tell what learning style a pupil has?

Some schools will give out questionnaires that are designed to measure aspects of learning styles. As a TA you can take advantage of this information. But perhaps more useful is to ask pupils how they would like to learn or to watch how they learn in

---

Case study

'I was working with Sam. Sam has difficulty with handwriting. Often he uses the pencil with so much pressure that he rips the paper. I have tried to talk to him about what is light and what is hard (I suppose I have tried an auditory approach). I have tried demonstrating to him what it is to write heavily and what it is to write lightly (a visual approach). But then the SENCO suggested that I play a game with him involving paper and carbon paper. We ordered the carbon paper on-line. Anyway, I pre-prepared a paper and carbon paper sandwich so to speak, that is, alternating layers of paper and carbon paper. The game involved that sometimes we would need to write heavily so a mark went through all the pages and sometimes we would need to write ever so lightly that a mark only went through the top copy. This approach (kinaesthetic) really seemed to work with Sam and his writing has improved.'

---

different environments and with different subjects. Most pupils, although having their preferences in how they would like to learn, are actually quite adaptable. However, some pupils who are struggling will only be able to learn using one style – this is where a knowledge of learning styles can be very useful.

All pupils will benefit from information being presented in a variety of styles. Though individuals will have their preferred learning style it is also important to be able to learn in a variety of ways.

School policy and practice in relation to the use of praise, assistance and rewards and how to use these to maintain pupils' interest in learning activities

Schools will recognise the importance of praise and have established systems of rewards. Challenges facing TAs include:

- trying to support pupils who are not interested or bothered;
- working with pupils who find work challenging;
- supporting pupils who give up when they encounter difficulties.

In these situations praise, assistance and rewards can be effectively used to motivate pupils and support learning.

Case study

Nicola works as a TA in a secondary school. She states:

'Often the pupils that I work with find work challenging, are not bothered and easily give up. I suppose the first thing I need to do is to make sure that the work set is at an appropriate level and that they can achieve. You cannot praise a pupil if they have no chance of success. I find knowing what interests the pupils useful in that I can use that information to try to relate the work to their interests. When the pupils want to give up – or they keep asking me to do the work for them – I remind them of situations where they have previously found work difficult but where after effort they have succeeded. In terms of assistance it would be easier sometimes to do the work for them, but that would not help them.'

For further information on the use of praise, assistance and rewards see pp. 87–8.

The importance of active listening and how to do this

Active listening is a skill that TAs will need to develop. Active listening is different from social listening. When we listen socially we might not really be listening as well as we could, for some of the following reasons:

Table 2.5 Learning styles

Variations		What am I?

Perceptual learning style – what senses are being used

Visual Individuals prefer to be taught and learn more when teaching activities involve visual materials (videos, pictures, maps)	**Auditory** Preference to learn by listening. Preferred teaching activities would include listening to tapes, and lectures	**Kinaesthetic** These individuals prefer hands on, physical involvement. Preferred teaching activities would include making things or role play

Preferences in processing information

Global When a topic is introduced, global learners need to see the complete picture before they can begin to look at the details	**Analytic** When a topic is introduced, analytic learners would prefer to proceed step by step. For them being presented with the big picture could prove too overwhelming and confusing	
Impulsive This refers to the preferred pace of thinking. Impulsive learners like to jump in, start activities, make decisions and finish work quickly. However, in the rush mistakes are often made	**Reflective** This refers to the preferred pace of thinking. Some pupils prefer to take their time over their work. They like to have time to think and consider the possibilities. However, it could be that the pupil spends so much time thinking that they don't get around to actually doing the work	

Environmental learning style

Preferences in background noise	**Silence** Some pupils prefer to work in absolute silence	**Some noise** Some pupils prefer some background noise	**Specific preferences in terms of noise** Pupils will differ in terms of what they would like to listen to when they learn, be it classical, jazz, rap, or hip-hop

Table 2.5 continued

Variations	Cool	Warm	Hot	What am I?
Preference in regard to temperature	Cool	Warm	Hot	
Preferred classroom design	Traditional desk and chair placed in rows	Chairs and tables arranged in groups	Desks arranged in semi-circle	Sitting or lounging relaxed on carpet or floor
Preferred level of lighting	Bright	Moderate	Subdued	
Emotional learning style				
Preferences in responsibility	Work independently without any supervision	Some adult supervision	Frequent adult supervision	
Preferences in structure	Need to be told in exact and precise terms what the task is, how to do it and what is expected		Student would prefer to be given the objective and then given the freedom to decide how they will accomplish the objective	
Physiological learning style				
Food and drink intake	Prefer to have no food or drink when learning		Prefer to have some food or drink when learning	
Time of day	Learn best in the morning		Learn best in the evening	
Need for mobility	Preference to sit still while learning		Need, sometimes unconscious, to move their body while learning Often these individuals cannot keep still	

- We might be busy doing other things or thinking about other things and not really listening to what is being said to us.
- We might be so busy thinking about what we are going to say and trying to get others to listen to our views that we don't really hear what is being said to us.
- We might let our emotions get in the way. If we are told something we don't want to hear we might get angry or upset. It is at this point we can stop listening. If someone we are talking to is upset we might try to cheer them up. Again, this could mean that we stop listening.

Active listening is about giving someone the chance to really express what is happening to them. It involves: *Observing the body language of pupils for clues to how they are really feeling.* For example:

- If a younger child has done something that they should not have done, often they don't look at you, they look at the floor or perhaps their face might turn red.
- Sometimes, a pupil might be on the verge of crying but still say that they are fine.
- Sometimes, you can tell by a pupil's posture, the way they are slouching over the desk, that something is the matter.
- Sometimes, when a pupil is just about to kick off you can see them tense up.

Encouraging the pupil to talk about how they are feeling

It is important to communicate to the pupil that you are there if they want to talk, that you are interested in them and what they have to say. It might be necessary to find the right place to talk. This might involve taking the pupil to a quiet area in the class or outside. In encouraging the pupil to talk it is helpful to use open questions, make encouraging sounds or nods and repeat key phrases. Sometimes it is necessary to be silent and sometimes it is important to give them the space to be silent.

Be aware of what your body language is saying

TAs need to be aware of their posture. Does your body language communicate to others that you are tense? For example, are your shoulders hunched or your arms crossed? These actions indicate tension. It is always helpful to get down to a pupil's level. For example, with a younger pupil you could kneel down besides them. As a TA you will need to be close to the pupil, but not so close that you invade their personal space and make them feel uncomfortable. You will need to show interest and understanding by engaging in eye contact, yet you do not want to seem that you are staring.

Active listening is a skill!

As we need to listen and communicate with pupils, we also need to encourage pupils to listen and effectively communicate with us and each other. This is particularly important when working with a group.

Strategies for challenging and motivating pupils to learn

When working in a classroom it is easy to see that some pupils are motivated and equally some are not. Sadly some pupils seem to have given up. Some believe that they can't do it, that they are going to fail anyway – so why bother. If you are a TA what you want to know is how to motivate pupils.

Self-efficacy (Bandura 1977, 1986) concerns the individual's belief that they have the capability to organise and perform the necessary actions to produce a required attainment. Simply, self-efficacy refers to the pupils' belief that they have the necessary ability to achieve. Many pupils who are not motivated have low levels of self-efficacy.

Praise is important and praising effort is more important than praising achievement. However, sometimes TAs will say that praise is not enough for some pupils. TAs will say that although they praise some pupils at every possible opportunity, it does not seem to make a difference.

In trying to make sense of what is happening for these pupils we need to consider *'enactive mastery'*. Enactive mastery involves a pupil reflecting on and judging how successful they have been on a task. So you might have praised the pupil for their effort but the pupil might have looked around at what the others have done and come to their own conclusion that they are rubbish. Again we come back to the question regarding how to work with such pupils.

Plan moderately challenging tasks

If you are working with a pupil helping them to understand the task, this is known as working at an instructional level. At this level, pupils will need to quickly recognise 90–95 per cent of the words in a text and understand 70–89 per cent of the text. If they have questions you are there to answer their questions. Here you are working with the pupil within their Zone of Proximal Development (see pp. 47–8).

If the pupil is required to work independently they will need to quickly recognise 96 per cent or more of words within the text and understand 90 per cent or more of the text (McCormick 1999).

If you feel the task is not suitably challenging or too challenging, then it is your responsibility to report this to the teacher. The task will need to be adapted.

Use suitable role models

Pupils who are de-motivated and struggling would benefit from role models. There are two types of models. *Mastery models* are pupils who can easily do the task. It is helpful to watch someone who is an expert, see how they do it and pick up tips. However, if there is too much of a difference between what the pupil can do and what the expert can do, then there is a danger that the less capable pupil could say to themselves 'I'll never be able to do that'. In this case it is perhaps better to use *coping models*. Pupils with low self-efficacy benefit from coping models. Coping models are pupils who the less able pupils can identify with. The coping models also have difficulties with learning, they too make mistakes, however they don't give up, they learn from their mistakes and move forward. By watching how coping models deal with their mistakes, struggling pupils realise that they too can achieve (Margolis & McCabe 2006; Zimmerman 2000).

Praise

Praise is important but with pupils who have low self-efficacy it should be used only when the pupil has earned it. If praise is not authentic then the pupil may not believe you or dismiss your comment as they think that you say it to everyone.

The importance of independent learning and how to encourage and support this in pupils

Supporting a pupil involves giving the pupil the study skills they need – so that they can learn and develop themselves. It is easy to fall into the trap of allowing the pupil to become dependent on you. Lorenz (2002) talks about three different types of TAs:

- There is the TA that is *Velcro'd to the pupils* they support. They are stuck to them like glue. However, this way of working with a pupil may not allow the pupil to relate to others in their class.
- The next type of TA has been compared to a *hovering helicopter*, the TA is always at hand if anything goes wrong or the pupil needs help. This approach is seen as preferable to the 'Velcro'd' approach. However, sometimes pupils need space and time to try to work things out for themselves. Sometimes it is important for pupils to make mistakes as making mistakes can be part of the learning process.
- The next type of TA is called a *bridge builder* – this type of TA creates, with the teacher, learning opportunities that the pupil can participate in and social opportunities where the pupil can interact in a positive manner with other pupils.

While learning to begin with is very much guided by the teacher it is hoped that over the school years the student will learn how to learn, that is, they will become an independent learner. To do this pupils will need to develop certain skills. They will need to know:

- what they need to do in order to complete the assignment or answer the question;
- how to ask for help;
- how to gather the needed information;
- how to present ideas;
- how to use their time effectively;
- how to review and evaluate their own work against what they have been asked to achieve;
- how to take responsibility for their learning.

Self-assessment questions

1   Find what your school has to offer in regard to study skills.

2   How can you incorporate these study skills into your everyday work with pupils?

REVIEWING AND REFLECTING

How to help pupils to review their learning strategies and achievements and plan future learning

On a general level a TA can help pupils to identify both strengths and areas to work on and plan for next time.

Identify strengths

You will need to help pupils to identify what they are good at and what they liked about the work that they have completed. As a TA you will need to affirm the pupils' strengths and advise them on how they could develop and build on these areas.

Identify areas to work on

You need to be both clear and constructive about areas that need improvement. A pupil needs to know why they achieved a certain level and what they need to do to get a better one next time.

Plan for next time

You will need to help the pupil to identify what they need to do next. Of course, when you do next work with the pupil you will need to talk to them about their targets.

For pupils to be able to review their own learning strategies, achievements and plan for future learning they need to be aware of:

- how they learn best – what strategies they use to learn – what are their learning styles;
- how they recognise when they have problems in learning – this involves self-monitoring;
- what strategies they can use when they are experiencing difficulties. These strategies might include re-reading the question or asking for support.
- what they can do by themselves and what they can do with assistance from others. In this way pupils can measure their own progress.
- the need for them to take responsibility for their learning.

A teaching assistant can help pupils review their learning strategies, achievements and plan for future learning by talking to pupils about their work. Sometimes this can be recorded formally and sometimes it may be discussed verbally with the pupils.

MONITORING AND MODIFYING

How to monitor the pupils' responses to teaching and learning activities

Part of what you do as a TA is to feedback to the teacher regarding pupils' responses to teaching and learning activities. Teachers need to know:

WHEREVER SECONDARY SCHOOL

Year 7
Maths Worksheet

Complete questions 1–5 from page 74 and write your answers on the space provided:

1 _____

_____

2 _____

_____

3 _____

_____

4 _____

_____

5 _____

_____

What I did well _____

_____

What I need to work on _____

_____

Figure 2.6 Worksheet with space for self-evaluation

- whether pupils achieved the learning outcomes;
- if pupils did not achieve learning outcomes, what could they do and what did they find difficult?
- what strategies did you use to support the pupils?
- what assistance was offered to pupils? Teachers need to know what part of the work pupils could do without assistance and what they could do with assistance.
- were there any pupils who found the work easy – if so were extension activities offered?

Sometimes the feedback regarding pupils' responses to teaching and learning activities may be informal – sometimes you may be required to complete formal documentation for the teacher. Feedback is necessary for evaluating the lesson and planning for future lessons.

ANYWHERE PRIMARY SCHOOL

Assessing speaking and listening

Name _____   Date_____

Record sheet	Details of activity	Assessment comments
Speaking for different audiences • clarity, intonation, pace • organisation, use of detail • use of standard English		
Listening and responding • understands main points • asks relevant questions • responds appropriately		
Group interaction and discussion • takes different roles • supports others, takes turns • makes contributions to sustain and complete the activity		

How to monitor and promote pupil participation and progress

Although teachers are concerned with pupils' responses to teaching and learning activities it is also important to monitor and comment on pupil participation and progress. Teachers need to know:

- How involved were the pupils in the activity – or to what extent did they participate?
- What strategies were used to encourage participation?
- What examples did you see regarding progress?
- How did you recognise and celebrate progress?

One of the real rewards of teaching and supporting learning is to observe that 'light-bulb' moment when a pupil who has been struggling to understand a concept finally gets it. Those moments are priceless! It is important to recognise individual progress, praise the progress and to share the news of the progress with the teacher. The teacher, too, will want to celebrate the progress.

When and how to modify teaching and learning activities

Part of supporting pupils' learning involves helping the pupil to achieve the learning objectives. Whereas some pupils will find learning easy others will struggle. If a pupil does not understand, you will naturally try to explain the task. But what if the pupil still does not understand after your explanation? Obviously you will need to try to explain the task again but in a different fashion. Hopefully, the pupil will now understand. But what if they don't? If they don't – then you will need to try a different approach. Examples of modifying teaching and learning activities can be found on pp. 39, 244–5. In trying to modify teaching and learning activities you will need to use all that you know regarding learning styles, scaffolding and discovery learning. Obviously the teacher will be very interested in the approaches you used and how you modified the activities.

WHEN THINGS DON'T GO TO PLAN

The sort of problems that might occur when supporting learning activities and how to deal with these

What is presented in Table 2.6 are the sorts of problems that might occur when supporting learning. Throughout this chapter we have talked about various ways to support learning and encourage independent learning. Using the tips and strategies from this chapter and other chapters, fill in Table 2.6. To help you get started a few suggestions have been given.

Table 2.6 Problems that might occur in supporting learning

Possible explanations	Ways forward – how to adapt or modify activities to achieve learning outcomes	When to report difficulties
Pupils may find the task too difficult		
Pupil may not be ready (maturational readiness)	Use discovery learning	As a matter of routine I would inform the teacher regarding how the learning session went and any difficulties or modifications that I made
Pupil experiencing cognitive dis-equilibrium	Stress to pupils that to experience difficulties is part of the learning process	
Task not presented at correct instructional level	Select appropriate task at appropriate instructional level	
Pupils may not understand the task		
Pupils may say they are bored and they don't want to do the task		
One pupil may not want to join in with the group		
Pupils may not be paying attention		
A pupil may say that they are stupid and that they cannot do a task		
Pupils may be distracted by other activities		

Checklist

✔ I understand that children need to be active in their learning.
✔ I need to match **teaching styles** to learning styles.
✔ I need to help pupils realise that getting stuck is an important part of the learning process.
✔ I encourage and promote independent learning wherever possible.
✔ I need to ensure that the task set for a pupil is set at the appropriate level.

GATHERING EVIDENCE

 Setting the scene

Miranda looked at the indicators for this unit, specifically in regard to reviewing learning targets. Miranda then wrote up the following account:

Writing personal accounts: collecting evidence

PERSONAL ACCOUNT

Name: **Miranda Appleton**
Date: **Tuesday 5 Dec.**

Activity: **Decorating individual Christmas cakes with Year 3 pupils**

I mentioned to my teacher that one of my hobbies was cake decoration and that I had taken several adult education classes regarding this. As it was approaching Christmas the teacher asked if I would take small groups out to work on decorating and icing their individual cakes. Each of the Year 3 students I was working with had to draw a picture of how they planned to decorate their cake. When the students arrived in the staffroom/kitchen where we were having our cake decorating classes I had each of them sit orderly around a table. I had been given a small amount of money to buy supplies and we had a range of coloured icing and novelty items to use. I had brought a range of equipment, cookie cutters, etc. from home. As the task was potentially quite messy, I had a number of other volunteer TAs to assist me.

   Before we started I asked each of the pupils to show the group their plan and to discuss what they hoped to do. On looking at the different coloured icing and novelty items to choose from the pupils soon started to ask if they could change their plans.

   I told them that they could change their plans but they would need to be able to justify or explain why they changed their plans. At the end of the session I asked each of the pupils to show again their original plan and to discuss their Christmas cake.

   I had thought about the questions I would ask:

- What did you plan to do?
- What did you do?
- Did you make any changes and why?
- What do you like the best about your cake?
- What would you like to do next time?

Signed: **J. Crowther HLTA**

I was very impressed with Miranda's work with the group and in particular her use of questions.

ASSESSOR COMMENTS

A very good example of reviewing work, however, more details are needed. Did you record any of this in terms of feedback to the teacher? Perhaps you could include as evidence a feedback sheet based on the performance indicators for this unit.

Signed: **Terrie Cole**, NVQ Assessor

Miranda later submits the following evidence:

ANYWHERE PRIMARY SCHOOL

Feedback sheet

Name: Amy S.

Activity: **Decorating Christmas cakes**

- *Provide information, advice and opportunities for pupils to choose and make decisions about their own learning*

- *Encourage pupils to take responsibility for their learning*

Amy's plan was to decorate her cake with an angel. Originally her background was going to be green and the angel was going to be white. However, after explaining the plan to the group Amy said she didn't want to do the angel anymore and that she didn't want to have a green background. Amy looked like she was going to cry. I told Amy that she could change plans but that she would have to explain why. Amy said that the angel was a good idea at first but it was too difficult to get it right. She wanted the wings to be golden and frilly and that was difficult to do with icing.

A Christmas tree shape would be easier to do and she could use the little golden balls as decoration.

I said that she had a good reason for changing her plan and that I thought the Christmas tree was a brilliant idea.

- *Give positive encouragement, feedback and praise to reinforce and sustain pupils' interest and efforts in learning activities*

I left Amy for a bit. When I went back I realised that she had cut out her Christmas tree shape in green and had covered it with so many golden balls that you couldn't see the Christmas tree.

- *Help pupils to review their learning strategies and achievements*

I asked Amy to stand back and say what she thought about her cake. Amy paused and said: 'I can't really see the tree.' I asked Amy to think about what she could do. Amy said that she would take some of the golden balls and use them as a border around the cake. I said: 'Well done.'

At the end of the session I asked her what was best about the cake.

Amy said that she loved the golden balls.

- *Listen carefully to pupils and positively encourage them to communicate their needs and ideas for future learning*

I asked Amy what she would like to do next. Amy said that she would like to make a bigger cake and perhaps try to do an angel but that she would need to look for gold icing.

Signed: **J. Crowther**, HLTA

I was very impressed with Miranda's work with the group, in particular her use of questions.

ASSESSOR COMMENTS

This is a very detailed feedback sheet that corresponds to the performance indicators for this unit. It is through the details of what you said to Amy and what she said to you that I can clearly see how you helped this pupil review her work.

Well done!

Signed: **Terrie Cole**, NVQ Assessor

Nicola Wilson, a secondary TA, having looked at this unit, focuses on the performance indicators relating to her role in supporting pupils engaged in learning activities and how this relates to the teacher's role. Nicola explains to Terrie that at her school they have been involved in a new initiative whereby the teacher and TAs are required to discuss and sign an agreement relating to roles and responsibilities. Nicola submits this as evidence.

ESTABLISHING ROLE AND RESPONSIBILITIES: TA AND TEACHER AGREEMENT

Please discuss the following points and note down any agreed points before signing the agreement. See notes for clarification.

Contribution to class work/discussion

Notes: *Can the TA join in a class discussion spontaneously? Can the TA contribute to asking and/or answering questions?*

I will encourage Nicola to contribute to class discussion. Nicola is encouraged to ask questions as this will help facilitate group discussions. Also to encourage the class to answer questions and not to be afraid of giving the wrong answer – Nicola has agreed to sometimes give the wrong answer on purpose.

Seeking clarification

Notes: *Can the TA seek clarification from the teacher in front of the class if they don't understand something or feel that certain students need clarification?*

If Nicola doesn't understand the task then I am sure that other pupils will not have understood. If this does happen, Nicola should ask me to re-explain the task to the class.

Marking work

Notes: *Can the TA give a verbal comment on the quality of the work? Can the TA mark written work where immediate feedback might be useful and/or where answers are easily marked? Can the TA provide formative comments when assessing work?*

Nicola always gives the pupils verbal feedback on the quality of their work. I have now asked Nicola to assist in marking the tasks set in class, for example, when I have set exercises from the textbook. Nicola is to focus on the pupils she supports and then if she has time she can mark other pupils' work. I have also asked Nicola to help pupils review their work and to help them make comments on what they have done well and what they need to do next.

Changing tasks set

Notes: *Can the TA alter the task set to enable students to complete it? For example: altering the wording of a question or simplifying the instructions for a task. If 'yes', does the TA need to check with the teacher first or can they do this independently?*

Nicola can alter the wording of a question or simplify the instructions – but she needs to include these details in her feedback to me.

Suggesting appropriate learning activities

Notes: *Can the TA suggest strategies that may suit the preferred learning styles of students? Can the TA suggest strategies that may suit students with particular learning difficulties?*

Hope to spend time discussing the need for appropriate differentiated learning activities with Nicola. We plan to discuss developing word searches, multiple-choice questions and writing frames for certain pupils.

Giving permission

Notes: *Giving pupils permission to: go to the toilet, get out of their seats for a legitimate reason, move places for a legitimate reason, or anything else?*

Nicola can give permission for pupils to go to the toilet, and move seats if she feels that there is a legitimate reason. I would appreciate if Nicola does this that she informs me to avoid any misunderstandings.

Managing pupils' behaviour

Notes: *Which pupils can the TA be responsible for? Allocated pupils? Other pupils? Whole class?*

Nicola has special responsibility for allocated pupils. Although, if necessary, Nicola needs to encourage all pupils to abide by the school's behaviour policy.

Sanction imposition

Notes: *What sanctions is the TA able to give? Who is responsible for issuing detention slips?*

I am willing to give Nicola the authority to issue detention slips.

Removing pupils from the class

Notes: *Under what circumstances can the TA remove pupils from the class? Which pupils will the TA be responsible for if they are removed from class?*

Nicola is responsible for working with the pupils who are on School Action Plus and for those who have statements. Nicola has built up a good rapport with the pupils and if she feels it necessary she can remove them from class and accompany them to the learning support unit. I would encourage Nicola to remove a pupil if they were becoming very agitated and disrupting the learning of other pupils in the class.

Intervening in pupil/teacher conflict

Notes: *Are you comfortable with the TA intervening under any circumstances, or specific circumstances, or not at all?*

Nicola and I have developed a good working relationship. If Nicola observes that I am having difficulty settling the group, then I would appreciate it if she could have a quiet word with those pupils who are causing a problem.

Signed: **P. Bradley**, Teacher

Signed: **Nicola Wilson**, TA

ASSESSOR COMMENTS

This is very good evidence clarifying your role in regard to supporting pupils engaged in learning activities and how this relates to the teacher's role and an example of good practice regarding teachers and teaching assistants working together. I would suggest, however, that you write a brief note to accompany this regarding your discussion with the teacher on these issues and have the teacher countersign your note. You will be able to use this as evidence for the unit on contributing to the review of team practice.

Well done!

Signed: **Terrie Cole**, NVQ Assessor

A template for discussing roles and responsibilities can be found on p. 263.

Chapter 3

Promote positive behaviour

In this unit there are two elements:

1   Implement behaviour management strategies.
2   Support pupils in taking responsibility for their learning and behaviour.

KNOWLEDGE AND UNDERSTANDING

Introduction

This chapter is concerned with the role that support staff have to play in promoting positive behaviour.

Policies, roles and responsibilities

The school's policies for the care, welfare, discipline and attendance of pupils including the promotion of positive behaviour

Every school will have policies. School policies are not written in isolation but relate to **local authority** (LA) and national or government guidelines. Some documents that are of interest to TAs are:

- The Children Act (2004)
- *Every Child Matters* (2004)
- Disability Discrimination Act (2005)
- Education Act (1996)
- Convention on the Rights of the Child, Unicef (1989)
- Circular 10/98, Section 550A of the Education Act 1996: *The Use of Force to Control or Restrain Pupils*
- Schools Standards and Framework Act (1998).

See Chapter 15 for a brief summary of some of these documents and useful references.

In terms of behaviour management, the **board of governors** of the school, in response to Section 61 of the School Standards and Framework Act (1998) will ensure that schools have and follow policies that are designed to promote positive behaviour. Specifically, a school will have policies on behaviour, bullying, child protection and equal opportunities. These policies will outline:

- the designated roles of staff, pupils, governors and parents/carers for promoting positive behaviour;
- how rewards and sanctions are used to encourage positive behaviour;
- support and training opportunities in managing challenging behaviour and encouraging positive behaviour that are available to staff.

As a TA it is your responsibility to read these policies.

The school's agreed code of conduct

In order for learning to take place, appropriate classroom expectations and rules need to be established and enforced. Pupils thrive in an environment where there are clear boundaries. To establish a co-operative learning community, 'behaviour plans', 'behaviour agreements' or 'codes of conduct' are formulated. Whatever terminology your school uses it is essential that pupils are actively involved in this process. If pupils understand why rules are important there is a greater chance that they will follow the rules. Being involved in this process creates ownership. To create a classroom code of conduct the teacher will discuss with the class:

- how pupils can learn well;
- how pupils can support and respect each other;
- what behaviours are right and fair;
- how pupils can feel safe.

Here we are talking about shared rights, shared responsibilities and shared rules (Rogers 1998, 1995).

Self-assessment questions

1   What is the code of conduct for the class you are supporting?
2   How were the pupils you work with involved in the process of establishing a code of conduct?

The school's policy and procedures for rewards and sanctions

To encourage pupils to choose to act in a manner that is focused on learning and that is respectful and co-operative, the school will produce policies and procedures on rewards and sanctions.

Positive rewards include:

- verbal praise;
- rewards such as stickers and house points;
- positive notes or phone calls home;
- special privileges, for example, a pupil being able to work on a favourite activity, being first in line or first out of the class;
- special recognition from class or school.

Sanctions

Pupils need to know that there are limits and that there is a structure within the school that will create a safe and productive learning environment.

A behaviour policy will outline what constitutes disruptive behaviour and what are the appropriate levels of intervention in your school.

POSSIBLE LEVELS OF INTERVENTION

1   Warning and reminder of appropriate behaviour.
2   If inappropriate behaviour continues a consequence is delivered. This consequence could be in the form of a detention or missing break-time.
3   If inappropriate behaviour continues to be an issue a letter is sent home and if deemed necessary meetings are held with parents. Very serious incidents of inappropriate behaviour may result in an exclusion.

Remember:

- sanctions are important in setting limits and boundaries;
- sanctions need to be something that pupils do not like;
- sanctions should never be psychologically or physically harmful;
- pupils need to perceive that sanctions are applied consistently and fairly;
- sanctions should be delivered in a calm manner;
- sanctions need to be focused on inappropriate behaviour and not the person;
- pupils need to know why they received a sanction and what they should have been doing;
- staff should know what sanctions are appropriate in what circumstances;
- pupils need to know how they can make amends and move forward.

Many schools will involve pupils in formulating fair systems of both rewards and sanctions.

The roles and responsibilities of yourself and others within the school setting for managing pupil behaviour

The importance of working within the boundaries of your role and competence and when you should refer to others

All school staff have a role to play in encouraging good behaviour and dealing effectively with disruptive behaviour. As a TA you will need to know what *you can do* to manage behaviour. Specifically, you will need to know the rewards, sanctions and strategies or techniques you can use. A TA will need to know when to consult the teacher and what strategies the teacher alone can use. In order to know what your role is in managing behaviour you will need to discuss this with the other staff. To help you do this, fill in Table 3.1. A template for teacher and TA discussion on roles and responsibilities to include behaviour management can be found on p. 267. To help get you started let's look at how one TA has started to fill in her chart.

Of course, how you fill in this chart depends very much on your role. Your assessor will probably ask you questions in regard to what you can do as a TA and when you need to transfer responsibility to the teacher.

The importance of shared responsibility between all staff for the conduct and behaviour of pupils in corridors, playgrounds and public areas within and outside of the school

The benefits of the consistent application of good classroom management and behaviour strategies

Pupils are very good at assessing teachers' and TAs' abilities to handle and manage a class. Some pupils will quickly realise what they can and cannot get away with. Some pupils will take advantage of situations. Some pupils will try to play one teacher/TA off against the other. For example: 'Miss lets me text in her class', 'Sir doesn't mind if I swear.'

Good behaviour management involves teamwork. Staff need to be supported and need to support each other. Rewards and sanctions need to be applied consistently.

Consider the following:

> 1 You are working in a Year 5 class. A pupil swears at another pupil. You, following the school's zero tolerance policy on swearing, tell the pupil that they will need to stay in at break. The pupil goes up to the teacher complains that it is unfair, says sorry and asks the supply teacher if she can go out to break with the others. The supply teacher agrees. As the pupil leaves the class for break she says to you quietly: 'See – I don't have to listen to you.'

- How do you feel?
- What are the consequences of the teacher's actions?
- What can you do to move the situation forward?

> 2 It is 4.00 p.m. and you are on the bus home. You notice a few pupils from one of the classes you support (in school uniform) a couple of seats ahead of you. They are playing music very loudly. An elderly gentleman asks them politely to turn down the volume. One of the pupils swears at the passenger 'Mind your f***** business, you old git.'

- What can you do?

Table 3.1 Roles and responsibilities relating to behaviour

| Routine | School and class rules | Role and responsibility of yourselves and others | | | The teacher will |
	Pupils are expected to	I (the TA) will intervene when	I (the TA) can use these strategies	I (the TA) will inform the teacher if	
In the playground	• Play safely • Play kindly with other pupils • Stay in designated areas	• A child is in out of bounds area • Not playing safely on equipment or leaving equipment lying around so that it is a danger for others • If a child is alone	• Remind them of the rules for play • Remind them of the consequences of not behaving • Praise good behaviour • If a child is alone encourage them to play with others	• A child refuses to behave after I have reminded them and told them of the consequences • Report any incidents of fighting, bullying or accidents	• The teacher has the authority to have pupils miss break and put their name in red book
Standing outside in the corridor waiting to come into class	• Stand in separate lines • Class helpers to go to front of line • Whatever line is the quietest gets to come in first	• The pupils are making too much noise or pushing in their line	• Remind them of the rules: be quiet, no pushing • Praise good behaviour	• A pupil refuses to get into line • If fighting occurs • A pupil refuses to behave when asked	

Table 3.1 continued

Beginning of the day	• Enter quietly • Hang coats up • Put book bags in right box • Put lunch box on shelf in corridor • Put water bottle in tray • Sit quietly on carpet	• Remind pupils to hang their coats up • Remind pupils not to step on others' coats	• Praise for good behaviour	• Report to teacher if any pupil was upset
Where to sit				
When wishing to participate in class				
When requesting help				
Going into assembly				
Walking in corridors				
Using ICT equipment				

Figure 3.1 Pupil's behaviour can sometimes present challenges

When working with behaviour – factors to consider

The stages of social, emotional and physical development of children and young people and the implications of these for managing behaviour of the pupils with whom you work

Stages in emotional growth

Erik Erikson (1982) developed a stage theory in regard to emotional growth. At each stage there is a conflict or challenge that needs to be addressed. This conflict can be resolved positively or negatively. If the outcome is not positive we carry this negativity over, making it more difficult to meet the challenges of the next stage. What is summarised in Table 3.2 relates to the stages of emotional growth up to 18 years of age.

As a TA your role is to support the pupils you are working with to resolve these conflicts or challenges in a positive manner. This is especially true for children who have difficult backgrounds that may include problematic relationships with parents. Many psychologists, including Erikson, believe that positive parent–child relationships are fundamental to healthy personality development. What this means is that when a child has had a difficult background the school may need to pick up the pieces.

Much recent research has been carried out into resilience. Resilience has been defined as the ability to deal positively with adverse life situations. A difficult background and problematic relationships with parents does not condemn an individual to a life of hardship. In fact, many children experiencing extreme hardship will rise to the challenge and make a success of their lives. Research on resilient children has found

Table 3.2 Psychosocial stages of development

Age	Psychosocial or emotional conflict		Description
	Resolved positively = Emotional growth	Resolved negatively = Emotional immaturity	
0–1	Trust	Mistrust	Trust is gained through the experience of being able to rely on others. At this stage the infant or small child needs to rely on its parents to provide food, warmth and care. If the child's needs are met the child learns to trust.
			If the child's needs are not met this legacy of mis-trusting others will affect the child's future emotional growth.
1–3	Autonomy	Shame and doubt	Autonomy refers to independence, a sense of being in control of and being able to control what happens to you. At this stage children must be given the opportunity to assert themselves and do things for themselves. If children experience constant criticism or are never allowed to try to do things for themselves they will learn to doubt their abilities and to anticipate failure.
3–6	Initiative	Guilt	At this stage children will develop initiative by being asked to carry out plans. These plans could concern what to paint or what to construct with a set of building blocks. The child, while putting their plans into action, will also need to respect the rights of others.
			The child who has in the previous stage learnt to doubt their abilities will find it difficult to try new tasks as they fear failure. As a TA you will need to encourage pupils to have a go.
6–11	Industry	Inferiority	At this stage school-age children will need to master academic and social skills in order to feel competent. If they feel they are not as good as their fellow pupils they will start to feel inferior. As a TA you will need to help children to recognise areas that they are good at.
12–20	Identity	Role confusion	Teenagers need to ask themselves questions about the type of person they want to become as an adult. This stage involves dealing with social relationships and, as they mature, sexual relationships. This stage also involves deciding on career goals, for example do they want to go to college or do they want to go to work. What is important at this stage is that the individual pupil really thinks about what they want to do. As a TA you can help them in the thinking process.

Source: Sigelman and Shaffer 1991

that these children are very good at finding supportive adults, such as teachers and teaching assistants to help and guide them.

You never know who you touch or the difference you can make (see Figure 3.2)

The story: Ten years after Rory has finished school, both Rory and Mrs Brightside reminisce on Rory's school days:

Rory: My life was difficult – I was a right so-and-so, but Miss made a difference. She believed in me. She was instrumental in turning my life around.
Miss: Yes, I remember Rory – he was a right so and so – I tried everything – it was like banging my head against a wall – I wonder where he is now?

Stages in friendship

- **Pre-school** – Friendships are based on physical aspects. Friends are those who play with you or who are physically near you.
- **Primary** – The key concept here is reciprocal trust. Friends help and support each other. Friends are those you can trust. In terms of play, children from the age of four become increasingly involved in complex games. It is within these games that skills involving taking on roles, giving directions and leading are learnt. From seven onwards friendships are formed through conversation, telling jokes and keeping secrets.
- **Secondary** – The key concept here is mutual understanding. Friends understand each other. Friends confide in each other, share their innermost thoughts and feelings and open their hearts to each other. From 12 onwards teenagers can become increasingly self-conscious. This is the stage where they must forge an identity that is separate from their parents. Betrayal of a friend at this stage can be devastating.
- **Late adolescence, early adulthood** – At this stage there is awareness that even a very good friendship cannot fill every need. An individual will realise that their friend needs other friends and that the nature of friendships change with time. A good friendship grows and adapts to changes.

(Selman 1980; Damon 1983; Berndt 1983)

Popularity

In a classroom pupils can be classified into categories reflecting social status. There are children who are:

Popular: well-liked by most children
Rejected: rarely liked and often disliked by most children
Neglected: children who are neither liked nor disliked but seem to be invisible
Controversial: children who are liked by many and disliked by many.

(Coie *et al.* 1982)

Figure 3.2 Touch the future: teach

Friendships are important. As a TA you can encourage friendships and friendly behaviour. You will also need to be on the look-out for pupils who seem rejected or neglected and pass this information on to the teacher or SENCO. These children might benefit from social skills training.

Supporting friendships

Consider:

> You are supporting a seven-year-old boy, Tyler. Tyler is quiet, sensitive and has problems making friends. In fact he is rejected by most of the other pupils. They call him names, they make fun of him, and no one wants him to be on their table. Of course when pupils are caught pushing Tyler or teasing him they are reprimanded, but this only seems to make it worse. The boys blame Tyler for being in trouble and pick on him even more. Instead of standing his ground Tyler retreats more inside himself. You hear an older member of staff comment that: 'he is a born victim'.

• What can you do?

Physical milestones

Physical milestones incorporate both gross and fine motor skills. Gross motor skills are the abilities required to control the large muscles of the body. Gross motor skills are involved in walking and running. Fine motor skills describe the smaller more precise motor skills that are involved in handwriting or tying up shoelaces. (See the top box on the facing page.)

It is important to realise that children will reach these physical milestones at different rates. When a child is considerably delayed in reaching these milestones then there is an issue of concern and this information needs to be passed on to the teacher or the SENCO. The SENCO might raise these concerns with the school nurse.

In addition to physical milestones there are physical aspects relating to maturation that will impact upon a pupil. (See the bottom box on the facing page.)

As a TA you have a role to play in boosting the self-esteem of the pupils you support.

The range and implications of factors that impact on behaviour of all pupils, e.g. age, gender culture, care history, self-esteem

- **Social-emotional development** – As children grow they learn how to relate to others around them and how to recognise and deal with their and others' emotions. When psychologists talk about social-emotional development they talk about age-related changes in empathy (showing concern for others), sharing, turn-taking and friendship skills.

- **Special needs** – Special needs has been defined as occurring when a child has significantly greater difficulty in learning than the majority of the children of his/her age or has a **disability** that prevents or hinders the pupils from making use of the educational facilities that are generally on offer within schools (Daniels *et al.* 1999). There are many specific types of special needs including: **dyslexia, dyspraxia, Autism Spectrum Conditions (ASC)** and **Attention Deficit Hyperactivity Disorder (ADHD)**. Children with special needs will require additional support. The SENCO within a school is there to advise both teachers and Teaching Assistants on how best to support a pupil with special needs.

- **Family/care history** – It goes without saying that what happens within family life will influence how a child behaves at school. A small number of children will, for a number of reasons, be in the care of the local authority. Sadly, for some children the reasons for being removed from the family are physical or sexual abuse. It is known that many children who are looked after will underachieve and leave school early. The government, in trying to address the needs of this group of children, have stated that each child in care must have a **Personal Educational Plan (PEP)**.

  For children who are living with their parent(s) issues of family bereavement, illness, divorce and general family dynamics will influence their behaviour in the classroom.

  Common sense tells us that if a child is emotionally unsettled then they will have difficulties settling at school.

- **Issues of stereotyping and labelling** – Stereotyping and labelling involves placing individuals into categories and making assumptions and judgements about these

AGE-RELATED ABILITIES

Gross motor skills	Fine motor skills
4–5 • Jump forwards 10 times without falling over • Do a roly-poly • Bounce and catch balls	• Cut on line continuously • Copy a cross and square • Print some capital letters
5–6 • Can walk on balance beam • Can skip on alternate feet • Can walk on tip-toes	• Cut out simple shapes • Copy triangle • Copy first name • Colour within lines • Has adult grasp of pencil • Has a well-established preference for being left- or right-handed
8–9 • Typically can ride a bike, swim, roller skate, ice skate, scale fences and play a variety of sports	

PHYSICAL ASPECTS RELATING TO MATURATION

Factor	Impact
Baby teeth fall out to be replaced by adult teeth. Pupils will differ in regard to athletic prowess and agility. Some children will excel at sports while others will struggle with any activity involving physical co-ordination.	This will influence a child's ability to pronounce sounds correctly. This ability or inability will impact on self-esteem and possibly on popularity.
Puberty There is a great variation between individuals. Both fast and slow developers may struggle. It is not easy being 1 ft taller than all your friends in Year 5 and likewise 2 ft shorter than all your mates in Year 9.	This will impact on self-esteem.
Appearance In a media-driven society appearance is important. Some pupils will judge themselves against the models they see on TV and in magazines. Eating disorders such as anorexia and bulimia are affecting younger and younger children.	This will impact on self-esteem and possibly physical well-being.

individuals. For example, if I said Mr Brown was an accountant you might have an image of what he is like without even meeting him. If I said Miss Smith was a circus trapeze artist you would have a completely different impression. Stereotypes are damaging when they lead to prejudice and discrimination. As a TA part of your role is to support equal opportunities for all the pupils you work with.

- **Self-esteem** – Self-esteem involves self-evaluation. This evaluation involves a comparison between your **self-image** (the way you see yourself) and your **ideal self** (the way you would like to be). As a TA your role is to help a pupil develop high esteem, that is, help the pupil feel good about who they are.

- **Age** – As an individual progresses through the school system, from pre-school to infants, to juniors to secondary they change in many ways. Knowing what behaviour is expected from a child, or what behaviour is age-appropriate helps you, the TA, understand the children you are working with. Knowing what is age-appropriate behaviour also makes it easier to identify those children who may benefit from additional support.

- **Gender** – Whether someone is male or female is a biological fact. Gender refers to how they *act* as a male or female, how masculine or feminine they are. In our society there are said to be sex-role stereotypes. Sex-role stereotypes state the behaviour that is believed to be appropriate for our sex or gender. Traditional stereotypes such as 'big boys don't cry' or 'girls are not good at maths' can limit

Figure 3.3 Recognising uncharacteristic behaviour

the emotional and academic development of pupils. As a TA your role is to discourage stereotypes that limit the development of pupils.

- **Culture** – Culture refers to the learned and shared behaviour of members of a society. Those individuals belonging to the same culture would have similar attitudes, values and beliefs. Sub-culture refers to those groups, who, though sharing many aspects of the mainstream culture, would have distinctive beliefs and values, for example, New Age Travellers. Ethnocentrism refers to the tendency of judging and evaluating another culture in terms of our own.

    Today the UK is said to be a culturally diverse society. As a TA your role is to promote mutual respect between various cultures and sub-cultures.

Stereotypical assumptions about pupils' behaviour relative to gender, cultural background and disability, and how these can limit pupils' development

When we make assumptions about what a pupil can or cannot do on the basis of gender, cultural background or disability we are setting limits on their behaviour both now and in the future. When a child hears what others say and internalises the belief, that is, believes it to be true, then the child is setting limits on what they can do. As a TA it is important to challenge assumptions and stereotypes and encourage the pupil to reach their potential and follow their dreams.

How the home and family circumstances and care history of pupils with whom you work may affect behaviour and how to use this information appropriately to anticipate and deal effectively with difficult situations

Knowing the background of pupils can help you understand why a pupil behaves in the way they do and hopefully help you to anticipate difficult situations.

Consider:

> You are accompanying Year 6 pupils back from a leavers' assembly. At the assembly many of the parents present were emotional and tearful regarding this important transition for their sons and daughters. Joel had noticed Malcolm's mother and others crying. Joel remarked: 'Your mother is a f***** loser!' At that point Malcolm pushed Joel and Joel retaliated by punching Malcolm in the face.

As a TA you had access to confidential information. You knew that:

- although Joel had previously been in short-term foster care he was now back with his mum;
- Joel, however, remained on the child protection register;
- Joel's dad was currently in prison;
- for all his time in the school Joel's parents had never attended an assembly, sports day, school fete or parents evening.

Self-assessment questions

1   Knowing this background information could you have prevented the argument between Joel and Malcolm?
2   Knowing this background information how would you deal with this situation?

Strategies – making it happen

The importance of modelling the behaviour you want to see and how to do this

As you go about your job you can demonstrate the behaviours you would like to see the pupils exhibit. For example:

- always saying please and thank you;
- talking to all pupils and staff in a calm and respectful manner;
- contributing to a lesson in a manner that has been established in the classroom code of conduct. For example, one TA reported: The teacher and I have an agreement. When I want to contribute to the lesson I sit up straight and put my hand in the air (as the pupils should do). The teacher then says: 'I see Miss Jones is sitting quietly with her hand up. Miss Jones – what would you like to say.'

Remember actions speak louder than words!

Figure 3.4 TAs beware: pupils will imitate your behaviour

The importance of recognising and rewarding positive behaviour and how to do this

Disruptive behaviour needs to be dealt with. However, the most effective way of dealing with disruptive or inappropriate behaviour is by encouraging and rewarding positive behaviour.

How to give praise

- Praise can be verbal. Praise can involve giving out a sticker or a house point. Praise can involve informing the teacher of pupil achievements. This allows the teacher the opportunity to praise the pupil. Praise can involve writing glowing comments in their homework or reading diaries. To be effective praise needs to be genuine. Praise also needs to be specific; that is, you need to tell the pupil what they did that was good. It has been said that those of us in the teaching profession do not praise pupils as much as we think we do. To determine how much you praise – make a note of how much praise you give during a day.
- Give praise in a suitable format for the pupils you work with. With older pupils a simple thumbs-up sign is often effective. One secondary TA remarked that she used 'walk-by-praise'. As she encountered a pupil she had worked with in the corridor she would remark in passing: 'Great work in class'. The TA said that she found this an effective way of giving praise to pupils who would find such praise hard to accept in a classroom situation.
- Another approach that is effective with pupils who find praise difficult to accept is crediting. With crediting you are not using congratulatory phrases such as: 'well done' or 'great' – you are simply stating what they have done. For example: 'Yes, that is the correct answer.'
- Make sure the task set is achievable. If the child achieves, it is easy to give praise. If, however, you feel that the work set is too much for the pupil then you will need to discuss this with the teacher. Sometimes you might be able to adapt or modify

Figure 3.5 Ahmed, I see you have been good today

the task so the pupil can achieve the work. If a pupil feels that they cannot do the work then the temptation for the pupil is to act up so that they do not have to do the work.

- Praising effort is important. Praising effort increases the motivation to continue working at difficult problems. It is not whether the pupil gets the question right or not that is important, it is the effort that they put into their work.

The importance of giving praise

- Praise gives pupils a feel good factor. Praise raises self-esteem.
- Praise is a powerful reward. Praise encourages the pupil to repeat the behaviour.
- Praise motivates a pupil to work.
- When you praise a pupil, other pupils might imitate the behaviour so they too can be praised.

The agreed strategies for managing pupils' negative or inappropriate behaviour

Be consistent – know and use your classroom discipline plan

Both staff and pupils need to know the rules. Rules need to be applied consistently. Here it is important to have a classroom discipline plan. What I mean is that you know what the rules are, the types of praise you can use and importantly the type and sequence of sanctions you can use. For example, the first time a pupil acts inappropriately you might remind them of the rules. What happens if they still misbehave? Perhaps the next stage is to give them choices and to state the consequence. For example: 'If you don't sit in your seat and do your work, I will need to talk to the teacher.' What if they say: 'No – you can't make me'? A classroom plan will tell you what you should do next. This could be to report the matter to the teacher. Or perhaps as a TA you have the authority to tell the pupil that they will miss break. With a classroom discipline plan you do not have to make choices on the spot regarding how to respond.

Encourage pupils to remember the rules

Remind pupils of the rules and expectations of behaviour before they begin an activity. If you notice a pupil misbehaving remind them of the rule or better still ask them to think about what they are doing. For example, ask the pupil: 'What are you doing? What should you be doing?'

Encourage pupils to think about their behaviour

Consider the following discussion where a TA helps a student to reflect on why he has been given a detention.

Oliver: Miss, it's so unfair – Sir gave me a detention.
TA: Are you saying you didn't deserve it?

Oliver: No!
TA: What were you doing?
Oliver: I was just wandering around.
TA: You weren't sitting in your seat.
Oliver: I didn't like where he told me to sit and if he thought I was going to sit next to . . .
TA: So, Oliver, you refused to do what the teacher asked?
Oliver: Well – yeah.
TA: Do we have rules in the school about remaining in your seat and doing what the teacher asks you? Do we have rules about what happens when you don't do as you are told? Could the teacher teach if everyone was wandering around the class?
Oliver: I see what you mean, Miss.

Encourage pupils to think about choices and consequences

For example, if you are faced with a secondary pupil who is becoming rude to other pupils, then you will need to remind the pupil of the expected behaviour in the class and the consequences, that is, a detention or being put on report for not behaving appropriately. Once you have informed the pupil about what happens if they do not do what they are told, then you tell them that it is their choice. This approach also encourages pupils to think about their behaviour.

If a reprimand is necessary – think about how you are going to give the reprimand

Sometimes it is helpful to ask the pupil to step outside or to come to the back of the classroom for a quiet chat. Important discussions are often best said in private. Giving a pupil a reprimand, or a telling off, in front of other classmates can sometimes backfire, as the pupil may feel under pressure to play to the audience.

In giving a reprimand it is important to consider the language you are using. You need to separate the behaviour from the person. Telling a pupil that they are 'naughty', 'that they will never amount to much' is not helpful, in fact it is counter productive in that the pupil can come to believe this of themselves and start acting accordingly. So if you observe a child snatching a ruler – rather than saying 'You are naughty', you could say: 'We have a rule for sharing in this classroom and I expect you to follow that rule.'

Remember, all pupils need to feel valued. All pupils need to be treated with dignity and respect.

Be pro-active

Another approach to managing negative behaviour is to take steps to avoid the negative behaviour in the first place. As you spend time in a class you will begin to really know the pupils you are working with. Try to find out the reason for the behaviour. Is acting out a way to avoid failure? Is playing up a result of being bored? Has the learner been set a task that is suitably challenging?

If you know that a certain pupil always arrives in class without their equipment and is always told off for this, perhaps you can find a way to make sure that they do arrive with the right equipment.

Ask for support

Promoting positive behaviour and dealing with negative behaviour requires teamwork! As a TA you have your role to play, but part of your role is to know when to ask for help and what incidents need to be brought to the attention of the teacher or head teacher. There is no such creature as the perfect TA or for that matter the perfect teacher. All staff, no matter how experienced, will need advice and support.

Agreed strategies for managing and meeting the additional needs of any pupils with behavioural difficulties

Behaviour Support Plans

Pupils who have specific issues related to behaviour may have a Behaviour Support Plan or behavioural targets written on an IEP. Below there is an example of a behaviour plan. Simply, a behaviour plan states the goal or target, in terms of desired behaviour the pupil should be working towards. In the example the target was to reduce 'running out of classroom behaviour'. In order to meet the target certain *strategies* are put into place and then after a certain time all those concerned meet to discuss whether the strategies have been successful and the targets have been met.

ANYWHERE PRIMARY BEHAVIOUR PLAN

Name	J.S.		
Area of concern	Running out of classroom		
Year group	1		
Class teacher	L.S.	Support began	Oct 2007
Support by	M.A.	Review date	Jan 2008

Targets to be achieved	To reduce running out of the classroom behaviour by 50 per cent
Achievement criteria	Five incidents a week (down from ten incidents) over a period of three weeks
Possible resources or techniques	Use of Special Box of rewards for remaining in class
Possible class strategies	Remind him of appropriate behaviour Reward him for appropriate behaviour
Ideas for Teaching Assistant	In quiet time, alone talk about appropriate behaviour Keep records
Outcome	Met achievement criteria

Activity

1 Think of a pupil who you work with who has behavioural targets written on either a Behaviour Support Plan or an IEP. List these targets.
2 For each target there should be strategies that will tell you how to deal with the pupils. For one target, list the strategies you might use.
3 How are these strategies different from the strategies that you use with other pupils?
4 How do you record the progress of this pupil? Is this different from other pupils who don't have behaviour plans?

The key to having a behaviour plan is devising suitable targets. According to current terminology these targets need to be SMART, that is, targets need to be:

Specific	They are a precise description of a behaviour you can observe. After reading the target you should fully understand what it is that the pupil is working towards.
Measurable	Targets take into account the number of times a behaviour occurs (frequency) and how long the behaviour goes on (duration).
Achievable	Targets set in the behaviour plan should be achievable for the pupil.
Relevant	Targets need to be related to the specific needs of the pupil.
Time-limited	A realistic time is given for the pupil to achieve the target.

As a TA you need to know:

• the behaviour targets of any pupils you are working with;
• the strategies to use with these pupils to help them meet their targets;
• who to talk to regarding the pupil's progress.

The performance indicators included within any Behaviour Support Plans for pupils with whom you work, and the implications of these for how you work with the pupil(s) concerned

Working with a pupil who has a Behaviour Support Plan means that there are specified strategies and measures of monitoring progress that you are required to follow. A template for a Behaviour Support Plan can be found on p. 272.

When things don't go to plan

How to assess and manage risks to your own and others' safety when dealing with challenging behaviour

Extremely challenging and aggressive behaviour from some pupils can pose a risk to other pupils and staff members. As a TA it is important to know what to do if challenging behaviour occurs. For example, what do you do if two pupils are fighting?

What do you do if these are secondary pupils and they are considerably bigger than you? What do you do if a pupil picks up a chair and threatens to throw it at the other pupils?

- In the first place it is important to know your school's policy in regard to extreme behaviour and reasonable physical restraint.
- Remember you are part of a team. In extreme situations there are procedures to follow. Schools will often have a procedure where you can call for assistance if needed. As a TA you need to know this procedure.
- Preventive measures are always best! If you have been working with a pupil who has extremely challenging behaviour you may be able to pick up on the warning signs such as a change in their body language. A noisy pupil may all of a sudden become quiet; a quiet pupil may become noisy. The pupil's face may redden; they may clench their fists. The key is to intervene early and remove them to a quiet place where they can calm down.
- If a pupil is very aggressive the advice is to ensure the other pupils' safety and your own, by moving out of harm's way. In terms of reacting to the pupil displaying the challenging behaviour remain calm and talk in a soothing voice.

The triggers for inappropriate behavioural responses from pupils with whom you work, and actions you can take to pre-empt, divert or defuse potential flash points

In order to effectively deal with major incidents of inappropriate behaviour it is helpful to understand the process.

The assault cycle (Breakwell 1997)

Trigger stage At this point something happens to ignite a person's fuse. As a TA you might notice this pupil becoming tense. If you are very knowledgeable of the pupil you may be able to identify what triggers their anger and intervene at this point.

Escalation stage At this stage an individual is preparing for flight or fight. There will be an increase in tension, though how an individual experiences this tension will vary from individual to individual.

Crisis stage At this point the individual explodes and is unable to make rational judgements, engage in a rational dialogue or demonstrate empathy or concern for others involved. Here you need to be concerned with the safety of the individual and other pupils. Following set procedures and working with other team members is crucial at this point.

Plateau or recovery Following the outburst the individual's anger begins to subside. The individual is still aroused and is likely to feel vulnerable and confused. Careful handling is needed to prevent further aggression.

Post-crisis depression stage   Here the pupil needs to rest and recover. The ability to think and listen returns. The pupil might feel unhappy or guilty about what has occurred. Again, careful handling is needed if calm is to be maintained.

Obviously, to avoid the 'assault cycle', the time to intervene is at the earlier stages (trigger and escalation stages). Extreme challenging behaviour is not inevitable if triggers or incidents that ignite the fuse are known, avoided if possible and strategies for handling situations are discussed and practised.

In order to intervene early it is necessary to know how to divert or defuse potential flashpoints. Some strategies that might be helpful include:

- distraction
- relocation
- change of activity
- reflection of feelings
- using humour
- offering choices.

It is important to act calmly even if you do not feel it. The difficulty is knowing what strategy to use. Talk to others about what strategies they have found to be effective.

The assault cycle talks about pupils moving through stages. However, there are some pupils who will go from a state of calm to extreme violence in a matter of seconds. Expert advice will need to be sought in order to work with such pupils.

Repair and rebuild strategies

On a final note, goodwill needs to be re-established. The individual needs to be helped to explore and understand their behaviour and find more positive and adaptive ways of dealing with anger and frustration. It is important that the individual realises that, though their behaviour was inappropriate, they are still seen to have potential and value by those working with them.

Specialist advice available

The specialist advice on behaviour management that is available within the school and how to access this if needed

Managing behaviour in a school calls for teamwork. If you are having difficulty dealing with a pupil then the first person to see is the classroom teacher. The classroom teacher will gain support and advice from the SENCO. In some instances the school will call on advice from outside support agencies. These agencies include:

- *The Behaviour Support Team*, which will be involved with schools and work with teachers to support pupils who have particular difficulties in behaviour.
- *The Looked after Children's Team*, which will provide support to children who are in children's homes or foster care. This team will work with the school to implement a Personal Educational Plan that is designed to raise educational standards for these 'at risk' children.

- *The Support Team for Ethnic Minority Pupils* aims to offer support to schools in regard to working with pupils from ethnic minority backgrounds, supporting bilingual learners, offering guidance on the needs of refugees and asylum seekers and welcoming new arrivals. The support could be in the form of offering practical advice on how pupils can be supported in learning English as an additional language.
- *The Traveller Education Support Service* aims to raise awareness and encourage understanding of the social and cultural traditions of this group.
- *The Education Welfare Service* monitors and promotes regular school attendance. This service will deal with pupils who have problems with attendance.
- *The Educational Psychology Service* where **educational psychologists** use knowledge of educational and psychological theory to advise and support schools in dealing with the specific concerns of pupils.

REVIEWING AND REFLECTING

School arrangements for reviewing behaviour including bullying, attendance and the effective use of rewards and sanctions

Pupil councils

Encouraging pupil voice is very important in schools. Often schools will appoint a member of staff to co-ordinate and foster the development of pupil councils. Pupil councils are composed of pupils who are representative of the larger school body. The council will be asked for their views on aspects of learning, behaviour policies and sometimes the appointment of new staff. The council's views will be fed back to the Senior Management Team and will inform their decisions.

Class reviews

As mentioned previously, classroom codes of conduct are formulated at the beginning of each school year.

Whole school questionnaires

These surveys are becoming more and more frequent in schools. These surveys usually consist of questions such as those shown in the Behaviour Questionnaire (see the box on the facing page).

In some schools everyone, including all staff members, pupils and parents are asked to fill in such questionnaires. Although there are problems with such questionnaires, for example, what one person sees as acceptable or OK behaviour may not be the same as the next, they are useful in that they can highlight issues that the school needs to address.

Whole-school policy reviews

Schools will set aside INSET days to review policies on behaviour. Feedback from pupil councils, analysis of attendance records, and wholeschool questionnaires will inform

BEHAVIOUR QUESTIONNAIRE

On a scale of 1–5 with 1= very poor, 2 = poor, 3 = ok, 4 = good and 5 = very good, how would you rate behaviour in the following.

(PLEASE CIRCLE WHAT YOU FEEL IS THE APPROPRIATE ANSWER)

Classroom	1	2	3	4	5
Playground	1	2	3	4	5
Corridors	1	2	3	4	5
Toilets	1	2	3	4	5

Do you have any comments you would like to make in regard to behaviour in the school and how this could be improved?

these reviews. In addition, some schools will have guest speakers come to discuss approaches and strategies to behaviour management. Behaviour management is an ongoing process.

School procedures for collecting data on pupils' attendance and behaviour, including the use of rewards and sanctions and tracking pupil progress, and your role and responsibilities in relation to this

Schools will collect a range of data on attendance and behaviour. An analysis of such data can highlight issues to which the school needs to respond, such as high numbers of unauthorised absences or an increase in exclusions. On an individual level such data can reveal concerns, progress and achievements. Teaching Assistants have a role to play in collecting this data.

Pupils' attendance

Registers will be kept and unauthorised absences noted. If unauthorised absences are an issue the Education Welfare Officer (EWO) will become involved. EWOs will often work with pupils who are school refusers. Part of your role might be to fill in the class register and you may be involved in helping pupils with a history of non-school attendance readjust to the school environment.

Recording sanctions

Schools will have various means of recording sanctions. Many schools will have a graduated approach to sanctions, such that pupils can be tracked according to sanctions administered both in terms of level of sanction and frequency of sanction. Some pupils will have behaviour targets on IEPs or behaviour plans that will be monitored and reviewed. Often, for serious episodes of inappropriate behaviour a school might require a behaviour incident form to be filled in. Perhaps you might be involved in filling out incident report forms or helping pupils to review their behaviour targets.

Recording rewards

As it is important to record sanctions, so it is also important to record which pupils are receiving rewards. Rewards needed to be fairly distributed to all pupils. What a school does not want is for the naturally well-behaved pupils to feel that their efforts are not recognised or rewarded.

Consider the following pupil comment:

> 'It's not fair – the teachers bend over backwards for the really disruptive pupils – they get away with murder and when they make an attempt to behave they get merits and if they go all term with only a limited amount of detentions they get to go to Westdown Adventure Centre for the day. I always behave, I always hand my work in on time – I always get good grades – but I don't receive merits and I never get to go to the adventure centre.'

Self-assessment question

I   Does your school have a system to track rewards and merits given to pupils?

Tracking pupil progress

To track progress in regard to behaviour, evidence needs to be collected. One type of evidence-gathering a TA may be involved in is a structured observation (see Figure 3.6 on facing page).

Figure 3.6 describes a TA recording a pupil's behaviour. In some ways it seems counter-productive to watch a pupil picking fluff and throwing it at other pupils. However, in order to change behaviour you first need an objective record of what the behaviour was to begin with. This initial record of behaviour is referred to as baseline data.

Once interventions and strategies are implemented behaviour can be assessed again to monitor progress. When recording behaviour it is also important to note the consequences of the behaviour. This brings us to the next type of observation where a TA is asked to record antecedents (triggers), behaviour and consequences. The analysis of such an observation record can give clues as to why the pupil is behaving in such a way.

Time	Written description of activity	Code
9.00–9.10	Sitting on carpet, picking fluff from carpet and throwing fluff at others	2 6
9.10–9.15	Supposed to be sitting at table – wandering around	4

CODE
1 = on task
2 = fidgeting
3 = talking inappropriately
4 = out of seat behaviour
5 = making inappropriate noises
6 = behaving inappropriately to others

Figure 3.6 Structured fixed interval observation

Time	Antecedent (trigger)	Behaviour	Consequence
10.00–10.15	Chris sitting with group	working on maths worksheet	
10.15–	John walks by and looks at Chris	Chris jumps up and pushes John over	Teacher intervenes and sends Chris out of the room

Figure 3.7 ABC observation

What can we make of this interaction?

1   There certainly is a dynamic between John and Chris that needs to be looked at.
2   Although Chris was working on task for 15 minutes there was no positive reinforcement for that behaviour. Possibly, what Chris will remember from the lesson is being sent out.

Standardised observation records

Perhaps as a TA you have seen teachers using the Connors' Teacher Rating Scale (Conners *et al.* 1998). Usually this index is used in the process of diagnosing ADHD. However, it can also be used effectively to systematically compare a pupil's behaviour across different classroom environments. This is particularly useful in secondary schools where pupils might behave better in certain classes.

How to support pupils in using peer assessment to promote their learning and behaviour

In much of what we have talked about in regard to behaviour policies, the role of the teacher and the TA is central. The role of the teacher and the TA is to remind pupils of appropriate behaviour and apply rewards and sanctions where necessary. The limitation with this approach is that a pupil could learn to behave well only when a TA or teacher is present. However, what we really want is to have the pupil internalise codes of behaviour, that is, to have pupils behave out of an inner sense of what is right and wrong. To encourage this, thinking skills need to be developed. Peer assessment involves pupils making judgements on standards of behaviour, rewards and sanctions. As discussed previously, this can happen in the classroom through pupils being involved in the establishment of codes of conduct. In addition, many schools are now involved in peer-mediation schemes.

Case study: Peer mediation in my school

In talking about peer mediation the first thing to say is that peer mediation is a whole-school initiative. As a school we had many training days devoted to this. In our school pupils were asked to apply for the position of peer mediators. Pupils were then selected and trained. The peer mediators were given special baseball caps and T-shirts. We had school assemblies that explained the process. Basically the scheme worked as follows:

Setting the ground rules
1 Conflict is acknowledged and brought to the attention of the peer mediator. To go forward through the mediation process both parties have to agree that they want to resolve the conflict. They have to agree that they want to solve the problem, be as honest as they can, to listen to each other and not interrupt.

Hearing the story – defining the problem
2 Once the ground rules have been established each person tells their story and how they feel and what they want.

Looking for solutions
3 This involves the peer mediator asking each party what they can do to solve the problem. The possible solution is discussed in terms of fairness and if each of the parties agrees the problem is resolved. The pupils involved are congratulated and asked what they would do differently next time and the peer mediator fills in an appropriate record form.

This is how it works at our school. Does it actually work? It really depends on the willingness of pupils to participate.

However, as a TA I find that I, too, can use the strategies used in this approach to deal with arguments between pupils. For example:

1   I ask the pupils together if they want to resolve the issue;
2   I have the pupils listen to each other's side or version without interruption;
3   I ask the pupils what they can do to solve the problem.

Supporting pupils in using self-assessment to promote their learning and behaviour

Self assessment involves *self-monitoring*, *self-evaluation* and *self-reinforcement*.

*   *Self-monitoring* involves the pupils observing and objectively recording their own behaviour. The key word here is objective. Objective implies that the observation is honest and realistic. To begin with, pupils may need help to achieve this. One strategy could be to have the pupils evaluate their own task behaviour when a bell rings. The pupils need to ask themselves, 'What was I doing for the last ten minutes?' The TA who has been observing the pupil's behaviour can help the pupil to reflect on their behaviour in an honest and objective manner.
*   *Self-evaluation* involves the pupil comparing performance against an agreed standard. It is important that the pupil has been involved in setting this standard.
*   *Self-reinforcement* involves the pupil giving themselves a reward if they have achieved the agreed standard.

How to support pupils with behavioural difficulties to identify and agree behaviour targets

As a point of principle pupils should be involved in setting behaviour targets for IEPs and behaviour support plans. Perhaps as a TA you are involved in such meetings. As a TA you can help pupils to:

*   negotiate targets;
*   reward pupils when they have reached their targets;
*   reassure pupils if/and when set-backs occur.

It is important to remember that even the smallest improvements can motivate a pupil. Of course a key skill for a TA to develop is to learn how to negotiate targets. This brings us to the next section.

How to encourage and support pupils to review their own behaviour, including attendance, and the impact of this on themselves, their learning and achievement, on others and on their environment

Again, the development of thinking skills is essential. One way forward would be to present the pupil with a scale (from 1–5) in relation to punctuality, attendance or movement in class and ask the pupil to rate their behaviour.

Reviewing the scale

For this approach to work the pupil needs to look at each point in the scale and discuss how this scale can be applied to their behaviour. As a TA, you can help the pupil to review their behaviour.

Consider the following case study:

Case study

I sat down with Ahmed and discussed his movement in class, in particular his out of seat behaviour. After discussion the figures in the section below are what we came up with.

Ahmed agreed that at present he was at number 1 in the scale; that is never in his seat, and by the end of the term he aimed to be in his seat for at least 50 per cent of the time.

Movement in class

1	Never in seat Wandering around the room Sitting on others' desks Jumping over desks
2	25 per cent of time sitting on chair
3	50 per cent of time sitting on own chair
4	75 per cent of time sitting on own chair
5	Sitting on chair throughout entire lesson

Negotiation

Here the TA needs to discuss with the pupil where they are and where they would like to be. It is helpful to set a time frame for improvements. It is also important to discuss what strategies the pupil can use to help them achieve their target. In reference to what we were discussing earlier it is also helpful to talk about how they can monitor, evaluate and reward their own behaviour.

One therapy that has applications for reviewing behaviour is entitled *Choice Therapy* (Glasser 1998). It involves helping the pupils to:

- Identify what they really want.
- Identify what they are actually doing.
- Evaluate whether what they are doing is helping or hurting.
- Plan and commit to what they should be doing.

Self-assessment question

Look at the Case study below. Assuming Max is motivated to change how would you:

1 Review his present behaviour?
2 Negotiate targets?
3 Set in place self-assessment (self-monitoring, self-evaluation and self-reward) strategies?

Case study

TA: How would you describe your behaviour in class now?
Max: It's not fair I always have detentions.
TA: Why do you think you have detentions?
Max: Ok. I talk a lot in class. Ok I talk when the teacher is talking.
TA: Do you want things to change?
Max: Yeah.

Checklist

✔ Be familiar with school policies regarding behaviour.
✔ Encourage pupils to remember the rules.
✔ Encourage pupils to think about how their behaviour affects other pupils.
✔ Encourage pupils to think about choices and consequences.
✔ If a reprimand is necessary – think about how you are going to give the reprimand.
✔ Know the behaviour targets of any students you are working with.
✔ Praise students.
✔ Remember managing behaviour involves teamwork.

GATHERING EVIDENCE

 ### Setting the scene

At the start of the day Mrs Goldbottom reviews the class behaviour strategies with Miranda – the teacher states that there are a few pupils in this class who can be challenging. At home that evening before writing up the session as a personal account, Miranda reviews *some* of the performance indicators she should cover.

Writing personal accounts: collecting evidence

PERSONAL ACCOUNT

Date: **25 January**
Activity: **Year 3 class participating in a numeracy session**

Who was involved: **I was working with a small group of pupils: Sharon, Michael, Kylie, David, Jason and Sinead. This group struggles with numeracy.**

What happened?

Before the numeracy session commenced I had a quick chat with the teacher regarding the lesson objectives and about Sharon. Sharon has been having difficulties in getting on with the other children in the class. The teacher and I talked about these difficulties and the teacher talked about ways of working with Sharon. Sharon needs to be reminded of the class rules and praised when she keeps to the rules. We also reviewed class strategies regarding behaviour for groups.

Mrs G in the session talked about different ways that you can add up. When the class divided for group work I was working with the yellow group. The group had to divide into pairs and each had a set of dice. They had to throw the dice and write the numbers down. Then they had to add the numbers together.

- *Apply agreed behaviour management strategies fairly and consistently*

- *Provide praise and encouragement to pupils to recognise and promote positive pupils' behaviour*

I began the group by reminding the pupils of expected behaviour, that they had to do their work, take turns rolling the dice and to listen to what each other said. For the first five minutes all the children were working well and I told them about how impressed I was with their behaviour.

Well, shortly after that Sharon grabbed David's pencil and would not give it back.

- *Use appropriate strategies to minimise disruption through inappropriate behaviour*

- *Provided praise and encouragement*

I reminded Sharon that one of the class rules was to share equipment and that I expected her to follow this. I asked her what she should do. Sharon gave the pencil back and said sorry. I praised her for this.

A few minutes later David complained that Sharon was not letting him have a turn at throwing the dice. I again reminded Sharon of the class rules. Sharon gave David the dice, but then Sharon grabbed the dice from the other group. I asked Sharon what she thought she was doing. Sharon said that she did not have to listen to me and that she didn't want to do the work anyway.

- *Applied agreed behaviour management strategies fairly and consistently*

Well, I had reminded Sharon about appropriate behaviour twice before but these reminders did not seem to work. The fact that Sharon was rude to me was the last straw. I reported the behaviour to the teacher.

Mrs Goldbottom told Sharon that her behaviour was out of order and that she would not be going out to break. Sharon apologised to me for being rude.

Evaluation

I think I was right to inform the teacher regarding Sharon's behaviour. To begin with, Sharon was working – but then her behaviour fell apart. Thinking about it I realised that she started being disruptive when we started to use the dice with the larger numbers. Perhaps Sharon was finding the work too difficult and felt that she needed to play up to get out of doing the work. I mentioned this to Mrs G.

I certify that this is a true statement of what occurred.

Teacher signature	Name (printed and role)
R. Goldbottom	Rosaline Goldbottom, Yr. 3 Class

Comments

I was aware of the problems Miranda was having with the Yellow Group. Miranda used a number of strategies that we had talked about. Miranda acted appropriately in this situation by informing me of Sharon's consistent misbehaviour. Miranda's observation of perhaps Sharon having difficulty with the larger numbers was a valid one and in future perhaps Miranda can suggest that they work through the difficult sums together.

Miranda when handing in this evidence includes a short note to her assessor, Terrie.

Dear Terrie

I am pleased with what I have written and with the teacher's comments. I am a bit concerned with how I am going to meet all the other indicators. I know I am going to have problems with 'Recognise and respond appropriately to risks to yourself/and/or others during episodes of challenging behaviour.'

I work in a primary school and on the whole the children are very good. Nothing ever dramatic happens – nothing like what the girls from the secondary school behaviour unit talk about.

xxx   Miranda

ASSESSOR'S COMMENTS

Miranda

This personal account is very good evidence. The way you structured your account using performance indicators as headings was very helpful.

Remember that NVQs are designed to adapt to the varying teaching environments that TAs work in.

What is challenging behaviour really depends on the pupils you work with.

What is challenging behaviour in a primary school will not necessarily be the same as challenging behaviour in a secondary school. However, saying that, it is important to know the school policies in regarding handling very serious incidents of challenging behaviour – should anything like that ever happen.

Also, remember that there are other ways of gathering evidence for this unit; witness statements, case studies and incident report forms.

Signed: **Terrie Cole**, NVQ Assessor

Miranda later hands in the following evidence:

Case study: Encourage and support pupils to regularly review their own behaviour, attitude and achievements

I have been working with J for two years now. J has a behaviour plan. One of the difficulties J has is with running out of the classroom and refusing to come back into the classroom after break. Initially the strategy was to remind J at the beginning of the day of the need to stay in the class. It was suggested that J had a special box of rewards. In this box were special activities and games he had chosen. If he behaves well then at the end of the day he can spend 15 minutes with me playing his special games. However, this strategy stopped working about two months ago. At that point it was suggested that the school use a 'video self-modelling technique'. This involved making a video of J behaving well. The video showed:

- J sitting at his desk working quietly.
- J playing nicely with his friends at break.
- J coming in after break when asked to.
- J working well.
- J coming back after lunch break when asked.

At the end of the day there is a clip of the Teacher saying: 'Well done J. You have behaved well, stayed in class and come in from break when asked and now you get to spend time with Mrs A on an activity of your choice.'

At the end of the video there is a lovely picture of J and a voice over of the whole class saying: 'Well Done, J' with lots of clapping.

Each morning I spend time with J talking about his behaviour. I ask him what happens when he comes in after break when he is asked to. He says he gets to choose a favourite activity. I ask him what happens when he doesn't come in after break time. I ask him what happens when he runs out of the class. He says he is sad. We then watch the video together and I praise J for his behaviour on the video. J then says he is going to behave. So far, this strategy seems to be working.

TEACHER'S COMMENT

Miranda has worked very hard at developing a positive relationship with J and her work with him has helped him to accept classroom boundaries.

R. Goldbottom, Class Teacher, 27 March

ASSESSOR'S COMMENTS

Miranda

This is good hard evidence.

Your account of helping J to review his own behaviour through watching 'his video' is impressive. However, if you include some more details regarding your discussions with J you may find that you can meet other performance indicators in this unit. For example:

- *Encourage and support pupils to consider the impact of their behaviour on others, themselves and the environment*

You could ask J what he thinks the teacher and other pupils think of him when he refuses to come in or runs out of class.

And

- *Support pupils with behaviour difficulties to identify and agree on ways in which they might change or manage their behaviour to achieve the desired outcome*

Here you might ask J if there are any strategies or things he can do to stop himself from running out of class or refusing to come in.

Signed: **Terrie Cole**, NVQ Assessor

Nicola, our secondary TA, also hands in evidence to the assessor:

INCIDENT REPORT FORM

Staff report of incident

Staff	**Nicola Wilson**
Time	**12.30 p.m.**
Date	**13 Oct**
Place	**Playing fields**
Pupil(s) names	**B.F and N.W.**

Brief description of incident

As I was walking through the field from Upper School to Lower School at lunch time I noticed NW (8b). NW was with a group of lads from year nine. NW looked upset – so I casually went over and asked if everything was all right. As I did, BF (9c) swore at NW and tried to push him over. I stood between the boys and said that was enough. The other lads started shouting 'Fight Fight' and a crowd soon gathered. BF was right in my face – screaming and he pushed me over. I picked myself up. I was shaken up – but not hurt. Miss Taylor (Head of Year 9) appeared at that time and everyone quickly disappeared. Miss Taylor asked me to write down what had happened.

Action

I reported the matter verbally to Miss Taylor and wrote up the incident.

Head of Year Action

Copy of report sent to Mr Dean, Head of the Behaviour Unit.

Meetings scheduled with both boys.

Signed: _____   Signed: _____

Nicola Wilson (TA)   **Tessy Taylor** (HoY)

After Terrie, the assessor, had read the incident report form he asked Nicola if they could have a quick chat about what had happened. She recorded her questions and Nicola's answers.

RECORD OF QUESTIONS

Date: **2 November**
Candidate: **Nicola Wilson**

Question: Why did you write up the incident?

Answer: It is school policy – that all incidents of a serious nature are recorded. It was just as well – I wrote what had happened and Miss Taylor collected other written reports from pupils involved as BF had gone home and told his parents that I had pushed him! Without the written reports and other witness reports I would have been in serious trouble! This just shows how important it is to follow school policies.

Question: What is the correct procedure for dealing with fights?

Answer: I know that in terms of controlling and restraining pupils the policy in my school states that staff can if necessary stand between pupils or block their path. We had specific training about what we should do under such circumstances and I am really glad that I had this training.

Signed: **Terrie Cole**, NVQ Assessor

Terrie commented that Nicola had handled a very difficult situation well and through her answers to the questions had demonstrated understanding of relevant underpinning knowledge in regard to behaviour policies.

Chapter 4

Develop and promote positive relationships

In this chapter we will look at four elements:

1 Develop relationships with children.
2 Communicate with children.
3 Support children in developing relationships.
4 Communicate with adults.

KNOWLEDGE AND UNDERSTANDING

The importance of good working relationships in the setting

Good working relationships are essential to the effective running of a school. Working relationships concern how staff relate to:

- each other;
- pupils in their care;
- the wider community, to include pupils' parents and guardians.

When staff work well together a secure atmosphere is provided where pupils can flourish both academically and socially. Effective staff relationships provide the pupils with role models regarding how adults communicate.

Staff members, through effective relationships with pupils, can communicate to pupils their high expectations in regard to behaviour. When staff members have an open, supportive relationship with parents, parents are more likely to share concerns with staff, to get involved with the school and be supportive of what the school is trying to achieve.

All this sounds wonderful – but working in a school it is important to work towards a match between the rhetoric (what is formally written in mission statements and school charters) and reality (what actually happens in the school). To achieve good working relationships it is often the small everyday actions that make all the difference.

For example:

> *TA*: I feel it is important to get to know the pupils I support. I try to find out what their interests are. Often I find that I can use their personal interests, be it, trains, hoovers or ultimate frisbee to support their learning. Once I designed a maths worksheet around hoovers. The fact that I will talk to them about what they find interesting is my way of showing that I am interested in them as individuals.

> *TA*: Sometimes in the course of my job I will need to phone parents. Whenever I make a phone call to parents I always check the contact form to ensure that I am using the preferred name and mode of address. Some parents prefer to be called by their title and surname while others prefer you to address them by their first name.

Relevant legal requirements covering the way you relate to and interact with children and young people

Relevant legal requirements covering the needs of disabled children and young people and those with special educational needs

In this textbook many legal requirements or documents are referred to:

- *Special Needs Code of Practice* (DfEE 2001)
- *Every Child Matters: Change for Children* (DfES 2004a)
- Disability Discrimination Act 2005.

(See Chapters 14 and 15 for further details.) As a TA you need to appreciate how these documents impact on your day-to-day practice.

The types of information that should be treated confidentially: who you can and cannot share this information with

At many times in this textbook we have talked about confidentiality. In terms of sharing information, information can be categorised in terms of which information is shared and with whom the information is shared. Some information is strictly confidential, other information is shared on a need to know basis and some information needs to be communicated to all staff members. (See Quiz on next page.)

For further detailed information on relevant legal requirements and procedures covering confidentiality and the disclosure of information see pp. 254–5.

The meaning of anti-discriminatory practice and how to integrate this into your relationships with children, young people and other adults

Discrimination can be defined as unfavourable treatment of an individual or group of individuals. Individuals, including pupils, can be discriminated on the basis of gender, ethnicity, sexuality, class or disability.

QUIZ

To what extent is the following information shared?

	Shared on a need to know basis Yes or No	Who needs to know and why?	Does everyone need to know?
IEP targets			
Behaviour targets			
Parent contact details			
Pupils' attainment on reading schemes			
Details of behaviour incidents			
Allergies			
Details of disclosures			
Details regarding parents' change of circumstance, e.g. parental divorce			

As a teaching professional you can integrate anti-discriminatory practice into your everyday relationships by:

- valuing diversity
- challenging stereotypes
- promoting self-esteem
- encouraging individuals to fulfil their potential
- working towards a more just and fair society.

Figure 4.1 Challenge stereotypes: my pupil's can't dance – or can they?

Self-assessment questions

1 How as a school do you celebrate diversity?
2 As a TA how do you challenge racist, sexist, homophobic and disablist name-calling? For example, how do you respond to the following:

- In the playground you overhear one pupil saying to another 'you're gay!'
- After a particularly close game in football between Germany and England, one pupil remarks that his father says that all Germans are tossers.
- You overhear in the playground a mother saying to her child that she is not to play with that child as her mother has learning disabilities.
- While trying to encourage all the pupils to be involved in making Christmas cakes, one male pupil comments that cooking is woman's work and that he and his brothers don't cook or have anything to do with cooking or cleaning at home.

How you adapt your behaviour and communication with children/young people to meet the needs of children/young people in your care of different ages, genders, ethnicities, needs and abilities

Regardless of age, gender, ethnic background, needs and abilities all pupils need to be listened to, valued and reassured. To do this TAs need to develop an awareness for what the pupil is experiencing and an empathy in relation to how the pupil feels about their world. In responding to pupils TAs need to use active listening skills (see pp. 55, 58 for further details).

Although all pupils need your attention and time – there are circumstances when your behaviour and communication needs to be adapted in line with the needs of the individual pupil.

Matching your communication to levels of understanding

In communicating with pupils it is necessary to use language that pupils can understand. Consider the following statements:

'Class, we need to ensure that everyone has equal access to the IT equipment.'

'Class, remember everyone needs to have a chance at using the computer.'

Both sentences are communicating the same message. However, it is doubtful whether reception children would understand the first statement. What is important to realise is that though we might be communicating in sentences, the individual who is hearing what we are saying may be understanding only a fraction of what is being said. It is always important to check for understanding.

Taking into account differences in learning

Some pupils will have additional needs. Often those pupils with additional needs will have IEPs that specify difficulties in learning and the strategies that need to be used to support such pupils. Some pupils will have limited short-term memories – that is, they do not easily remember instructions. With such pupils you may need to keep instructions short, repeat instructions and always check for understanding.

Being aware of the influence of an audience

As pupils develop, the opinions of their peer group become increasingly influential. When you have difficult things to say to a pupil it is best to choose a quiet moment away from earshot of other members of the class. Telling a pupil off in front of the class could mean that the pupil, as well as responding to you, is performing to the wider audience.

The development of gender roles

An issue that has been raised is the impact that sex stereotyping can have on pupils' understanding of what it is to be male and female and their subsequent choice of career. Sex stereotyping can lead to occupational segregation – for example, women becoming nurses, while men become doctors. What is important here is that pupils see that there is a choice – that they could either be a doctor or a nurse. As a TA it is important to challenge traditional sex stereotypes.

Strategies you can adopt to help children/young people to feel welcome and valued in the setting

The *Index for Inclusion* (Booth *et al.* 2000) was written to help schools reflect on how they support learning and participation for all. Within this document, a number of questions are listed that consider ways in which pupils are made welcome and valued.

Let's look at some of these questions and the role that TAs can play within the school.

Figure 4.2 All pupils have that extra factor

- Is the school welcoming to all pupils including pupils with additional needs and transient pupils such as Travellers?
- Are there positive rituals for welcoming new pupils and marking their leaving?
- Are there induction programmes for new pupils?
- Are there programmes to help assist the transition between primary and secondary schools?
- Are new pupils paired with supportive experienced pupils?
- Do new pupils know who to contact if they are experiencing difficulties?
- Do pupils offer help and assistance to each other when needed?
- Is the work of all pupils displayed within the class and the school?
- Are the achievements of all pupils equally valued?

Again, it is the small everyday actions that are important. As a TA you can make a point of getting to know all pupils you work with. It is important that as a TA you are seen as approachable. You can offer genuine praise for individual achievements. You can encourage pupils to value each other and support each other. Perhaps you are given responsibility for displaying pupils' work; the care and attention you put into these displays communicates to the individual pupils that they are valued.

What is meant by 'appropriate' and 'inappropriate' behaviour when interacting with children and young people; the policies and procedures to follow and why these are important

As a TA in a school it is essential to discuss what appropriate and inappropriate behaviour is. Issues of concern relate to touch, being alone with a pupil, disclosing personal information and seeing pupils outside of school time. These issues relate to policies regarding child protection and to what it means to work in a professional manner. (For further information see Chapter 1.)

Touch

As a TA you need to discuss with other professionals in your school what appropriate touch is in regard to the pupils you work with. Very young children like a cuddle especially if they are upset. Younger pupils may like to hold your hand in the playground. But does there come an age when this would be considered inappropriate? Can female teaching assistants engage in more demonstrative behaviour than male teaching assistants?

Being alone with a pupil

What is your school's policy regarding being alone with a pupil or groups of pupils? How would you respond to an allegation of child abuse?

Disclosing personal information and seeing pupils outside of school time

Through working with pupils we develop relationships. In such a relationship we might choose to share personal information. We might talk to the pupils about our children, our pets, our likes and dislikes. But what would you do if a pupil asked for your e-mail or phone number? What would you do if a pupil invited you to their birthday party, to meet them at a Burger Bar on a Saturday or come to the park and play with them? These issues need to be discussed within a school and lines set regarding what is professional behaviour.

The importance of encouraging children and young people to make choices for themselves and strategies to support this

The importance of involving children and young people in decision-making and strategies you can use to do this

Giving pupils choices are said to have a number of advantages. Choice is seen as empowering and can lead to a sense of self-determination. Further, daily decision-making opportunities assist both personal and academic growth. However, choices and decision-making opportunities need to be considered. Too many choices can lead to confusion and less participation. Some individual pupils may feel uncomfortable with choices and prefer to be told what to do. The first point to consider is what choices are available to the pupils you work with. The box on p. 115 presents types of choices available. What you will notice is that the examples given of choices involve small everyday interactions.

Modelling choices can be helpful

Some pupils have limited experiences of making choices. Other pupils may lack the confidence to make a choice and prefer to be told what to do. With such pupils TAs can model or show what is involved in a choice-making process (Sanacore 1999). For example, consider the choice of selecting a book to read.

TYPES OF CHOICE AVAILABLE

Choices available	For example	Examples of choices I can give pupils in my school
Where to work	The pupil may choose to work on their maths sheet at their table or they can do their work at a quiet area at the back of the class.	
What materials to use	When working on a maths sheet pupils can choose the materials or resources to support them. Some pupils might want to use number lines or they might choose to use multi-link.	
When to start to work	You have chosen your book – are you ready to start to read?	
Who to work with	In some activities – group projects – pupils can select the members of their team.	
What activity to do first	What do you want to do first – your maths work sheet or practise your spellings?	
When to finish an activity	Have you finished your painting?	
What activities you wish to do next	What do you want to do next – your spellings or work on the computer?	
The right to refuse to do an activity	Do you want to continue to play football?	
The right to choose an alternative activity	If you don't want to read this book – what do you want to do?	

(Jolivette *et al.* 2002)

Case study

Sandy – a TA in a primary school explains:

'I work with a small group of pupils who have been described as reluctant readers. When I took the group to the library to help them select a reading book I decided to show them how I selected a book to read for pleasure. I told them that first I think about what books I enjoy reading. I said: "I like to read about horses." I then picked up a book about ships and quickly looked at it saying, well, this is not about horses – I need to find another book.

'The children found this amusing. I repeated picking up the wrong book and realising that it was the wrong book for me several times to show the pupils that it takes time to choose books. Then I found a book on horses. As I picked it up I pointed out that the book had no pictures and lots of words. I said that although this book was on horses I wanted a book with words I could read and pictures. Eventually I found my book.

'Then I asked the pupils what books they liked to read. I gave them ten minutes to look for a book. I also asked them to bring back to the table not only the book that they had chosen but the books that they looked at but decided not to choose. I asked each pupil to describe how and why they chose their particular book.'

Pupils need the opportunity to learn from making the 'wrong ' choice or decision. To truly appreciate what choice involves, pupils need experience of making choices. Likewise, to appreciate the consequences of making decisions pupils need to experience the consequences of their decisions. A widely used behaviour strategy is to state choices and consequences to pupils. For example, a TA may say to a pupil: 'If you continue to disrupt the others in your group you will receive a detention – the choice is yours.' If the pupil makes the wrong choice, and continues to disrupt other pupils, then they will face the consequences. Hopefully, the pupil will learn through the process of making choices and facing consequences.

Often to make an informed choice pupils need to have an opportunity to try out a variety of activities or options. Consider a pupil who always chooses to select books on dinosaurs and states that he doesn't want to read anything else. To truly make a choice the pupil needs to have the experience of reading or being read other books on a variety of topics.

How to negotiate with children/young people according to their age and stage of development

The aim of negotiation is to come to an agreement or compromise. Negotiation skills can be seen early on in a child's development when they are involved in trying to decide what to play or who gets to play with what toy. Very young children find this difficult and will often fight over the right to play with one toy. 'It's mine – I was here first!'

A TA working in Early Years could step in and settle the disagreement for the pupils – but it is better if the TA encourages and supports pupils in finding a way to share. For example:

Sam:	It's my tractor – I got it first (hugging tractor).
Jim:	That's not fair! I never have a turn.
TA:	What have we said in class about sharing – what should we do about the tractor?
Jim:	Take turns.
Sam:	It's my turn.
TA:	All right, Sam, it is your turn first – but when will it be Jim's turn?
Sam:	Never!
TA:	What did we say about sharing?
Sam:	When I have gone around the playground five times.
Jim:	No once!
TA:	How about after two laps around the playground it is Jim's turn! All right boys?
Sam:	OK.
Jim:	OK.

Although this example of negotiation applies to pupils in the Early Years, the strategy of having the pupils talking to each other to agree a compromise applies to all year groups. However, as pupils mature, hopefully they can better understand concepts such as fairness and compromise. Your role as a TA is to help pupils develop an understanding of these concepts and help them apply these concepts to their everyday interactions.

As a TA you may be involved in supporting pupils on a one-to-one basis. With some pupils who are reluctant to work or find work challenging, negotiation can be a strategy to get the pupils involved. For example:

Belinda:	I'm not doing it!
TA:	Come on, you know we need to read this book.
Belinda:	I'm not doing it. It is too long.
TA:	How about I read some and you read some.
Belinda:	You can read it all.
TA:	Let's be fair – I will read one sentence and then you can read the next. What do you say?
Belinda:	If you start?
TA:	Right, let's begin.

Strategies you can use to show children and young people that you respect their individuality

Getting to know the pupils you work with

Part of the inclusion agenda involves celebrating diversity. All children and young people are unique. As a TA part of your role involves finding out about the pupils you work with. For example: What are their interests? What is their background? What makes them tick?

Pupils need to be encouraged in their interests and helped to feel proud about who they are.

Using differences in culture, background and language to enrich curriculum development and teaching

Differences can be used creatively to expand teaching opportunities as the following case study exemplifies:

Case study

Sheelagh explains that at her school there are now a number of Polish and Russian pupils. As a class all pupils are now learning a few basic phrases in Polish and Russian.

At morning register the class in addition to saying 'Good morning' to Mrs Spencer in English, say 'Good morning' to each other in Polish and Russian. Sheelagh states that the class enjoys learning new words and this has made the new pupils feel special, welcomed and valued.

In addition, some of the Russian and Polish parents have volunteered to come in at Christmas and talk about how Christmas is celebrated in their native countries and to help all the pupils prepare special Polish and Russian biscuits and cakes.

Encouraging respect for differences and alternative views

As a TA you can model the behaviour you would like to see in the pupils you support. Therefore it is essential that you are seen to show respect for alternative views and differences. At times this may involve challenging pupils who are not respectful, as the following case study demonstrates:

Case study

Dermot, a secondary TA, was approached by a Year 7 pupil who had just joined the school. The pupil in question was from a Traveller family. The pupil was very upset and angry as she had been called some very unpleasant names by a number of other girls in her class. Dermot replied that the behaviour of the girls was not acceptable and they would be dealt with. Dermot also told the pupil that she should be proud of her background. This was obviously a case of bullying but it also showed a lack of respect for differences in regard to lifestyle and background. Dermot confronted the girls in question. The girls did not deny what had happened and Dermot immediately took them to the Head of Year.

Why it is important to listen to children and young people

Listening communicates value

It is not only important that we listen to what pupils have to say but that we listen in such a way that pupils feel they have been listened to. When individuals feel that someone has taken the time to listen to them and has really heard what they have had to say they feel supported and valued. Active listening skills involve: making time to listen, giving your full attention to listening; and use of the appropriate body language and giving supportive feedback are important. For further information on these techniques see pp. 55, 58.

Listening allows pupils to share concerns

When pupils feel they have been listened to they are more likely to come back to that person for further support. Pupils who feel that they are listened to are likely to feel more comfortable in discussing problems they are encountering. These problems could involve difficulties with not understanding work, in relating to other pupils or staff or could involve serious matters regarding bullying or abuse. (For further information on disclosures see pp. 22–4.)

Listening gives information on pupils' thinking processes

When we listen to pupils explaining how they have solved a problem we get a glimpse of their thinking processes and the strategies they have used. If pupils are having difficulties in understanding, then knowing how they are approaching a problem can give a TA useful information necessary to help move the pupil forward.

Consider the following:

TA: What is the answer to 12×12?
Pupil: 23.
TA: How did you get that?
Pupil: 12 plus 12 = 23, no 24.
TA: Does the question ask you to add or multiply the numbers?

In terms of listening to children and young people there can arise specific challenges. For details regarding issues relating to clear communication in bilingual and multi-lingual settings see Chapter 12.

Why it is important for children/young people to ask questions, offer ideas and suggestions and how you can help them do this

Listening to children and young people is crucial; but to listen the TA first needs to encourage the pupils to communicate. One strategy that a TA will use on a day-to-day basis is questioning. In reference to Piaget and Vygotsky's theories (see pp. 42–8) the use of carefully considered questions can aid cognitive development. Considered questions can lead to cognitive disequilibrium and the development of new schemas. Considered questions can help develop a shared understanding of new terms. Work on questioning has revealed that there are different types of questions.

Open vs closed questions

Open questions

There is no one right answer to this question. This type of question encourages the students to talk:

> *Example*: What did you do over the summer holidays?

Closed questions

In this type of question you are requiring the pupil to give a specific answer:

> *Example*: Is the world flat?

Here there is a correct answer:

> *Example*: Do you like pizza?

Here there is no correct answer. The pupils could say yes, no or sometimes. Closed questions have a disadvantage in that they may not encourage much discussion.

Recall vs thought

Recall questions

These questions check on existing knowledge:

> *Example*: Was schema a concept that Piaget used?

> *Example*: How did Piaget define schemas?

Thought questions

These questions stimulate the development of new ideas and aim to develop new knowledge:

> *Example*: How could Piaget's concept of discovery learning be applied to your classroom?

> *Example*: Do you help develop new schemas in the pupils you work with?

Questions are complex

However, this analysis of the types of question used can become more complex when you realise that these two dimensions of questions, open vs closed and recall vs thought can be combined. For example, you can have: open-recall, closed-recall, open-thought and closed-thought. Further, when we use questions in the classroom we might need to adapt the questions we are using.

Prompts or probes

Prompts or probes are defined as follow-up questions that you give pupils when the answer you get from them is not quite what you are looking for. Prompts can involve:

- re-phrasing the question in simpler language;
- breaking the initial question into smaller and simpler questions that eventually leads back to the initial question;
- reminding the pupil of the information they need to know in order to answer the question.

(Brown and Wragg 1993)

Although the strategy of asking questions seems simple, Brown and Wragg identified a number of common errors in questioning:

- not giving pupils enough time to think about the answer to a question;
- always asking the same pupils;
- asking too many questions;
- asking a question only to answer it yourself;
- asking too easy or too difficult questions;
- not responding to wrong answers;
- ignoring answers;
- failing to build on or link pupils answers to questions.

Activity

1   Listen to a teacher deliver a lesson. Note the types of question that are asked and fill in the box on p. 122.
2   Work with an individual pupil. Afterwards try to remember the questions you asked. Fill in the box on p. 122.
3   Which questions do you think were most successful and why?
4   Do you think that certain questions are suited to certain students and why?

WHAT QUESTIONS DO YOU USE?		
Type of question	How often was this strategy used?	Examples of questions
Open-recall		
Closed-recall		
Open-thought		
Closed-thought		
Prompts – using simpler language		
Prompts – breaking initial question into smaller questions		
Prompts – reviewing or reminding pupils of information they need to know in order to answer the question		

How to respond to children and young people in a way that shows you value what they have to say – and the types of behaviour that could show that you do not value their ideas and feelings

Children and young people need to feel that they are valued in order to thrive. Value can be expressed by praising pupils for their contribution. For a full discussion on praise see pp. 87–8.

Valuing pupils means finding the time to really listen. Often in the hub-bub of school life it is easy to say: 'Not now – I'm busy – can it wait?' What is important is to find the time to go back to the pupil and listen to what they have to say. Active listening is crucial – there is nothing worse than just pretending to listen. For further information on active listening see pp. 55, 58.

How you can help children and young people to understand the value and importance of positive relationships with others and develop respect for other people's individuality and feelings

Why it is important for children and young people to understand and respect other people's feelings and how you can encourage and support this

As a TA you can help pupils understand the value of positive relationships and develop the underlying skills by demonstrating these qualities in your everyday interactions. For example, a TA can:

- make a point of being friendly and courteous to all pupils;
- always say please and thank you;
- be seen to share equipment and resources;
- be aware and concerned for others' feelings;
- be prepared to say sorry and to accept others' apologies.

Some pupils will automatically watch your behaviour, learn from your behaviour and imitate the desired behaviour. However, for some pupils you might need to draw their attention to what are appropriate ways of relating and why these ways are important.

Consider the following case study:

Case study

I was working with another TA. The group we were working with had recognised problems in behaviour and managing their emotions. In the group we were making posters about road safety. To draw the group's attention to the importance of sharing, the other TA and I had an argument about who got to use the red felt pen first. The argument went like this:

I said:	It's my red pen – I saw it first.
TA said:	No, I saw it first.
I said:	I need it more as I am the better artist – your drawings are too messy.
TA said:	I don't like the way you draw. Your drawings are rubbish!

The group were shocked to see us argue and after about a minute we stopped and said that we knew that this was not the right way to behave. We then asked the group to talk about what we should be doing. The group said that we needed to take turns, that we were being silly, that we were wasting time and that we needed to apologise to each other as we had hurt each other's feelings. One member of the group said that there was no one right way to draw. We then had a discussion regarding how what we drew was a unique expression of who we were. We could have reminded them of appropriate rules before we started the group – but I think what we did had a real impact on the group.

As well as being a role model for appropriate relationships, there are currently structured programmes that focus on aspects of what is now referred to as emotional intelligence. Programmes dealing with social and emotional aspects of learning (SEAL) (DfES 2005) have been developed. These programmes consider self-awareness, managing feelings, motivation, empathy and social skills. SEAL sets out whole-school initiatives focusing on emotional well-being as well as small groups and individual work for those pupils who have recognised difficulties in these areas. Key themes within SEAL include new beginnings, getting on and falling out, say no to bullying, going for goals, good to be me, relationships and changes. Many TAs have been involved in these programmes.

Self-assessment questions

1   How has your school implemented the SEAL programme?
2   How, as a TA, have you been involved in the programme?
3   How, as a TA, have you helped pupils to understand the value and importance of positive relationships with others and develop respect for other people's individuality and feelings?

Why positive relationships with other adults are important

Positive relationships with adults are important as pupils thrive both academically and socially if they feel they are valued by the adults who work with them. Children or young people need to feel that adults believe in them and that other adults are there to support them when there are difficulties. This is especially true for children or young people who are looked after or are at risk of exclusion.

Why it is important to show respect for other adults' individuality and how to do so

As we have stated, it is important for pupils to feel welcomed, valued and supported and so it is for adults. Adults working with other adults, as professionals in a school, need to respect and value the diversity and individuality of each member of the team. To do this, adults within the school need to share their experiences and expertise with each other. More is said regarding aspects of teamwork including communication and conflict resolution techniques in Chapter 5.

Checklist

✔ Remember positive relationships are based on small everyday acts of kindness.
✔ In terms of confidentiality know who you can and cannot share information with.
✔ Value diversity, challenge stereotypes and promote self-esteem.

This chapter has covered many aspects of promoting and developing relationships. However, there are some areas of required knowledge within this unit that are extensively covered within other chapters. See the index for further information.

GATHERING EVIDENCE

Setting the scene

Nicola reads over the performance indicators for this unit and submits the following evidence:

Writing personal accounts: collecting evidence

PERSONAL ACCOUNT

Name: **Nicola Wilson**
Case study: **Developing relationships**

One of the students I support is Zoë. Zoë is bright and is in the top set for most subjects. However, Zoë has dyslexia and does need extra support with her spelling and essay-writing organisation. I have been supporting Zoë for several years but have noticed a huge difference since she started in Year 9.

Whereas Zoë would always greet me warmly in the corridors and welcome my support in the class – now she wants nothing to do with me and just blanks me when I greet her in the corridor.

Last week in science she asked me if I really needed to sit beside her.

I said that I didn't have to sit there but that I would be available for her when she needed and that I would be at the back.

- *Adapt your behaviour to the age needs and abilities of individual children and young people. Recognise when there are communication difficulties and adapt the way you communicate accordingly*

I felt that she needed more independence now that she was in the upper school and I would sit at the back. However, I did go to her desk several times in the lesson and ask her if she needed help. She said she was fine and covered her work so that I couldn't see. After class Zoë stopped and said that she did not need my help any more as she was not stupid and that no one else in the class had support.

I mentioned my problems in talking to and supporting Zoë both to the science teacher and the SENCO. Both have picked up on Zoë's change in attitude and have noticed that her work has suffered. Zoë is bright but due to her dyslexia she does need support.

I reported that I thought Zoë's attitude had been adversely affected by a group of girls who sat near her and that the only time that I had managed to get Zoë to do any work was one day when all three girls were absent from class. The teacher decided to alter the seating plan so that Zoë would not be sitting next to these girls.

When I went into class over the next two weeks I had hoped the change in seating arrangement would make it easier to work with Zoë. However, Zoë was very angry. Often she would ignore me, and yesterday as I approached her she said in a loud voice so that all the class could hear; 'Oh no, it's brick face'.

- *Support children/young people in understanding other people's feelings*

I knew that Zoë was saying this for the audience – but the comments still hurt and I took her aside and I said that I wanted to support her but it was difficult when she was rude to me. I asked her how she would feel if someone called her 'brick face'. Zoë said that she wouldn't like it and apologised for hurting my feelings and being rude. I then asked Zoë how I could support her. I realised that previously I had made decisions about what I thought was the best support for Zoë, without consulting her.

- *Negotiate with children/young people about their needs and preferences and involve them in decision making as appropriate to their stage of development*

Zoë said that she *did* want support but the other girls said she was stupid when she asked for help. I said that perhaps I could come over to her table and help all of the pupils on the table. Zoë said she would like that as she could then ask for help but it would not seem like it was just her who needed support. When we finished our conversation it was smiles all around!

ASSESSOR'S COMMENTS

Well done, Niki! For this to count as evidence you now need to have this signed by the teacher. Also much of what you have mentioned can be cross-referenced to Unit: Promoting Positive Behaviour.

Signed: **Terrie Cole**, NVQ Assessor

Chapter 5

Support the development and effectiveness of work teams

In this chapter we will look at two elements:

1　Contribute to effective team practice.
2　Contribute to the development of the work team.

KNOWLEDGE AND UNDERSTANDING

Introduction

Schools are said to advocate a collegiate approach, that is, they believe that it is essential to work together. As discussed in a previous chapter, giving a group of pupils a task to collectively work on and hoping for the best is not always the best strategy. This brings us to what personal characteristics staff members need to develop to work effectively as a team.

The principles underlying effective communication, interpersonal and collaborative skills and how to apply these within the teams in which you work

Effective communication and interpersonal skills involve:

- **Trust**　For members of a group to communicate honestly there needs to be an atmosphere of trust and respect. Obviously, confidentiality is important.
- **Listening skills**　Members of a group need to listen to each other. It is important to let other members have their say without interruption. Have you ever tried to get your point across only to have others butting in? How does this make you feel? Have you been guilty of doing this yourself? Sometimes when you are bursting to add your view it is really difficult to wait for your turn to speak. However, listening to others is an important skill to develop.

It is easy to fall into the trap of being so busy thinking about what you want to say that you don't actually listen to what others have to say. Here it is helpful to write down key ideas.

A member of a group needs to listen to exactly what is being said. It is important to be objective rather than subjective and to listen to all sides of an issue and not just to the views that you agree with. If we don't do this we might be guilty of selective listening, that is, hearing only what we want to hear.

As a group member we need to deal effectively with our emotions. Often, disagreements within meetings and disagreements between colleagues result from reading personal messages into comments or statements.

Case study

Sandy, a secondary TA reported: 'The **SENCO** asked me twice in the meeting if I had finished the reports – I felt like she was saying I was unreliable. I felt that she was having a go at me.'

There could be many reasons why the SENCO reminded Sandy of the reports. Perhaps the SENCO was herself forgetful and didn't realise that she had reminded Sandy of the report twice in the same meeting.

Good listening skills involve being seen as approachable and open-minded. Here it is not only what you say but how you say it – this is an issue of body language. An approachable person appears friendly; they smile, they maintain eye contact and they have a relaxed posture.

What makes for an effective team?

An ethos of collaboration

An obvious point being that group members are willing and committed to working together.

Clear objectives and focus

It is helpful if the group identifies and sets targets.

Agreed roles and responsibilities

Depending on the nature of the group there can be various roles such as team leader and secretary.

Necessary skills and knowledge

What is deemed necessary skills will vary according to the group. If the group's focus is to review IEPs of students, a personal knowledge of relevant pupils and the SEN Code of Practice would be necessary.

Set procedures for working together

Often meetings will have an agenda to follow.

Ways of reviewing and evaluating group progress

Often the outcomes of meetings are a set of action points. A review of whether the action points have been met can indicate the effectiveness of the group.

Conducive working environment

An obvious but important point being that a group needs an appropriate place to meet that is free from interruptions and the necessary time to cover the required topics.

Self-assessment questions

1   How effective is your team?
2   To what extent does your team work collaboratively?

Collaborative skills involve working together as a team with each member contributing. So far in this chapter we have discussed interpersonal and communication skills and what makes for an effective team. In a previous chapter relating to the teamwork skills of pupils we talked about stages in group formation to include: forming, storming, norming and performing (see pp. 51–2). These stages of group formation can equally be applied to adults working within teams.

1   Think of a group that you are a part of. The team might be focused on a particular project, for example planning a summer fete, or be involved with ongoing reviews of pupils' needs. Describe this team.

The relationship between your own work role and the role of other members of the work team

Before you can consider how your work role relates to the role of other members of the work team, it is important to be clear about what your role entails. To this end, every member of staff will have a job description that is given when they commence employment in a school. As the time goes by often further responsibilities are added in recognition of experience and knowledge gained. A review of a job description or role can be an important part of an appraisal or performance management review.

A summary of a typical job description for a primary teaching assistant could look like the one shown in the box on p. 131. Many job descriptions will include more details than this.

A summary of a typical job description for a secondary teaching assistant could look like the example shown in the box on p. 132.

QUIZ What type of team member am I?

Task	I do this well	I could do better	Help! There is definite room for improvement My action plan is:
I contribute to meetings			
I express my views in a way that my colleagues understand			
I am confident in expressing my views			
I wait until others finish speaking before responding			
I listen to what others say			
I make notes of key points in meetings			
I express my feelings in a professional manner			
I use appropriate body language (smiles, encouraging nods, relaxed body posture)			
I accept constructive feedback from others			
I encourage others to contribute			
I offer constructive feedback to others			
I carry out my team responsibilities			
If I can't carry out my team responsibilities I inform relevant people			
I am positive and enthusiastic			

ANYWHERE PRIMARY SCHOOL

Job title: Teaching Assistant

Job purpose: To ensure, in collaboration with other teaching professionals that the aims and objectives of the school are achieved through the delivery of the National Curriculum and the provision of other activities that promote optimum child development.

Responsible to: Initially to class teacher and ultimately to Headteacher/ Deputy Headteacher/SENCO.

Accountable for: Providing classroom small group and individual support as required.

Key accountabilities:

1 To assist with the organisation of the classroom and preparation of activities.
2 To observe pupil behaviour and to share in the responsibility for the well-being and discipline of all pupils.
3 To assist in the teaching and learning process as required.
4 To work in co-operation with other teaching professionals to ensure that equal opportunities and equal access to the curriculum exist for all pupils across all age groups.

Teaching assistants do not work in isolation. An effective school relies on teamwork. The following list shows 'Who's who' in a school and gives examples of how TAs interact with other staff members.

- **Governors**

Duties   The governors with the Head Teacher make the final decisions about how the school is run. The governors will deal with issues relating to finance, curriculum and special needs. The governors will include members of the community, parents, teachers and representatives from the local authority.

Examples of how a TA could interact with other staff members   The governors are there to give assistance and advice as required. As a TA you might meet one of the governors when they visit the school. Some TAs themselves are governors and gain a useful insight on the school from this role.

- **Headteacher**

Duties   The headteacher is responsible for managing all aspects of the school. The headteacher needs to ensure that the curriculum is effectively taught and that the well-being of the pupils is ensured.

Examples of how a TA could interact with other staff members   Headteachers are busy people, but they make time to listen to all those involved with the school.

WHEREVER SECONDARY SCHOOL

Job title: Teaching Assistant

Job purpose:
- To support teachers and students in the classroom.
- To support students in examinations.
- To help with clerical work in the department

Accountable to: SENCO

Key accountabilities:

1   To support pupils in the classroom.
2   To read texts and scribe responses for designated pupils as appropriate.
3   To help pupils plan and organise their work.
4   To explain work to pupils as necessary.
5   To give social and emotional support to all pupils and in doing so help to build positive self-esteem.
6   To work with individuals, groups or class as required.
7   To assist teachers with the differentiation of work.
8   To keep necessary records as required.
9   To support designated pupils in exam settings as required.
10   To help with clerical work in the preparation, photocopying and organising of materials as required.
11   To communicate effectively with pupils and all members of staff.

- **Deputy head teacher**

Duties   The deputy headteacher is second in command. The deputy is there to assist the head in managing the school and will take the responsibility for the school when the head is absent.

- **SENCO**

Duties   The **Special Educational Needs Co-ordinator** is responsible for all pupils registered as having special educational needs. The duties of the SENCO will involve monitoring pupils, writing, updating and reviewing IEPs.

Examples of how a TA could interact with other staff members   SENCOs are very busy people. They also have a wealth of information regarding how to deal with pupils who face particular challenges. They will offer advice to teachers and teaching assistants on what strategies could be used with pupils who are having difficulties.

- **Secretarial and administration staff**

Duties   These members of staff are responsible for greeting visitors, answering phone-calls, typing, sending out required correspondence and maintaining necessary records.

- **Bursar**

Duties   The bursar is in charge of the finances of the school.

Examples of how a TA could interact with other staff members   The bursar will know how much money the school has available to spend on training and continuous professional development.

- **Curriculum co-ordinators/subject managers**

Duties   These are teachers who are given special areas of responsibility. In this case the teachers will be responsible for a certain subject or curriculum area. In primary school this could be Key Stage 2 Maths or it could be Head of Maths at a secondary level.

- **Heads of year/key stage**

Duties   These are teachers who are given the responsibility of meeting the pastoral needs of pupils within a year group or key stage.

Examples of how a TA could interact with other staff members   At a secondary level if a pupil you are working with starts behaving in an uncharacteristic manner, the head of year is a good person to talk to. The head of year may be able to talk to the pupil's family to see if there are any issues going on that are affecting the pupil.

- **Classroom teachers**

Duties   Each teacher will have responsibility for planning, preparing, delivering and evaluating the learning for the classes that they support.

Examples of how a TA could interact with other staff members   As a TA most of your work will be with the class teacher to whom you are assigned.

- **Senior teaching assistants or HLTA**

Duties   In some schools where there are a large number of TAs there may be one senior TA who has responsibility for organising the work of all the TAs within the school. Some TAs will have gained the status of HLTA and will be given extra responsibilities.

Examples of how a TA could interact with other staff members   Senior TAs or HLTAs can offer valuable advice and training to TAs who are just starting out.

- **Teaching assistants**

Duties   Teaching assistants can be assigned to work with a specific class or assigned to work with a specific pupil with special educational needs. In secondary schools TAs may be assigned to work with a specific year group supporting those pupils within the year group who are on the SEN Register. Some TAs at secondary school are assigned to work within departments.

Examples of how a TA could interact with other staff members   The advice, encouragement and support you get from your fellow TAs is invaluable.

- **Cover supervisors**

Duties   Cover supervisors are often employed by large secondary schools. Their job is to fill in for absent teachers.

Examples of how a TA could interact with other staff members   If the regular teacher is absent you might find yourself working with a school's cover supervisor.

- **Before and after school supervisors**

Duties   In response to the government's vision for extended schools some schools now cater for working parents who need to drop off their children early for school and pick them up after they have finished work. These supervisors will look after such pupils and deliver appropriate activities.

Examples of how a TA could interact with other staff members   Some pupils in your school may attend such facilities. They may be dropped off for school and collected after school by these staff members.

- **Volunteer TAs**

Duties   Volunteer TAs are dedicated individuals, who are interested in education and are giving up their free time to help teachers to effectively manage their classroom.

Examples of how a TA could interact with other staff members   Often volunteer TAs go on to full or part-time employment within a school.

- **School nurse**

Duties   This member of staff is responsible for dealing with minor accidents, making decisions regarding when to call for further medical assistance and for administering necessary medication.

Examples of how a TA could interact with other staff members   As a TA you will need to know who these individuals are.

- **First Aiders**

Duties   These are members of staff who have taken courses in First Aid and know what to do in the event of medical emergencies.

- **Cleaning staff**

Duties   These members of staff start to work before other staff arrive for the day or when the teaching staff prepare to go home. They ensure that the working environment of the school is in a clean state.

- **Site security**

Duties   These members of staff are often found in large schools. These staff members are there to ensure the premises are safe from unwanted intruders. These staff will often have the duty of ensuring that the buildings are secure at the end of a teaching day.

- **Premises staff**

Duties   This member of staff is responsible for the maintenance of the school building.

- **Mid-day meal supervisors**

Duties   These individuals are responsible for setting up the dining hall for many hungry pupils. They are responsible for ensuring appropriate behaviour is maintained during the lunch hours and they are responsible for clearing up afterwards.

Examples of how a TA could interact with other staff members   Some TAs may also work as mid-day meal supervisors.

Self-assessment questions

1   What is your role within the school? Do you have more than one role?
2   In a typical week what other members of staff do you work with?

Figure 5.1 It is important for staff to work together

The value and expertise you bring to a team – your role within the team and how you contribute to the overall group process

The value and expertise brought by your colleagues – the importance of respecting the skills and expertise of other practitioners

As it is important to recognise the skills and expertise you have, it is also important to know what others have to offer. An effective school makes the most of the skills and talents of its most valuable resource, its staff.

An example of good practice:

> We have just had a new head appointed. At our first staff meeting all staff – teachers, teaching assistants, cleaners, mid-day meal supervisors, volunteer TAs, secretaries and governors – attended. As an ice-breaker we all had to write down on a piece of paper our name and what we were good at. It is strange – I have worked in this school for five years and I thought I knew everyone – but there were surprises. I didn't know that one of the TAs was a former swimming coach, that our cleaner was the secretary of the local horticultural society and that one of our mid-day meal supervisors was involved in the local operatic society. Well, the new head was thrilled with all the talent in the room and made a point of suggesting to every one of us other areas of the school in which we might wish to be involved.

The range of interactive styles that individuals have and how these may affect ongoing work

Often in teams there will be issues that provoke discussion. Occasionally there are issues that cause widespread disagreement and conflict. Conflict is not necessarily a bad thing. If handled correctly, conflict and heated discussion can lead to new understandings and lead to improvement in day-to-day practice. Obviously, conflict and disagreement that is not resolved will make the team and the school less effective.

Smith (1996) talks of a number of ways in which individuals can approach conflict.

- *Non-assertive approach*   This individual is both unassertive, unco-operative and avoids conflict if possible. An individual with this interactive style when confronted with conflict could state that it has nothing to do with them, that they don't want to get involved, and could they talk about it later.
- *Agreeing/co-operative approach*   This individual is unassertive but will co-operate with others and follow their ideas even if they don't agree or don't want to. Individuals agree as they don't want to make a fuss or cause problems. This individual puts others' needs before their own.
- *Compromising approach*   This individual is somewhere between the unassertive and co-operative approaches. This individual strives to keep everyone happy and works very hard at trying to meet others half way.
- *Competitive approach*   This individual needs to win the argument. An individual following this approach is extremely assertive and wants their ideas implemented. Such an individual is convinced that they are right and will use their expertise and power to achieve their ends.
- *Problem-solving approach*   This individual is assertive and co-operative. This individual will emphasise the need to get everyone on board and working together. This individual will use their emotional intelligence to convince others that it is in their and the school's best interest to find a solution.

Smith (2002) argues that a problem-solving approach leads to effective staff relationships and better chances of resolving conflicts should they occur.

Another approach to describing interactional styles is Eric Berne's (1991) view of transactional analysis. Berne argues that every individual has three ego states and that when they communicate with others they talk from the perspective of one of these ego states. These ego states are:

- *Adult*   The adult ego state is the rational and thinking part of us. When we are talking from this perspective we might use phrases such as: 'I think', 'In my opinion' or 'After considered reflection it would seem'.
- *Parent*   This ego state is the voice of authority and represents an internalised parental figure. When we are talking from this perspective we might use phrases such as: 'Don't do that', 'What did I tell you?' and 'Do as you're told'.
- *Child*   This ego state is the emotional part of us; the inner child that never grew up. When we talk from this perspective we let our emotions rule. We might appear sulky. We might have a tantrum. We might be silly. We might use phrases such as: 'That's not fair' and 'You're always picking on me'.

The theory of transactional analysis is complex. Not only do we talk from one of these ego states but the person with whom we are talking with is also using one of these ego states. This theory can be applied to the conversations we have with team members.

Case study

One TA has been signed-off sick for six weeks. In a meeting with other support staff the SENCO is discussing who will cover the TA's hours. Consider the following possible transactions:

Transaction – Adult ego state to Adult ego state:

SENCO:	Can I ask the group for suggestions regarding how we should cover Year 1 for the next half term?
First TA:	I think we could develop a rota system and take turns spending one week in Year 1.
Second TA:	I think Year 1 needs continuity, how about we ask one of the volunteer TAs to help out?

Transaction: Parent ego state to Child ego state

SENCO:	As you know Millie has been signed off for the rest of the term and I have decided that Angie will move from year three to year one
Angie:	What! This is news to me! No one asked me . . . But! . . .
SENCO:	No buts . . . No discussion . . . I have made up my mind – just do it!

In general, when communicating with colleagues an adult ego state to adult ego state is desirable.

The range of learning styles and preferences within the work team and the implications of these for the ways in which you offer support to colleagues

In Chapter 2 we talked about learning styles and the importance of matching teaching styles to learning styles (see pp. 54–7). Just as this is true for working with pupils, so it is also true for working with colleagues.

Self-assessment question

I   Imagine that you were asked to deliver a five-minute presentation on effective team building to your work colleagues. Taking into account perceptual learning style (visual, auditory and kinaesthetic), how would you plan your presentation?

The differences between work relationships and personal relationships and how work relationships can be maintained effectively

Many people will say that they have made close personal friendships with those they work with. Further, many will spend time socialising with their colleagues outside of work hours. Although personal friendships exist, staff know that within working hours they need to act in a professional manner.

Being a professional and acting as a professional requires:

- following a code of conduct;
- being accountable for your actions;
- being competent at your job;
- being worthy of trust;
- acting in a manner worthy of respect.

On a day-to-day level this means acting as a role model, addressing your work colleagues in a respectful manner, dressing appropriately and knowing what information needs to kept confidential.

Case study

Norma, a TA at a large primary school states that her sister works at the same school as a teacher: 'Obviously we do not work in the same class – but we always come into work together. As sisters we are very close. However, I know that there is information my sister knows about pupils and the school that is confidential. I wouldn't dream of compromising my relationship with my sister by asking her for information that she is not at liberty to discuss.'

Situation	I would personally give help and advice such as:	I would refer this to another member of staff Yes/no and why
Another TA states that she is finding it difficult working with a particular pupil as they don't want to accept any help		
A TA confides that she is finding it very difficult working with the teacher in her class. The TA states that she is always being told what to do and that the teacher is not interested in her ideas or suggestions		
A volunteer TA confides that another volunteer TA has talked about pupils' IEP targets to mothers in the playground		

Figure 5.2
It is important for TAs to
seek advice from others

The sorts of situations where team members may require help and advice and how you should respond to these

As an experienced TA in the school you will probably be able to think of many occasions when you have been asked for help and advice. However, in offering help and advice it is essential to know what you can offer personally and when it is important to refer issues to other team members.

The indicators of problems with teams

Possible indicators of problems:

- *Tension between group members* – members not wanting to talk with, sit with or have anything to do with certain other members.
- *Emotional outbursts* – this can be outbursts of temper or tears. In extreme cases relationships between colleagues will be characterised by sarcastic comments, shouting matches and verbal bullying.
- *Increase in confrontations with pupils* – often when there is tension in the group, group members can, without realising, be short tempered with the pupils in their charge.
- *Infrequent meetings* – not enough time is given to group meetings.
- *Meetings are seen as ineffective and a waste of time.*
- *Difficulties in regard to sharing and delegation of tasks* – some individuals will justly claim that they are doing more than others.
- *Individuals members feel unsupported, not valued, stressed and exhausted.*

Methods of handling and minimising interpersonal conflict and actions you should take in response to problems with teams

Smith (2002) states that there are three usual ways of dealing with conflict, and these are:

- Ignore it.
- Have a solution imposed.
- Create a process whereby all those involved are able to work out a solution. This may be achieved by the team or an external facilitator may be needed in certain situations.

A number of ways of resolving group conflict have been proposed. Chivers (1995) suggests:

- defining the nature of the conflict;
- identifying the causes of the conflict but in doing so to avoid seeking scapegoats;
- describing the effect the conflict has on the team and the work the team is involved in;
- defining and listing the benefits of the team resolving the conflict;
- deciding who to discuss the issue with and involving other individuals if appropriate;
- taking time to listen to and understand conflicting views.

At this point we are back to trying to facilitate a solution. As stated previously, some conflicts are not easy to deal with and will need the skilled expertise of a team leader or outside facilitator. However, the best method of dealing with conflicts is to interact with other team members in such a manner that all potential disagreements are discussed and resolved at an early stage.

To act in a professional and amicable fashion with other team members TAs will need to use active listening skills (pp. 55, 58), interactive styles such as problem solving (pp. 136–7) and adult-to-adult discussions (p. 137).

School policies and procedures for dealing with difficulties in working relationships and practices, including confidentiality requirements

All schools will have disciplinary and grievance procedures. As a new member of staff you should be given a copy of your school's procedures in these matters.

Taking out a grievance procedure against another member of staff or being yourself the object of a disciplinary process is stressful and is a situation every employee hopes to avoid.

If you have a problem, the first step is to clearly define what the problems are and to talk to your line manager. Most work-related problems can be resolved informally. However, it is recommended that an employee take written notes of what occurs in the eventuality that they may need to prove what has been said at a later point in time. The Advisory Conciliation and Arbitration Service (ACAS) offers free, impartial and confidential advice regarding employment rights.

In today's climate it is important to know what to do should a complaint or allegation be made against you. ACAS have published a Code of Practice in regard to disciplinary and grievance procedures. The Code states that employees:

- should be informed of allegations and provided with copies of the evidence against them;
- should be given the opportunity to discuss issues with someone who has not been involved in the matter;
- be provided with information regarding allegations and supporting evidence in advance of any meeting;
- have opportunities to challenge the allegations before any decisions are reached;
- have the right to appeal.

(Pilkington 2007)

It goes without saying that in dealing with grievance or disciplinary procedures confidentiality is key. For a further discussion on confidentiality see p. 25.

The broader contexts in which everyone works and the particular situations of colleagues that might affect both how they work and tackle problems at particular points in time

There are a number of factors that will affect how individual staff members work and tackle problems.

Factors operating at an individual level

This level relates to personal circumstances and family dynamics. A staff member who is going through a divorce or is busy supporting an elderly relative could be experiencing stress that will impact on their ability to do their job. Such a staff member will need support from colleagues.

Broader context factors relating to catchment areas

The area in which the school is located and the relationship with the surrounding community will impact on staff members. Those schools situated within what is referred to as 'areas of socio-economic deprivation' may face particular challenges, such as disaffection, high truancy rates, higher levels of behaviour problems and exclusions. Some schools may find themselves taking on an extensive number of pupils who have English has an additional language. Additional support in terms of resources and training may be given to such schools.

Broader context factors relating to local and national initiatives

In recent years the workforce remodelling agenda has had an enormous influence on schools. In some school TAs and HLTAs have taken on additional responsibilities to allow teachers to have their designated Planning, Preparation and Assessment (PPA) time. All schools have felt the impact from the inclusion agenda and have had to increase their skills in regard to dealing with pupils with additional needs. For further information on workforce remodelling see p. 260.

Self-assessment question

I   What factors have impacted on your work? Consider individual factors, challenges resulting from the catchment area and local and national initiatives.

The sorts of information and expertise you have that could benefit team members and how to share them with others

As stated earlier, an effective school recognises and utilises the skills and expertise of its staff. As a TA you might have expertise in IT skills or be gifted in sewing. The first point in regard to sharing your expertise is to let others know you have something to offer. An effective team member does not 'hide their light under a bushel'. Once others know that you have skills and expertise to share then you need to find a way of sharing this information. One way of contributing is to offer to do tasks for other members of staff. For example, an expert in IT could make themselves available to sort out any IT difficulties. However, when we were talking about working with pupils we mentioned that if we always solved their problems for them, then they would not learn how to solve the problems for themselves. So following this logic, the IT expert can best share their expertise by teaching other members of staff how to become more

---

Case study

Jean, a TA at a small primary school was sent on an INSET day entitled 'Smarter Marking'. As Jean explained to the head teacher, the session described techniques that the teacher and the TA could use, such as discussing the assessment criteria in language the pupils could understand before the task; telling pupils that mistakes to be corrected will be marked by a coloured dot; and that for each assignment pupils should be given no more than three specific points to work on. Smarter marking techniques stated that it was important to celebrate the successes made by the pupils and to note clearly how they could improve. Jean was so enthusiastic about the session, the head teacher asked her to give a brief presentation with examples at the next staff meeting.

---

proficient at using the relevant technology. Likewise, many experienced TAs will be offered the opportunity to attend INSET days and asked to share what they have learned with other members of staff.

The value of sharing how you approach your role with other members of the team

What has been stressed within this chapter is the importance of working as a team. All members of the team will have expertise and skills that they can offer. As well as sharing what you know it is also helpful to share the nature of how you approach your role. In a sense you are sharing with others how you act professionally.

Acting professionally involves:

• participating in group decision-making processes;
• recognising and valuing the expertise others have to offer;
• being a role-model for the standards of behaviour you are expecting from the pupils;
• helping to create a culture where all staff members work together for the common good of pupils.

Checklist

✔ Be clear about the relationship between your work role and the role of others.
✔ Acknowledge your areas of expertise and those of others.
✔ Strive to be a good team player.
✔ Act in a professional manner.

GATHERING EVIDENCE

 Setting the scene

Nazreen Begum, a junior school TA, reads the performance indicators for this unit and scribbles a quick note to her assessor.

Writing personal accounts: collecting evidence

PERSONAL ACCOUNT

Hi Terri

I was looking at the performance indicators for this unit – and thinking about what real work evidence I have – I have included copies of the minutes of our staff team.

Will this do?

Nazreen

School Support Team Minutes   *Date:* 5 November

Present:

Miss Ambley (TA), Mrs T. Bell (HLTA), Mrs Rider (deputy head), Mrs Daneen (HLTA), Mrs Jennings (TA), Mr Ewing (TA), Mrs S. Chade (TA), Ms N. Begum (TA)

1   Welcome to new members of team.

2   Peer-mediating scheme.

   • Mrs Tina Bell recapped for all present the details of the peer- mediating scheme.
   • It was mentioned that though the new peer-mediating scheme had met with some success, the pupils who were the most difficult were not interested in resolving their disputes.
   • Some pupils' behaviour was seen as a real concern. Miss Amberley, being new in the post, expressed a desire for further training on behaviour. Help in terms of behaviour management was offered by Ms Begum.
   • Ms N. Begum expressed concern over the fact that mid-day meal supervisors on duty were not aware of the individual pupils who had behaviour targets and specific strategies. A discussion followed.
   • Mrs Rider agreed to raise these concerns at SMT meeting and report back.

3   Setting date for Christmas evening out. It was decided that Mr Ewing would look into various venues and report back at the next meeting.

4   Date for next meeting set for Monday 3 December.

ASSESSOR'S COMMENTS

Dear Nazreen

What you have presented potentially is very good evidence. However, minutes of school meetings are confidential records; so ask your Head for permission to include this document in your portfolio. You will also need to annotate this record to show exactly how you have met the performance indicators.

For example, I imagine that you communicated with other team members openly and honestly and I am sure that you acknowledged the views and opinions of colleagues constructively.

But you need to say how you did this and get your comments witnessed by the Deputy Head who attended the meeting.

All the best.

Signed: **Terri Cole**, NVQ Assessor

PERSONAL ACCOUNT

Candidate: Nazreen Begum   *Date:* 12 Nov

Annotations to Support Staff meeting of 5 November and work that I conducted in response to that meeting.

- *How I communicated with other team members openly and honestly*
- *Identify and share information on opportunities for improvement in team practice in a constructive manner*

At the meeting I mentioned the fact that mid-day meal supervisors were not informed of behaviour strategies on IEPs. I personally feel that they should be. Some of the TAs present said that if mid-day meal supervisors knew pupils' behaviour targets and diagnosis such as ADHD they might label them and treat them differently.

- *How I acknowledged the views and opinions of colleagues constructively*

Although I feel that all relevant staff need to know behaviour strategies, I acknowledged that there were other views and that the other TAs who talked about the dangers of labelling have a point. I said this to them in the meeting.

- *Work in ways that conform to decisions taken by the team*

I was put forward to help Miss Amberley, who is a new member of staff, in dealing with behaviour issues. I agreed with the decision on whether or not mid-day meal supervisors should have knowledge regarding behaviour issues and that details of SEN status should go to the Senior Management Team. I will await their feedback.

- *Give clear and accurate and complete information to other team members as needed for them to work effectively*

As a consequence of the meeting I have observed Miss Amberley working with pupils in various situations and have given her advice.

Since the meeting we have had another new TA join the team. I have given her advice regarding behaviour.

- *Offer help and advice to colleagues when they ask for it, when this is consistent with your other responsibilities*
- *Demonstrate a willingness to share information and expertise which could benefit other team members*

The help and advice I have given Miss Amberley, in regard to behaviour management, is in line with my role. I have attended many INSET sessions on behaviour management and have now discussed with Miss Amberley strategies such as using 'the look' and 'giving choices and stating consequences'.

Since the meeting we have had feedback from the Senior Management Team and mid-day meal supervisors who now will receive information on behaviour targets in regard to IEPs. I have started assisting the deputy head in delivering INSET sessions to the mid-day meal supervisors.

- *Provide positive feedback to other team members for activities which they have undertaken effectively*
- *Recognise and value the strengths which each team member can bring to a situation*

In the staff meeting Mrs Bell explained to us the details of the peer-mediating scheme. Though the scheme was not working with everyone, it was still working with many pupils. As some of the others in the group were focusing on things that weren't working within the scheme, I didn't want Mrs Bell to get the impression that we weren't appreciative of all the work she had put in. I made a point of thanking her for all the work she had put in.

With my more recent work with Mrs Rider on training mid-day meal supervisors I have said to her that it was a pleasure working with her and that I have learnt a lot from her.

Witness: Mrs Rider (Deputy Head) 20 Nov

Ms Begum has been a real asset. She is a real team player

ASSESSOR'S COMMENTS

Hi Nazreen

As I said, the minutes of the meeting were potentially very strong evidence – but what they needed was annotation, filling in the blanks so to speak. What you have now written and have had witnessed clearly shows how you work as a team member and how you contribute to the effectiveness of the team. Well done!

Signed: **Terri Cole**, NVQ Assessor

Chapter 6

Reflect on and develop practice

> **In this chapter we will look at two elements:**
>
> 1 Reflect on practice.
> 2 Take part in continuing professional development.

KNOWLEDGE AND UNDERSTANDING

Introduction

This unit concerns the skills that are needed to be able to reflect on practice. Reflection, as we shall see is an important part of continuing professional development.

Why reflection?

Why reflection on practice and evaluation of personal effectiveness is important

Reflection is defined as the process of thinking and critically analysing your actions with the goal of changing and improving occupational practice. To highlight why reflection on practice and evaluation of personal effectiveness is important, consider the following two imaginary teaching assistants.

Impulsive Imogen	**Ponderous Penelope**
Imogen is always on the go. Imogen is a whirlwind of energy and enthusiasm.	Penelope too has energy and enthusiasm but is more considered in her actions.
Imogen rushes from one activity to the next without spending time to review what happened.	Penelope likes to take time to pause and think about what has occurred. Penelope writes down key ideas and thoughts in a notebook she keeps handy.

Imogen always has great ideas of what she could do next time but never puts her plans into action.

Imogen loves going on INSET days and courses and raves about how much she has learnt – but by the next week (sometimes the next day if she is honest) she has completely forgotten everything.

Imogen knows in her heart that she could progress but doesn't quite know how.

Penelope notes what she could do differently next time and does put her plans into action.

When Penelope goes on a course, Penelope takes notes and files all the handouts away. Penny also writes notes about how she could apply what she has learnt to her work in the classroom. Penny shares her ideas with other colleagues. Penny learns from experience.

Penelope has set herself both personal and occupational goals. Penny celebrates when she achieves her goals. Penelope is going places. Penelope feels good about who she is.

Penelope is reflective. Imogen wishes she was. But in truth there is probably a bit of Penelope and Imogen in all of us. Reflection is a skill that can enable us to become better at what we do. Reflection requires commitment!

Figure 6.1 Impulsive Imogen vs Ponderous Penelope

How learning through reflection (thinking about what we do) can increase professional knowledge and skills

Schön (1983) contrasts the abilities of *reflection in action* with *reflection on action*. *Reflection in action* can be equated with thinking on our feet. However, *reflection on action* involves considering an event after it has occurred. Reflection on action can also be defined as an in-depth consideration of the characteristics, successes and weak points of a teaching or learning activity.

Further, Schön speaks of tacit knowledge. Tacit knowledge is knowledge of how to do a complex activity that is developed over time and through experience. However, often, tacit knowledge is unconscious in that we are unable to describe how we do what we do. Often it is in the moments we are thinking on our feet that we are making use of this tacit knowledge. As one TA said: 'I don't think about what I do – I just do it.'

Reflection involves making our tacit knowledge conscious and available to others. If an experienced TA can think about how they do what they do, for example how they deal effectively with disruptive pupils and how they motivate those pupils who do not want to learn, then they can share their professional knowledge and skills.

In order to increase professional knowledge and skills we need guidance and support. To understand and make sense of our experiences we need constructive feedback.

A TA'S CHARTER ON REFLECTION

To make sense of and learn from classroom experiences I can:

- Discuss and talk through issues with colleagues. I can ask for and seek advice.
- Gather feedback from others. Feedback could be comments from observations made on my practice. Feedback could be in the form of pupils' comments
- Relate current classroom experiences to my personal history of experiences that I have had in the classroom.
- Relate classroom experiences to general life experiences as a parent and as a responsible adult.
- Relate classroom experiences to what I have learnt on courses, training and INSET days.
- Read books, articles and conduct Internet searches.

In a previous chapter we discussed how children learn. The same principles apply to us. We can learn:

- through discovery learning, that is, through trial and error;
- through being guided by a more experienced individual;
- through the process of assimilation and accommodation, remembering that we need to be aware of what we don't know in order to learn.

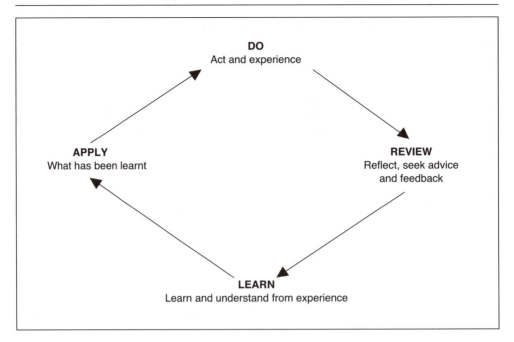

Figure 6.2 The Do, Review, Learn and Apply Cycle

Often the development of knowledge and skills has been seen as a cycle. Dennison and Kirk (1990) talk of a cycle of 'Do, Review, Learn and Apply'. Figure 6.2 illustrates this cycle.

Professional development is a cycle, in that we never stop learning – thus the term continuous professional development.

How reflection can enhance and use personal experience to increase confidence and self-esteem

Schön (1983) distinguishes between two types of knowledge, these are:

1 Technical and rational

This involves abstract knowledge that we learn from outside sources, for example facts and theories presented in textbooks.

2 Experiential knowledge

This is knowledge developed through everyday work experiences and engagement in professional activities. When we reflect on classroom experience we utilise both types of knowledge to try to understand and learn from the activity. In this textbook there have been many examples of TAs reflecting on their practice. These examples highlight how reflection can increase confidence and self-esteem.

Techniques of reflection

The following case study will be used to illustrate techniques of reflection:

Techniques of reflective analysis

Case study

I was asked to work with a small group of pupils. The objective of the session was to go over the answers and strategies used in a maths test. In preparation for the session I had paper, pencils, number lines and multi-link available. However on reflection, I feel we didn't accomplish much. The pupils were extremely restless and fidgety and not much was done.

---

1 *Questioning what, why and how. The process of reflection involves asking questions.*

In reference to the case study we could ask:

Question:	What happened?
Answer:	Pupils were not concentrating.
Question:	Why were the pupils restless and not concentrating?
Answer 1:	Prior to the session the pupils had to sit for an extended period on the carpet. For 20 minutes they had to sit very still and be totally focused on what the teacher had to say.
Answer 2:	We were in the library and there were other groups coming and going. This was distracting for the pupils.
Answer 3:	One of the lads is always restless. He is currently being assessed for ADHD.

In evaluation, it is important to realise that there can be multiple answers to any question. For example, to the question, 'Why were the pupils restless?' there are a number of possible reasons. Perhaps the most important question is, 'How do you take this information forward to support teaching and learning?' This brings us to the next technique.

2 Seeking alternatives

This implies searching for a range of possible ways forward. Let's refer back to the case study example. If the environment, a table in the library, was not conducive to learning then perhaps a different learning environment needs to be found. If the pupils were finding it difficult to focus after an extended period of time on the carpet then perhaps beginning the session with a few 'brain gym' activities would help.

3 Keeping an open mind

An open-minded approach involves being prepared to ask difficult questions and being committed to learning from the process of asking these difficult questions. Being open minded implies going beyond what is immediate in the situation or experience – it involves looking in depth at a situation. Being open minded can also involve asking questions regarding the theoretical material you might be required to read and applying this new knowledge to practical situations. Here we see that technical and experiential knowledge need to be used in combination.

Much has been written on learning styles. In reference to the case study, a possible explanation for the pupils' restless behaviour could be that the teaching style was not directed to learning styles. Here we see that we are using technical knowledge to help find a way forward in our everyday experiences.

An open mind also involves:

- a willingness to continue to learn and acquire new skills;
- an awareness and acceptance of the perpetually changing world of education and a willingness to adapt to new changes and ways of thinking;
- an awareness of your own and pupils' changing needs.

(Collins and Simcoe 2004)

4 Viewing from different perspectives

When reflecting on a situation or experience it is helpful to consider:

- How you felt.
- How you think the pupils involved felt.
- How do you know what the pupils felt?
- Did all the pupils feel the same?

In reference to the case study, the TA might say that she felt frustrated at her inability to focus the group and that this frustration made her question whether she should be a TA. It is important to note that feeling frustrated at the inability to deal with a situation is part of being involved in teaching. It is a feeling that even the most experienced teacher feels from time to time. Learning to accept and deal positively with these feelings is essential.

The TA in this example might say that she asked all the pupils how they felt the session went. The TA might say that she used the class technique of thumbs up and thumbs down and all the pupils displayed thumbs up. How can the TA interpret this? Perhaps all the pupils enjoyed the session. Perhaps the pupils enjoyed the session as they enjoyed mucking around – but did they learn? Perhaps one pupil put their thumbs up – because everyone else did. The difficulty with asking for opinions is that there are times when pupils don't always say what they feel. An intuitive TA will use not only what pupils say but take into account pupils' body language and observations of pupil behaviour to inform judgements and evaluations.

5 Thinking about consequences

Here you need to consider the consequences of possible alternatives. In reference to the case study – perhaps the TA could have told the pupils that they would have to stay in at break if they didn't start to work. Would the consequences of this be that the pupils would work harder and focus – or were they just too tired to work?

6 Testing ideas through comparing and contrasting

This involves comparing the present experience to past experiences. Have there been similar situations that you have dealt with? What did you do then? Would the same strategy have worked this time?

7 Asking 'what if?'

This involves thinking about what would have occurred if only I had done this. . . .

In reference to the case study regarding reviewing test answers with a group of pupils, the TA could say:

What would have happened if I had:

- moved location;
- altered the activity to look at just one problem and not the whole test-paper;
- used a brain gym activity first?

8 Synthesising ideas

This involves putting all these ideas thoughts and feelings together in order to make sense of and understand the situation. In reference to the cycle of activity: we do; we reflect; and we review in order to understand and learn from the experience. We then can use this new understanding to plan for the next time. Then the cycle starts all over again.

9 Seeking, identifying and resolving problems

We mentioned earlier that for reflection to occur we needed feedback and advice from others. Reflection can be a solitary process but the reflection needed to seek, identify and resolve problems requires a school that is committed to a rich professional dialogue where everyone is engaged in asking deep, searching questions (Collins and Simcoe 2004).

Reflection on action

Reflection as a tool for contrasting what we say we do and what we actually do

Often we may think we know how a lesson went. Often we may think we know what a pupil's capabilities are. Often we say to others: 'This is what I do' – but do we actually do what we say we do? How can we be sure that we know how the lesson went? How can we find out? Again we need to reflect. Reflection involves seeking advice and feedback from a range of sources.

Consider the following case study:

Case study

As a TA I feel I always pay equal attention to the boys and girls in my class. After a session on reflection at college I asked myself how do I know that I do this and how can I find out? I decided to ask another TA to observe my interactions with a class. I was shocked to find out that actually I spend more time answering and helping the boys. Thinking about this – or reflecting – I realise that the boys ask more of me than the girls. The girls just get on with it. But perhaps the girls too need help but they are just more reluctant to ask. Now I make a point of going around to everyone. I have since discovered that though some girls say they know what to do, when I question them in detail it is clear that they don't. Reflection has helped to improve my practice.

The difficulties that may occur as a result of examining beliefs, values and feelings

As we can see in the example of investigating the statement: 'I spend an equal amount of time with girls and boys in my class', the TA did not find out what she thought she would. This revelation can be distressing as you can find that you are acting in a way that is in direct opposition to your beliefs and values. Self-knowledge and awareness can be painful. However, this self-knowledge is important if we are to move on and improve practice.

Reflective questions

Supporting learning

- Do I fully understand the teaching and learning objectives?
- Do I provide the necessary levels of individual attention?
- How do I promote independent learning?
- How do I motivate reluctant learners?
- Are my comments to pupils perceived as constructive?
- Are my comments to teachers regarding pupils' learning sufficiently detailed?

Building relationships

- How do I make pupils feel valued and welcomed?
- How do I allocate my attention between pupils?

- How do I encourage inclusive and anti-discriminatory practice?
- How do I encourage pupils to be considerate of others?
- How do I encourage friendships between pupils?

Working with colleagues

- Do I make the time to listen to and support colleagues? How do I do this?
- Are my comments to colleagues always perceived as constructive?
- Am I aware of my limitations?
- Do I know who to go to for advice and support?
- How do I define constructive feedback?

How to use reflection to challenge existing practice

It has been said that a good school never stands still. Staff within schools need to be open to new ideas. Obviously a head teacher is in a position to influence change and challenge existing practice – but everyone has a role to play. As a TA you can make considered, constructive and tactful comments in regards to how learning and teaching can be moved forward. These reflections may be related to working with an individual or a class or they may involve a whole-school issue.

Consider the following case study:

Case study

PPA time, that is planning, preparation and assessment time for teachers came into effect in September 2005. This plan was intended to give teachers the time they needed to plan and prepare lessons. Our former head believed that PPA time should be covered by qualified teachers. However, our new head, Mrs Johnson, is in favour of HLTAs covering this time. When Mrs Johnson introduced this idea she stated that at her previous school the HLTAs reported that they felt they had grown in confidence. Mrs Johnson asked for our opinions. The HLTA in our school has only recently been appointed. She mentioned that she had covered PPA time at her previous school and felt that this experience had given her a wider understanding of the curriculum and had improved her time- and class-management skills.

However, I asked the head that if HLTAs were to take over from the teacher, who would take over from them in supporting individual pupils and groups? Here, my reflection on the possible consequences of HLTAs taking over the class added to the discussion on the proposed changes to practice.

What next?

How to assess further areas for development in your skills and knowledge through reflection, feedback and using resources such as the Internet, libraries and journals

To improve on practice an employee needs to consider both what they can do and what skills and knowledge they need to develop further. Information found through resources such as the Internet, libraries and journals, can highlight new ideas and initiatives that could impact on your role. Journals that a TA may find of value include:

- *Support for Learning*, Nasen Journal, Blackwell Publishing
- *Special*, *Supporting and Developing Good Practice*, published by Educational Solutions in association with Nasen
- *Supporting Learning*, The National Association of School Teaching Assistants.

Self-reflection and feedback from others can also guide you in identifying areas for further development. Central within this process is the role of appraisals.

Appraisals or review systems

How to develop a personal development plan with objectives that are specific, measurable, achievable, realistic and with timescales

In the changing world of education, TAs need constantly to think about how they do their job and in what ways could they do their jobs better. One way of doing this is by having an official review with their teacher or SENCO on a regular basis. In some schools these reviews are called professional discussions and in other schools they are called appraisals. An appraisal looks at:

- How you are progressing in your duties. What duties are you doing at the moment? Does your job description match what you are currently doing?
- The areas in which you feel confident.
- The areas you find difficult.
- The areas in which you need further training.

In order to answer these questions you will need to:

- Complete a self-appraisal.
- Ask relevant school staff to fill out an appraisal regarding your work.
- Possibly participate in a formal observation with feedback.

Once the information has been collected there is time to reflect on the information and to use it to identify both strengths and areas for improvement. This process will involve you having a formal meeting with your relevant line manager. The outcome of this meeting will be the setting of targets for the upcoming year, or to be more precise, developing a personal development plan with objectives that are specific, measurable, achievable, realistic and with timescales. A clear example of the paperwork and thinking involved in this process will be given in the second part of this chapter.

*The availability and range of training and development opportunities in the
local area and how to access these*

What is out there?

1   Your first point of contact is your line manager. Talk to them and ask about
    courses on offer.
2   Your local authority will be involved in organising and delivering courses for TAs
    and support workers in schools. Often local authorities will distribute a book or
    index of training events to schools.
3   Other providers such as FE colleges and adult education services may offer
    courses that are of value.
4   Access the training and development website (www.tda.gov.uk) for details of
    training opportunities.

Figure 6.3 TA training: mission impossible

*The importance of integrating new information and/or learning in order to
meet current best practice, quality schemes or regulatory requirements*

Continuous professional development is about a commitment to integrating new
information and learning into practice, such that what we do in schools is seen as
reflecting current ideas of best practice.

There are now specific requirements in regard to what teaching assistants and
support workers in schools need to know. These regulatory requirements are known
as the National Occupational Standards. At the time of writing, the latest version of
the standards was published in June 2007 and reflects the changes to the role of the
Teaching Assistants and the wider school workforce as a result of the re-modelling

agenda. This textbook and NVQ 2 and 3 qualifications for TAs follow the National Occupational Standards. In addition, many schools now have applied for and have been awarded quality marks.

Consider the following case study:

Case study

I work as a TA in a Reception class. My school was recently involved in a quality improvement scheme. The first part of the scheme involved gathering evidence of all aspects of the learning environment. For our year group we were looking at such questions as:

*   Are learning opportunities maximised in outdoor areas?
*   What opportunities are there for exploring other cultures?
*   How is self-esteem nurtured?

There were so many questions.

After collecting all the information we had a staff meeting to look at the results and identify areas to be developed. After a meeting with the Quality Scheme consultant an action plan was developed. One of our action points involved providing a consistent approach to children's successes and to raise self-esteem. To meet this action point the school decided to create a golden book where staff noted positive behaviour. Further, to provide a personalised and instant reward system we decided that staff should use blank stickers to write personal and positive comments.

We all thoroughly enjoyed working on this scheme and it made me personally feel that I was making a difference. All our hard work paid off as our school was awarded the quality mark.

Figure 6.4 TAs are busy people – if only they had more hands

GATHERING EVIDENCE

 Setting the scene

Miranda presents her evidence to her assessor.

PERSONAL ACCOUNT

Self-appraisal form for TAs

Name: **Miranda Appleton**
Position: **TA**

What I feel have been the key tasks/responsibilities of my job in relation to:

*   Supporting the school
*   Supporting the pupils
*   Supporting my colleagues
*   Supporting the curriculum.

My key task within the school is to assist the teacher and to support the pupils as required. This may be listening to individuals read, working with specific groups on social skills or helping the less able groups with work. This year I have been working with pupils who have challenging behaviour.

*   *Aspects of my work I'm most pleased with and why*

I find working with the pupils most rewarding. It is great when they experience that 'light bulb' moment.

*   *Aspects of my work I would like to improve and why*

I know that several pupils who are to begin school next year have a diagnosis of autism. As I will be supporting these pupils I would benefit from further training.

- *Things preventing me working as effectively as I would like*

Though I talk to the teacher about lesson plans and pupil progress I feel that I would benefit from having more time to discuss such issues with the teacher.

- *Changes I feel would improve my effectiveness*

Finishing my NVQ 3 course will help me understand the relevant knowledge and skills that I need to have to be a TA.

- *My key aims for next year*

Attend specialist training on autism

- *Training I would like to have*

Training on autism

- *How I would like my career to develop*

Eventually I would like to work towards an HLTA and when my children get older I would like to go to the local university and enrol on a foundation degree.

Signed: **M. Appleton** (TA)   *Date:* 16 May

APPRAISAL WITH TEACHING ASSISTANTS

Name of TA: **Miranda Appleton**
Name of appraiser: **M. Higglesmith (SENCO)**
Date of current appraisal: **10 June 2008**
Date of previous appraisal: **22 May 2007**

Targets set at last appraisal	Outcomes
1 First Aid training	Completed
2 Training in ICT and interactive white boards	Completed
3 Attend further inset on behaviour	Attended sessions

Achievements over the past year with regard to:
(i.e. what has gone well, what the TA is most pleased with)

- *Support for the pupil*

Miranda relates well to all pupils. The further training on behaviour management has really boosted Miranda's confidence.

- *Support for the teacher(s)*

Miranda is very good at using her initiative. If something needs to be done, Miranda gets on with the task. Miranda's comments on pupil progress are considered and reflective.

- *Support for the school*

Miranda was very involved in preparation for the school's Christmas play and I am pleased that Miranda has volunteered to chair the committee for organising the summer fete.

Type of training received (with dates)	Summary of what was learned
Sept./07 Healthy Eating Session	Advice on healthy diets
Oct./07 Primary Framework	Awareness of changes to curriculum

Impact on what the TA does	Further considerations
As we have started a Healthy School Initiative the information on healthy diets has been important as Miranda has been part of a team to write a handbook for pupils and parents.	

Areas for development
(i.e. what may not have gone so well or what needs to be learnt/taken on board)

- *Support for pupils*

It would be advantageous for Miranda to attend training on autism. There are some sessions on Social Stories coming up that might be very useful.

- *Support for the teacher(s)*

Miranda has expressed an interest in displays and again might benefit from training in this regard.

- *Support for the school*

There is a vacancy for a school governor coming up and Miranda should seriously consider applying.

Career aspirations and possibilities

Finish NVQ 3

Targets for the next year

1   Training in autism
2   Training in presenting displays

Action to be taken

What action?	By whom?	By when?
Training in autism	SENCO to arrange	ASAP
Training on display presentations	SENCO to arrange	Autumn 08

Date for next appraisal: June 2009

Signed: **M. Higglesmith** (Appraiser)

M. Appleton (TA)

DIARY OF TRAINING EVENTS

(compiled by Miranda Appleton)

Date	Event	Witness signature and position	Evidence unit
Sept 27	Healthy Eating	**J. Harris** School Nurse	
Oct 30	Primary Framework	**G. Talbot** Trainer	
Nov 24	County training day for teaching assistants at professional development centre. At the day we had a chance to meet 60 other TAs from across the county. We had specific workshops on negotiating roles and responsibilities.	**G. Taylor** County advisor	
Jan 10	Training afternoon with TAs from neighbouring schools.	**G. Taylor** County advisor	
Feb 26	Input at college on Assessment for Learning.	**D. Wills** College Lecturer	
Mar 17th	Advanced Training on Interactive Whiteboards at college.	**D. Smith** Trainer	

ASSESSOR COMMENTS

Miranda, your self-appraisal and appraisal provide very good evidence for this unit. Your diary of training events clearly shows how you have made effective use of developmental opportunities and support available to you.

   Miranda, what you need to do next is to write up your personal goals for next year. Remember they need to be written in such a way that they can be seen as realistic, achievable, specific, measurable and time-related.

Signed: **Terrie Cole**, NVQ Assessor

MY PERSONAL DEVELOPMENT PLAN

Miranda Appleton

After re-reading my self-appraisal and appraisal and reflecting on the comments made, I set myself personal goals to improve my practice as a TA. These goals are realistic, achievable, specific, measurable and time related

Goals	What I need to do to meet my goal	Measurable I will know that I have reached my goal when:	Time-related I hope to achieve this goal by:
To be more knowledgeable about autism	Attend further training Research topic online	When I begin to feel competent at supporting pupils with autism	May 2009
To develop skills relating to display presentation	Attend training Go to local library	By feedback from pupils and teachers regarding the quality of displays	May 2009
To finish the NVQ 3 course	Continue to put together my portfolio	I have finished and been awarded an NVQ 3	July hopefully!!!

Chapter 7

Common themes
In alphabetical order

ACTIVE LEARNING

'**Active Learning**' is a generic term that links with a social constructivist theory of the development of cognition and learning such as developed by Vygotsky and Bruner (see pp. 47–8, 216).

What is active learning?

Active learning means children being involved in their own learning. Children are not passive objects in school who have something 'done to them' in order for them to be educated. In order for effective learning to take place, children need to be actively and consciously involved in their learning – both in the content of learning and in the process of learning.

Rather than simply being present in class like absorbent sponges, children need to be involved. They need to be consciously aware of the learning process; of what they are being asked to participate in and they need to be able to have some control over what is being asked of them. Having said that, children are not mini-adults and they will require adult involvement to give direction and purpose to their learning.

Means of promoting active learning

Where adults talk to the class for extended periods of time, expecting them merely to listen and absorb the information presented to them, active learning will not take place. Where children are presented with endless series of worksheets to complete, active learning will not take place. Where the subjects taught bear no relation to the reality of the lives of the children in the lesson, active learning will not take place.

Both teachers and TAs can promote active learning by:

- extending the learning of the children through questioning and discussion;
- planning for individual children rather than the class as a homogenous whole;
- creating an atmosphere of acceptance whereby children feel confident to experiment, to 'have a go', even if they make mistakes;
- presenting children with learning activities with which they connect and that make sense to them;

- presenting children with genuine choices in their learning; and
- taking time to reflect upon their own teaching in the light of what children are learning.

ASSESSMENT

The need to identify need

Learning can only take place where the teaching connects with the pupils in a way they can understand and relate to. Teaching must also move the pupils on in some way, i.e. it cannot be too far ahead of them so that they do not understand what is being taught, but neither can it be something that they already know.

To pitch the curriculum at an appropriate level, teachers need to assess their pupils. Assessment can either be formal, such as via tests, or informal, such as through teacher observation. Within schools, a combination of both is undertaken.

Diagnostic assessment

Ordinary assessment will yield information regarding the pupils' current learning levels and needs, but for some pupils, more detailed diagnostic assessments will need to take place. These will normally be on an individual basis conducted by either the school's SENCO or external agents such as educational psychologists. Diagnostic assessments attempt to identify specific areas of difficulty experienced by the pupil such as limited working memory, left–right orientation confusion or difficulty with **phonological awareness**.

Role of TAs

A combination of in-class observation, regular ongoing analysis of work (both in class, homework and **summative assessment**) and diagnostic testing will normally yield a detailed picture of a pupil's cognition and learning need. As a teaching assistant, you can play a vital role in this assessment process. You may well be in a position to conduct more detailed observations than the class teacher. You could, for instance, undertake an observational checklist of how much a pupil participated verbally in class or group discussions over a particular period of time. Alternatively, you could conduct a reading or spelling test of high-frequency words with the pupil either individually or in a small group when such a test would not be appropriate to give to the class as a whole.

Knowing the needs of the pupils with whom you work

Whatever information is gleaned regarding a pupil, that knowledge must be communicated in some form to those with responsibility for that pupil's teaching. You will need to be familiar with the records kept for the pupils you support so that you are kept informed of the latest analysis of their learning needs. Each school will have its own system and procedures for this, but most will use something like an Individual Education Plan (IEP) for those whose learning needs are greater than the norm.

Validity and reliability

'Accuracy' in terms of assessments relates to two concepts – validity and reliability. Essentially, validity relates to what the assessment states it will do. If, for instance, it says it tests reading, then, to be a valid assessment, that is what it should measure and not some other factor such as cultural awareness.

To be reliable, a test must be able to be replicated – i.e. another assessor will reach the same conclusions with a particular group of pupils using the same assessment as the original assessor. Assessments results must not vary according to who administers them. This is one reason why, in certain tests, it is important that assessors follow the exact wording of questions.

Results of assessments

Assessments yield a range of results. Some information will be in the form of scores – reading ages, vocabulary ages, spelling ages and so on. These scores need to be treated with some caution as they tend to give a more definite result than is justified by the assessment. However, they do give an indication of the needs of a pupil.

DISABILITIES

Definitions of disability

Under the Disability Discrimination Act, 2005 (DDA), the definition of 'disability' is very broad and includes those with 'hidden' disabilities such as autism or ADHD and dyslexia as well as those with physical, sensory or mental impairments. The essential factors are that, for the child to be disabled, the impairment must be *substantial and long-term* (i.e. lasting longer than 12 months). Chronic illnesses such as diabetes or epilepsy may also be considered a disability.

Visual impairment

'Visual impairment' refers to a range of loss of sight up to and including blindness. It does not include difficulties with sight that can be corrected with the use of spectacles or contact lenses.

Hearing impairment

'Hearing impairment' refers to a continuum of hearing difficulties up to and including total deafness. Common forms of impaired hearing in children are *otitis media* (middle-ear infection) and *otitis media* with effusion, sometimes called glue ear, in which sticky fluid collects in the middle ear. Most commonly this is treated by inserting grommets (ventilation tubes) into the tympanic membrane to keep the middle ear ventilated. More serious conditions may require the fitting of hearing aids.

Physical disabilities

Physical disabilities may be the result of accident, illness or congenital factors. These include disabilities affecting the use of limbs, the absence of limbs themselves or damage to the brain controlling nerves and muscles. Under the umbrella of physical disability are conditions such as cystic fibrosis, epilepsy, diabetes, asthma, cerebral palsy, motor neurone disease, muscular dystrophy, spina bifida, Battens disease (a degenerative disease affecting the brain and muscles), Down's syndrome and Sotos Syndrome (what used to be known as cerebral gigantism). Any chronic condition such as cancer or HIV is defined as a disability, even if the effect has yet to be felt by the person concerned. Facial disfigurement is also defined as a disability.

Reasonable adjustments

All schools have a legal obligation to promote disability equality and to 'take such steps as it is reasonable to take to ensure that disabled pupils are not placed at a substantial disadvantage' (Disability Discrimination Act, (DDA), 2005). This is known as the 'reasonable adjustments' duty.

Schools also have a 'general duty' to take into account the time and effort required by pupils with disabilities to access school life and to ensure that such pupils are not subjected to indignity or discomfort and do not experience loss of opportunity to make progress.

Disability Equality Scheme

Schools must prepare a Disability Equality Scheme (Disability Discrimination Act 2005). This is a three-year action plan detailing the steps to be taken over time to increase access to the curriculum and to improve the physical environment of the school for disabled pupils. Your support for pupils with disabilities will be given in the context of this scheme. You therefore need to be aware of its content and its impact on the school.

Medication

Some pupils may require medication to be taken in school. Part of your role may be to administer these medicines. If this is the case:

- it should be written into your job description;
- you should receive appropriate and sufficient training from medical professionals such as the school nurse;
- you should be aware that staff can volunteer to administer medicines, but cannot be required to do so;
- you should understand that, if schools do not allow members of staff to volunteer to administer medicines, they are liable to be practising discrimination (The Disability Rights Commission Code of Practice, 2003).

Quality of life

It is stating the obvious to say that a long-standing or progressive disability is going to have a profound effect on a child. However, the actual effect is conditional upon a number of factors and will vary from child to child. When supporting a pupil with disabilities you need to take cognisance of these factors and the influence they have on the child's response to the disability.

The child themselves

A child's character and personality will be a large factor in influencing the effect of the condition. Two children with the same disability may respond in very different ways – one resenting it, becoming depressed and giving up on life; the other embracing it as the 'way things are' and living life to the full, making the most of what opportunities there are.

Family support

Where the child is surrounded by a close-knit, supportive and well-informed family, the effect of a disability may be less than where that disability is a source of conflict and tension within the family. The emotional and psychological support provided by loving parents and siblings cannot be overemphasised.

School environment

The school can make a great deal of difference to a pupil with disabilities. Much will depend upon how the school as a whole views disability and the provision they need to make for pupils with disabilities. There are a number of different models held regarding disabilities:

- *Medical deficit model* – there is something 'wrong' with the pupil that must, to the best of the school's ability, be 'remedied'.
- *Charity model* – 'disabled pupils' must be pitied, all sympathy shown to them and their courage esteemed. School provision is there to 'support' them and make them as comfortable as possible.
- *Social model* – disability is seen as difference rather than something of less value, often as much the result of the physical and cultural environment as something stemming from the individual person . Provision in this model seeks to adapt the environment to make the person with disabilities be as included and independent as possible.
- *Bio-psycho-social model* – social factors and 'within' impairment both contribute to the disability.

Pupils are likely to experience less of a negative impact of a disability where schools adopt a social or bio-social model of disability.

Provision

Access to appropriate provision, both within school and outside of it will have an important effect on the impact of the disability on the pupil. Counselling can help raise self-esteem. It may help in the transition to recognising and accepting deteriorating sight, hearing or muscle tone.

INCLUSIVE EDUCATION

Inclusion

One of the main driving forces behind education is the principle of inclusion. Essentially, this means that every pupil, no matter what their need, has the right to be educated in their local mainstream school. Although it is usually acknowledged that there will always be pupils for whom some form of special school is needed, the underlying presumption is that all children will be educated together.

The implications for mainstream schools are enormous. Rather than try to help the pupil adapt to the school (the principle of integration), the school needs to adapt to meet the needs of its pupils. This may mean adapting the learning environment as well as the curriculum to meet the needs of pupils with a range of needs including those with disabilities, physical and/or sensory impairments, communication and interaction difficulties and those for whom English is an additional language.

The role of the TA in promoting inclusion

As a TA you can:

- encourage all children to have a sense of pride in who they are;
- encourage friendships between all children;
- help pupils meet their learning goals and targets;
- challenge negative attitudes and low expectations;
- use a range of strategies that help all pupils to develop their potential.

It is important to remember that, in order to treat all pupils and staff 'equally' sometimes this requires putting in place unequal factors such as levels of adult support. Treating all equally does not mean treating all the same.

INDIVIDUAL EDUCATION PLANS (IEPS)

Pupils on the SEN Register at School Action or above will have individual targets set towards which they will be working. Since the first SEN Code of Practice in 1994 these targets have been written on Individual Education Plans or their equivalent. IEPs are no longer a statutory requirement, but there must be some kind of working documentation in place, setting out pupil targets, the provision to be made for the pupil, the success criteria and a review date.

To be effective, the pupils need to know the targets on their IEPs, indeed, for older pupils they should have been part of the process of reviewing their progress and drawing up the targets in the first place. Part of your role will be to support the pupils in achieving those targets.

SPECIAL EDUCATIONAL NEEDS (SEN)

Based on the findings of the Warnock Report (see p. 257) and building on the first SEN Code of Practice (DfE 1994), the government published the *Special Educational Needs Code of Practice* in 2001 (DfEE 2001). All schools must 'have regard to' this Code of Practice. The Code states the legal definition of special educational needs – pupils have special educational needs if special educational provision needs to be made for them in order for them to access the curriculum.

This Code develops two principles more fully than previous documents:

- partnership with parents; and
- pupil participation.

It identifies four main categories of special need – cognition and skills for learning, physical and sensory impairments, social and communication interaction difficulties, and emotional and behavioural difficulties.

The staged approach

The Code of Practice recognises that there is no distinct 'cut-off' between children with SEN and those without. Every school should have in place stages relating to degrees of provision. The Code of Practice describes these stages as Early Identification (EI), School Action (SA) and School Action Plus (SA+), with slightly different terminology being used for the Early Years.

Early Identification is the most basic level of intervention and occurs when a class teacher identifies a child as experiencing a measure of difficulty in school. Intervention at this stage is organised by the class teacher within the class using resources generally available.

At *School Action* the class teacher identifies a pupil experiencing SEN and devises interventions *additional to* or *different from* those provided as part of the school's usual curriculum. The class teacher and SENCO are jointly responsible for drawing up a programme of intervention. They will write an Individual Education Plan (IEP) that specifies targets for that pupil and outlines what provision will be put in place to meet those targets. The IEP should only record that which is *additional to* or *different from* the differentiated curriculum plan, which is in place as part of the provision for all children. IEPs should be reviewed at least twice a year.

The highest level of intervention within school is *School Action Plus*, when the school, in consultation with parents, asks for help from external services such as educational psychologists.

Statements of special educational need

If a child's needs are so severe or complex that provision at School Action or School Action Plus will not be sufficient, or if a child has been supported at those stages and has still made little or no progress over a period of time, then consideration may be given to providing that child with a **Statement of Special Educational Need**. This is a legal document that sets out the needs of a child and the provision to be made for that child by a local authority, which has to be reviewed at least annually.

THE SCHOOL'S SYSTEM AND PROCEDURES FOR RECORDING AND SHARING INFORMATION

It is important that each school has clearly defined roles and responsibilities for maintaining and updating its records. Class or subject teachers are responsible for maintaining records kept in their classes and for ensuring that this information is passed on to the school office, head teacher or head of year to enable whole-school analysis of data.

Further records will be maintained by members of staff with specific responsibilities for areas such as SEN, ethnic minorities and **gifted and talented pupils**. Some kind of whole-school register should be kept by the person(s) responsible for these areas, which is updated termly.

You need to find out what specific roles and responsibilities you have as a TA to maintain records. It is likely, for instance, that if you are working with pupils who have

Figure 7.1 Don't let paperwork overwhelm you

statements of special educational need you will be required to keep records of your work with them so that you can contribute accurately to their **annual reviews**. Ask the teacher(s) you work with or the school's SENCO to clarify any uncertainties.

The sorts of information to which you will be required to contribute will vary from situation to situation, but is likely to include records of individual pupil progress, particularly in relation to IEP targets. You may, for instance, be required to regularly test how many high-frequency words a pupil can read or spell and to record this in an agreed format.

Pupil records must be both valid and reliable. To be valid, information must be appropriate to the requirements of the records and to be reliable the information must have come from a source that is dependable and accurate. Reliable information is normally written information from a credible source such as a professional agency or signed minutes from review meetings. It is good practice for notes of conversations with parents or carers that are written up afterwards, to be signed by both staff and parents who agree that they accurately express what was discussed.

Chapter 8

Use information and communication technology to support pupils' learning

---

In this chapter we will look at two elements:

1   Prepare for using ICT to support pupils' learning.
2   Support pupil's learning through ICT.

KNOWLEDGE AND UNDERSTANDING

Policy and legislation

National legislation

All members of staff are required to be aware of the implications of legislation when using ICT. Schools are covered by legislation such as the Data Protection Act (1998), the Children Acts (1989, 2004) and the Freedom of Information Act (2005). Copyright legislation and software licensing law will need to be followed so that all computer programs are used legally.

ICT policies

Each school will have a policy for ICT. There will be 'Internet rules' along the following lines:

- I will never give out my home address, personal email address or telephone number or arrange to meet anyone over the Internet.
- I will only use the Internet and search engines when I have permission to do so.
- I will only e-mail people that I know or who my teacher has approved and when I have been given permission.
- Any messages I send shall be polite, respectful and sensible.
- I understand that the use of chat rooms is not allowed under any circumstance.
- If I am uncomfortable or upset by anything I see on the Internet I will immediately tell my teacher.

- I will not download files without my teacher's permission.
- I understand that the school can check my computer files and the Internet sites I visit.

Benefits of ICT

Supporting learning

ICT involves both the discovery of information and the communication of knowledge gained. The skills developed within the ICT curriculum can have enormous benefits on pupils' thinking and learning in every area of the curriculum. Skills acquired during ICT include:

- finding and processing information;
- analysing and interpreting information;
- presenting information for a variety of reasons;
- enquiry and decision-making;
- making judgements about the appropriateness and value of information;
- problem solving;
- creative thinking;
- synthesising information from a variety of sources;
- reviewing, modifying and evaluating work on an ongoing basis.

Pupils need to be taught the knowledge, skills and understanding within a specific IT curriculum and then given the opportunities to apply these skills in other curriculum areas.

Figure 8.1 Pupils need to be taught ICT skills

Websites can be a highly motivating tool to help develop higher-order thinking. The benefits of interactive whiteboards in classes include motivating pupils who are inspired by the graphics and range of material available on them.

How ICT promotes pupils' physical, creative, social and emotional and communication development

Alongside developing thinking and learning skills, ICT can help promote a wide range of skills needed by pupils, including:

- collaborative working;
- communicating via a wide range of media and with a variety of people often in various parts of the world;
- sensitivity to the rights and feelings of others, for example in respect of privacy.

Using a search engine can help promote pupils' skills of inquiry and analysis of information. There are many search engines to choose from, the most well known being Google. But there are also specifically 'child-friendly' search engines such as 'Yahooligans' or 'Ask for Kids' that are worth exploring.

ICT is particularly adept at developing pupils' skills in narrative story telling. This can apply cross-curricular and not simply in literacy. Story telling using animation, cartoons, sound effects, dialogue, importing backgrounds from the Internet and scanning in pupil drawings or artwork can be applied equally effectively in subjects such as history and R.E.

Contributing to teaching and learning objectives

One obvious contribution ICT can make towards meeting planned teaching and learning objectives is providing information for teachers and teaching assistants via the Internet. Two useful websites are curriculumonline.gov.uk and teachernet.gov.uk.

Software packages can enable teachers and teaching assistants, as well as pupils, to produce excellent graphics that enhance teaching and learning via templates, inserting visuals, animation, multimedia writing frames and many more. Some suggestions for the use of ICT in lessons include:

- displaying the work of a particular artist the class are studying to support their own work in that artist's style;
- visuals of historical artefacts allowing pupils to gain a deeper perspective into life in the past;
- scientific experiments shown via the Internet enhancing pupils' understanding of potentially complex issues.

Identifying the benefits of ICT materials

Not all software and Internet sources are of equal benefit. You need to be careful what you use; certainly what you spend money on. As a TA you will probably not be in a position to purchase software, but you can recommend or warn against those you have knowledge of. Similarly you may know excellent websites that can be visited by pupils to support their learning.

Identifying sources of information and advice

Within school, information and advice may be gained from ICT technicians or managers employed in the school. One key to the successful development of ICT within a school is positive leadership given by those who know what they are talking about. Such people are invaluable to members of staff and pupils alike.

Outside of the school, your local authority may have advisors or experts who can give advice. There are also numerous websites to visit, such as that of Becta (British Educational Communications and Technology Agency) – www.ictadvice.org.uk.

Safeguarding pupils using ICT

Health and safety

The school's ICT policy should make reference to health and safety aspects of using ICT, such as:

- Children shall not be responsible for moving equipment around the school. They may load software under supervision, but should not be given the responsibility of plugging in and switching on machines without a member of staff present.
- Food and drink may not be consumed near ICT equipment.
- It is the responsibility of staff to ensure that classroom ICT equipment is stored securely, cleaned regularly and that the ICT suite is tidy after use.
- Staff should ensure that children are seated at the computers comfortably and must be aware of the dangers of continuous use (e.g. eye/wrist strain).

Risks associated with ICT equipment

All electrical and electronic equipment carries a certain amount of risk. It is the duty of the ICT manager or technician to ensure that all equipment is regularly checked and adequately maintained; however, all staff and pupils have a responsibility to be on the lookout for faulty wiring, unsafe cabling and so on. Any risk needs to be communicated to the appropriate persons as soon as possible.

Screening devices for the Internet

Schools are likely to be protected by a 'firewall' from harmful Internet sites, but adult supervision is usually going to be required as well. Schools are likely to be relatively 'safe areas' for pupils using the Internet, but they need to be taught how to use it safely so that they are protected off-site, too.

Becta and the government have drawn up 'The Internet Proficiency Scheme', which aims to support teachers by providing advice on the safe use of the Internet in schools. Becta also provides advice for schools on Internet safety via their home page (look for the link to 'e-safety'). A useful website giving advice on Internet safety and security for children is www.childnet-int.org/.

Misuse of ICT

A minority of pupils misuse ICT, either using it against fellow pupils or against members of staff. Although much of this happens outside of school, it will have an impact within the school. For the pupils and staff members at the receiving end of threatening, bullying or humiliating text messages, e-mails or messaging services, this can be an extremely damaging experience.

Known as 'cyber-bullying', there are calls for closer monitoring by Internet providers to ensure this type of activity does not take place. School anti-bullying policies should relate to bullying via mobile phones or the Internet and should also have rules as to the possession and use of mobile phones in school.

'Cheating' on learning

Concern has also been expressed, by adults and pupils alike, that ICT can be misused in the learning process. Rather than aiding enquiry and research, pupils can simply 'cut-and-paste' from the Internet and cobble together a piece of writing that they then pass off as their own. Searching via Google may save time, but it can also be a form of cheating. Consider the following extract from a conversation between a researcher and a Year 9 pupil:

Researcher:	Does the Internet make school easier?
Pupil:	Yeah, cos you can copy and paste.
Researcher:	Tell me more.
Pupil:	Well, say you've got a history essay on Winston Churchill, or something like that. You just go to Google, type in Churchill, and World War 2, and then you get a load of information and then you like, 'I'll pick that' and put it in, 'I'll take that' and put it in. And it's really easy and all you do is slightly alter it to be your sort of language and you've got an easy level 6 or 7.
Researcher:	Wow. So, do you think pupils are learning anything doing it this way?
Pupil:	Not really.

(Flanders 2008)

Problems using ICT

Three practical problems present themselves to staff and pupils alike:

- It does not work – the hardware or software does not function properly.
- It is not available – the ICT suite is booked when you want it, there are not enough computers for everyone in the class to use at the same time and so on.
- I don't understand it – staff and pupils may not be technologically proficient enough to access what they want.

Although proceedings can be put in place to overcome these, the likelihood is that ICT, despite all its many benefits, will continue to be a source of frustration for some time to come.

Learning with ICT

ICT curriculum

ICT is a central part of the National Curriculum for both primary and secondary schools. The knowledge, skills and understanding for ICT are set out under four headings:

- Finding things out.
- Developing ideas and making things happen.
- Exchanging and sharing information.
- Reviewing, modifying and evaluating work as it progresses.

Age-related expectations

Throughout their schooling, the majority of pupils are expected to reach certain standards in ICT.

Foundation Stage

Children in Reception/Early Years will begin to use computers and programmable toys such as Roamers. They will begin to use appropriate vocabulary.

Key Stage 1

Children will use a range of ICT equipment both in literacy and numeracy. They will begin to learn the basics of word processing and use a variety of ways to present information.

Key Stage 2

Pupils will become more capable in the use of ICT and develop skills in working with a greater range of software, including word processing, audio-visual presentations and the Internet. The aim is that using ICT becomes both natural and normal and can be applied in a variety of subjects.

Key Stages 3 and 4

Students are expected to develop knowledge of technical aspects of how ICT works. They need to become proficient in the use of multimedia presentations and to collaborate in presenting information in a wide range of formats. They are expected to develop a good understanding as to when using ICT is appropriate and when it is better to use something else.

The National Curriculum Level Descriptors give an indication of the standards expected at different ages.

Monitoring and assessing ICT

Part of the ICT curriculum involves pupils being taught to review, modify and evaluate their work as they undertake it. They are encouraged to do this collaboratively so they develop their ideas together. The aim is that they improve future work and become increasingly effective in using ICT.

Alongside pupil and peer evaluation, teaching staff need to monitor ICT so that they ensure the full range of the curriculum is being taught and experienced and using ICT is suited to the needs and levels of the pupils. Assessment through observation and setting targeted learning challenges on a regular basis, usually at the end of each taught unit within the IT curriculum, will give staff an understanding of pupil progress.

As in any subject, assessment in ICT is most useful and accurate when considering a number of pieces of work over a period of time rather than making a decision on one 'snap-shot' activity. Evidence upon which staff base their assessments can usefully be gained through observation of and discussion with pupils.

Supporting the curriculum with ICT

It is a statutory requirement that ICT supports every curriculum subject apart from physical education. In this way ICT becomes not just a subject taught in its own right but a means of learning other subjects as well. From the beginning of their school careers pupils should be given opportunities to apply and develop their ICT knowledge and skills to support their learning in all subjects.

Evaluating resources

Although the software used by pupils you support is likely to have been chosen by the teacher, part of your role is to monitor how effective that software is. It may be that, for some of the pupils you support, the loading process is too complex or the level of English used in it is too advanced for them to access independently. If you find this to be the case, you need to inform the class teacher. Discussion with the ICT manager or with the SENCO may give you some ideas about more appropriate software.

Responding to ICT

Selecting ICT

A valid question has been asked of ICT – 'Is education driving technology or is technology driving education?' How software and hardware is selected goes a long way towards answering that question.

All schools will have similar criteria when it comes to selecting software that will be used by pupils. This will include:

- being age-appropriate;
- being of sufficient substance and accuracy to promote learning;
- being 'user-friendly';
- being legal – i.e. not pirated;
- not being violent or immoral;
- not being stereotypical or racist.

Pupils must be able to access and control software themselves and it must be something that actively promotes their learning rather than simply engages them in activities of stimulus-response.

Range of material

One of the issues regarding ICT is that there must be a sufficient range of material available to pupils in order for them to meet the requirements of the curriculum. There is a minimum of hardware and software material needed, included in which is:

- access to networked computers;
- access to e-mail and the World Wide Web;
- multimedia machines;
- printers – both colour and black and white;
- access to scanners, digital cameras, video cameras;
- software that enables pupils to word process, use data bases and spreadsheets, develop graphic and painting skills;
- music software.

Familiarisation – the pupils and you

Pupils need to have time to become familiar with the ICT they are being asked to use. This is not simply playing around on it, but it may well involve exploring what the equipment or the software can do.

To effectively support pupils in the use of ICT you also need time to become familiar with the software and programs they are being asked to use. Only when you are familiar with them can you explain to the pupils how to use them. This has obvious implications for planning and preparation.

Adapting ICT

One of the benefits of ICT is that it can often be more readily adapted to meet the needs of pupils than standard reading and writing materials.

Assisting equal opportunities and inclusion

The school's ICT policy should expressly state equality of opportunity in accessing ICT along these lines: 'All children have access to the use of ICT regardless of gender, race, cultural background or physical or sensory disability.'

The National Curriculum states that for inclusion to happen in a lesson, staff need to:

- set suitable learning challenges;
- respond to pupils' diverse learning needs;
- overcome potential barriers to learning and assessment for individuals and groups of pupils.

ICT offers an excellent opportunity to promote inclusion as:

- **differentiation** is often more easily achieved with ICT than with traditional learning techniques;
- hardware and software can be adapted to meet the needs of individual pupils through the use of an enlarged font, speaking text, larger mice or keyboards and screen magnifiers;
- ICT can be used to provide resources for specific pupils such as printing text in Braille;
- many pupils who find writing difficult will be more confident using a word processor;
- pupils are often highly motivated by ICT.

Most computers in schools come with software installed that allows access for pupils (and adults) with special needs and disabilities. Among these features are accessibility options such as a screen magnifier and an on-screen keyboard.

Age, gender, needs and abilities

ICT can provide support for pupils with SEN and be used to challenge more able pupils. Many software packages contain a range of levels for each activity, such as learning spelling rules or multiplication tables. For instance, when using these within one spelling lesson, some pupils may be learning to spell cvc words while others are working on the '-ious' pattern.

Tools and techniques

In order to adapt ICT to the needs of pupils an essential prerequisite is that staff themselves are familiar with and confident in using the particular hardware and software they are being asked to adapt. You need to be able to explain how pupils should do things and why they should do them. Techniques and tools in adapting ICT include:

- choosing one technique at a time to work on with pupils, for instance highlighting text and then learning how to change the font size or colour;
- combining several techniques to produce a completed piece of work;
- making sure icons are understood and used by pupils;
- ensuring pupils know how to do the basic techniques of ICT such as opening files and saving work.

Supporting pupils

Depending on their age, you can support pupils in their use of ICT by helping them develop a number of skills:

- learning to turn on the computer, log on, use a mouse and keyboard;
- selecting and using software packages – choosing those that will best help them learn in a particular lesson;

- using CD ROMs, the school intranet and the Internet to access programs, using these programs as independently as possible;
- using all of the above knowledge to gain information for other subjects;
- using the Internet and communicating via e-mail.

Promoting independence

When supporting pupils in ICT it is easy to do the work for them, particularly in the early stages. Your role is to tell them how to develop the skills they need and, where appropriate, model this for them. At all times you should encourage them to 'have a go' themselves and to develop their independent skills. You should remind them to continually save their work so it is not lost if something goes wrong.

Many pupils are more willing to experiment using ICT than when writing as they can edit errors out with ease. However, it is important to encourage them to keep records of their progress through saving work, even in the draft stages.

Keeping up!

One of the challenges and exciting features of ICT is that it is constantly developing and changing – hopefully improving! In order to be able to use ICT to support pupils' learning you need to keep up.

There are a number of ways to do this depending on how keen you are. You could subscribe to one or more of the many computer magazines available; you could spend all your spare time surfing the net; or you could ensure that you meet regularly with your friend who is an ICT nerd.

However, as a TA you probably do not need to know about all the latest design techniques in ICT across the world, but you do need to know what is being introduced in your school. Sufficient time needs to be given to all staff to train and experiment with new ICT before being asked to support pupils with it. If you are not sure about anything – ask.

Checklist

✔   I am aware of the benefits ICT can bring to learning.
✔   I am familiar with school procedures for safeguarding pupils when using ICT.
✔   I understand how ICT can promote learning.
✔   I can select and adapt ICT resources to meet the needs of the pupils with whom I work.

GATHERING EVIDENCE

 Setting the scene

Mr Palmerston's Year 6 class have begun to study the Tudors in history and Miranda has been asked to support them in the ICT suite where they are to use the Internet to help research information about Henry VIII. Prior to the lesson, she and Mr Palmerston met up to discuss the ICT implications of the teaching programme.

Writing personal accounts: collecting evidence

PERSONAL ACCOUNT

Candidate: **Miranda Appleton**
School: **Anywhere Primary School**   *Date:*   **2 May**

Prepare for using ICT to support pupils' learning

- *Identify and agree with the teacher the opportunities for using ICT to support pupils' learning within the overall teaching programme*

Mr Palmerston and I discussed how ICT might be used to help the class develop their knowledge of Henry VIII. We agreed that the most obvious way was by using the Internet for research. We agreed that we would focus on aspects of Henry VIII that are connected with our city; so as part of the preparation for the lesson it was agreed that I would find out a few websites to which the pupils could be directed as an introduction to their research.

- *Discuss and agree with the teacher the criteria for ICT resources to ensure the appropriateness for all pupils with whom you work*

We discussed the criteria I would use to evaluate appropriate websites and agreed the following:

- they would need to be readily accessible by all pupils;
- they would need to be geared to junior school children rather than older students;
- they would need to contain good visuals that could be downloaded or copied without breaking copyright;
- there should be opportunity for the more able pupils to go to other links leading them to more detailed information.

- *Explore and evaluate available ICT resources and consider how these can be integrated into the planned teaching and learning programme*

Earlier in the day I explored various websites. I started with Google UK, tapped in 'Henry VIII' and found there are over one million sites! I chose sites that I thought would be the most helpful, such as a BBC site. Gradually I narrowed the field down to four. All of these I felt achieved what we wanted them to – linking the topic with what the pupils were familiar with, and allowing those who wanted to, to explore further. During lunch I showed Mr Palmerston what I had found and he agreed with my choices.

- *Plan to use ICT to support learning in ways that are stimulating and enjoyable for pupils, according to their age, needs and abilities*

There are a small number of pupils in the class who find reading difficult, but who enjoy ICT. I had found a website for younger children that used larger format print and less technical vocabulary. The links were via pictures that the pupils were likely to recognise – some of them are only just round the corner from the school!

- *Identify sources of ICT materials that meet the needs of the pupils and the teaching and learning programme*

The websites I found should allow all the pupils to conduct research at their different levels, but they will all need to record what they have found out in some way. In the school all the computers in the ICT suite have several packages loaded on to them that support pupils' written communication. I made sure that I knew how all these operated. Before the lesson I practised copying and pasting pictures from a website to these programs (Textease, Word and PowerPoint) so that in the lesson I could support pupils if needed.

- *Ensure a range of ICT materials are available that meet the needs of all pupils including those with learning difficulties, bilingual pupils and gifted and talented pupils*

These three packages offer a range of ways that pupils can present their findings. Although all can access them, those who are gifted in ICT can develop them a lot further than the others. Textease enables all pupils to present their findings very effectively with relative ease, but the more able pupils can use PowerPoint to produce even more complex presentations. The beauty of Textease is that there is a word–sound facility on it so that each phoneme, word or sentence a pupil types can be spoken aloud by the computer. This is very helpful for those pupils with learning difficulties and those who are new to English.

- *Adapt ICT materials as necessary to meet the needs of the learning objectives and pupils' age, interests and abilities within copyright and licence agreements*

I spoke with the school's ICT technician about the needs of some pupils regarding reading text on the websites and he showed me how to use Windows Narrator. Prior to the lesson I spent time adapting two computers to access this accessibility support programme. During the lesson the two pupils who find reading the hardest will be able to use this to turn text into speech if they want to so they can listen to information about Henry VIII rather than read it all. I checked with our ICT technician to make sure this program is part of Microsoft's package and using it does not break any copyright or licence agreements.

- *Discuss and agree with the teacher how pupils' progress will be assessed and recorded*

Mr Palmerston and I agreed that during this lesson the focus of my observations and assessment would be the pupils' ICT skills and progress. I will assess three aspects – how pupils access and use the Internet to log on to appropriate websites; how well they use the websites to find out information; and how effectively they begin to write up what they have found out. These learning objectives will be given to the class at the start of the lesson. All the pupils have had a lot of experience using the Internet, so this is building on previous knowledge and skills. I will record my observations in a tick list for each pupil.

TEACHER'S COMMENTS

I certify that this is a true account of what happened. Miranda has shown herself very capable in preparing ICT and in thinking through how ICT can support learning. She has also shown that she is willing to learn from other people to develop her own ICT skills.

Staff signature   Name (printed and role)

N. Palmerston   Nicholas Palmerston, **Class Teacher**

ASSESSOR'S COMMENTS

This account shows that you have carefully thought through many aspects of ICT. Once the lesson has been conducted it would be useful to include some examples of pupils' work showing how your preparation supported their learning – please try and include examples from pupils who are gifted as well as those who have some measure of learning difficulty. It would also be helpful to have a copy of your tick list.

Signed: **Terrie Cole**, NVQ Assessor

Chapter 9

Support literacy development

In this chapter we will look at three elements:

1   Support pupils to develop their reading skills.
2   Support pupils to develop their writing skills.
3   Support pupils to develop their speaking/talking and listening skills.

KNOWLEDGE AND UNDERSTANDING

The school's literacy policy

Your school's policy for literacy will outline the way literacy will be taught throughout the school, linking with the National Curriculum, which sets out **Programmes of Study** of English for each of the Key Stages under the headings of speaking and listening, reading, and writing. You will need to be familiar with this policy if you are to support pupils in literacy.

Strategies and resources for developing reading, writing and listening and speaking skills

Primary Framework for Literacy

The Framework for Literacy was introduced to primary schools during 2007 as part of the **renewed Primary Framework**. This builds on and replaces the **National Literacy Strategy (NLS)**, which had been in place since 1998. The Framework takes into account the latest research into the early development of reading as outlined in the **Rose Report** (DfES 2006c) and is described as an 'interactive planning tool', largely being accessed online. Within literacy, the Primary Framework emphasises what is termed the 'simple view of reading'.

The 'simple view of reading'

This understanding of reading development identifies two factors as being crucial for children to become fluent readers – word recognition and language comprehension:

- Word recognition is a matter of coming to know, understand and be able to use the full range of **phonic skills**, beginning with basic phoneme–grapheme correspondence (i.e. being able to read and write the letters of the alphabet).
- Language comprehension is children understanding what they both hear and read.

Word recognition and language comprehension are related and both are essential if children are to learn to read, however, the balance should increasingly shift as children grow older and learn more. Whereas during Key Stage 1 the emphasis will be on word recognition, during Key Stage 2 this should shift to language comprehension. As stated in the Rose Report, 'learning to read' should give way to 'reading to learn'.

Implications for teaching

All children within Early Years and Key Stage 1 must experience 'high-quality' phonic teaching. This teaching should be discrete, daily and time-limited. Such phonic sessions should be systematic, structured and **multi-sensory**, with the progress of the children being frequently monitored and lessons adjusted accordingly. The aim is that by the end of Key Stage 1 the vast majority of pupils will be able to read and spell accurately.

Throughout Key Stage 2 the emphasis on teaching should be on developing children's understanding of texts. This will include specific teaching on aspects of reading such as deduction (reasoning) and inferencing (reading 'between the lines').

The Literacy Hour

A major part of the NLS was the daily Literacy Hour. Although this is not as rigidly followed by schools now, as it was when it was first introduced, the four-part structure of the literacy hour continues to shape much lesson planning:

- *Shared Text work* – when the teacher works with the whole class looking at texts and through this teaches reading and/or writing skills.
- *Shared Word/Sentence work* – when the teacher works with the whole class on phonics, spelling, grammar and/or punctuation.
- *Guided/Independent work* – when the class is divided into groups and the teacher and teaching assistant each work with a group of children on reading or writing while the rest of the class work independently.
- *The Plenary session* – when the whole class gathers together to discuss and reflect upon the lessons learnt.

Framework for teaching English

This is the national strategy covering the teaching of English in Key Stage 3. Like the Primary Literacy Strategy, it divides the subject into word-level, sentence-level and text-level work and recommends what should be taught in each year group. TAs working in the secondary sector need to be familiar with this Framework if they are supporting students in English.

Resources for supporting literacy development

For individual pupils and small groups numerous intervention programmes are available. These include reading schemes, phonic schemes, spelling programmes, activities to promote **phonological awareness,** social skills and speaking and listening skills. As a TA you need to familiarise yourself with what is available in your school. If in doubt, ask your SENCO. If you are asked to support pupils with any of these programmes you need to be fully trained in their use to gain maximum benefit.

Your role and responsibility in supporting literacy development

The exact nature of your role and the extent of your responsibility will differ according to the type of support you are being asked to provide. If you are generally supporting literacy in a class you are likely to have less responsibility than if you are specifically teaching a group of pupils basic phonic skills on a regular basis. In this situation you may well be responsible for collating resources, marking pupils' work and keeping records alongside actual teaching.

Whatever your role, the teacher is ultimately responsible for all pupils in the class or lesson. Your role and the limits of your responsibility will therefore need to be agreed with the class or subject teacher before the lessons begin. Your role will also likely be negotiated with the SENCO or another member of the learning support team.

Figure 9.1 TAs can encourage reading

Teacher's programme and plans for literacy development

All teachers have plans regarding the teaching of literacy, which, from 2007, will come from the Renewed Framework.

Planning falls into one of three categories – long-term plans indicating what is intending to be achieved in each year group; medium-term plans showing half-termly objectives and strategies; and short-term plans – what is going to be done on a day-to-day basis in lessons. The short-term plans should indicate what support the TA is expected to provide and which pupils the TA is to work with.

Plans are not something set in stone – they are there to be changed as situations require. It may be, for instance, that one literacy lesson plan aimed for pupils to learn to use 'powerful verbs' to make sentence writing more dramatic. On the actual day, however, very few pupils grasped this concept. The teacher's plans should reflect this and the next day's plans should be changed to reinforce the topic rather than to move on to something else.

It is helpful for TAs to be aware of the teacher's plans – short-, medium- and long-term. By becoming familiar with the plans and programmes it should be possible to see where each lesson fits into the 'big picture' and to identify the areas of support the TA is to provide in any one lesson.

How children develop literacy skills

Cognitive development

Just as there is physical development in children, so there is learning development – called *cognitive* development. An outline understanding of how children develop the skills they need to make progress in literacy will help in supporting them.

Speaking and listening

We learn how to speak through imitating those around us. This has significant implications for school life. Some children begin school already using a wide range of words and being able to express themselves very well. Others have a much more limited vocabulary. Encouraging pupils to express themselves verbally, and to listen to others in constructive ways, is an important aspect of developing their sense of identity and their self-esteem.

Reading

To become fluent readers, four qualities are needed. Children need to know what the book is about (content); be skilled at decoding (**phonics**); understand the structure of the language used (grammar); and be able to read words on sight (word recognition). All these factors are interrelated, but different ones have more impact on reading development at different ages.

Younger children are more reliant on simple word recognition and begin to read high-frequency words such as 'mummy' or 'daddy'. They also need to learn decoding skills – to recognise the names and sounds of individual letters and begin to put these together in phonically regular words, such as being able to read the sounds /c/-/a/-/t/ and put these together to make the word 'cat'.

As they get older, content understanding (comprehension) and grammatical understanding become increasingly significant in the development both of reading and of writing. Fluency in reading will only come with understanding of meaning and an ability to make sense of the grammar of a text.

Memory plays a large part in the development of all aspects of literacy, and this, too, develops with age. Typical four-year-olds will be able to remember two to three items of information said or shown to them; this increases to six items by the age of 12 and, at 15 and beyond they should be able to recall seven or so items. Older children develop more strategies for aiding memory than younger ones – this is a process that can continue throughout school life and into adulthood.

Neither reading nor writing is gained merely through imitation. Pupils make progress through interaction with others, particularly significant adults who teach them the skills and the knowledge they need to make that progress. Children need to be taught to read and write using apparatus that they can see and touch before they can progress onto more abstract ways of learning. This is called 'multi-sensory' teaching and is a crucial part of most reading programmes.

Children can be helped to make sense of texts by the use of pictures, suitable print size, the spacing of lines, the amount of words on a page, the complexity of sentences and the type of font used.

Writing

Writing, similarly, develops in stages. Beginning with scribbles on paper, children learn how to manipulate pencils and crayons. They move on to emergent writing when they begin to realise that they can convey ideas through putting pen to paper. Gradually they learn the shape of letters, the sounds they make and the way to sequence letters into words and groups of words so that others can read what they write without having to have it interpreted for them. Once this stage is reached, children need to learn the rules of grammar, sentence construction, punctuation and how to construct different types of writing. They also need to learn how to spell, which is easier said than done given the complexity of written English.

The stages of development expected of, and achieved by, the pupils with whom you work

Children develop their literacy skills at different rates. For primary schools, the renewed Framework for Literacy sets out learning objectives for each year group with the expectation that the majority of pupils in those years reach that standard. Some pupils will be working ahead of the expected levels for their age group whereas others are going to be working at lower levels.

There are certain age expectations to do with the acquisition of language and literacy skills; for instance, children of five years old, i.e. those starting school, should be able to pronounce all sounds correctly, they should be able to listen and to name which words sound the same and which are different. They should be able to make themselves understood orally by speaking in complete sentences.

The nature of any special educational needs or additional support needs of pupils with whom you work and the implications of these for helping them to develop literacy skills

Records of need

Not all children find learning to read and write easy. Teachers will keep records relating to the special needs or additional needs of pupils in their classes that should indicate both the nature of the need and the level of difficulty experienced in that area. These records will have been drawn up in consultation with the school's SENCO and will normally be in the form of IEPs.

Specific learning difficulties

The implications of pupils' special needs are many and varied. For instance, pupils with a specific learning difficulty, such as dyslexia, may well be functioning within the average or above average range for science and numeracy, but struggle with reading and spelling. Other pupils may have plenty of ideas to write about and can structure a story verbally using a range of vocabulary but find it extremely difficult to physically write the words as they have dyspraxia (more correctly termed 'Development Coordination Disorder').

Phonological processing

Pupils with dyslexia are likely to be experiencing difficulties with phonological processing – they may, for instance, be unable to recognise vowels in the middle of words (medial vowels) or syllables in words they hear. They are also likely to experience difficulties with short-term memory. They are almost certainly going to find decoding hard. However, many of these children may have strengths in other aspects of reading, such as comprehension. It may be, therefore, that for a pupil with dyslexia their comprehension age is higher than their reading-accuracy age and they compensate for their difficulties in phonic skills with their understanding of the content of texts and the context of words. They may also have strong visual-processing skills and are able to build up a large word-bank learnt purely through sight recognition and memory.

Not all pupils with dyslexia find reading difficult, but all will have problems with spelling. Those whose difficulties focus on spelling rather than reading may better be described as being 'dysgraphic' rather than dyslexic.

Understanding

On the other hand, pupils may be skilled in decoding, in that they can read words and texts accurately, but they may not be able to understand what they read. Pupils at the extreme end of this type of difficulty are said to have 'hyperlexia' as opposed to dyslexia; but both are specific learning difficulties. Many children on the autistic spectrum function in this way, but this is not to say that all pupils with autism have hyperlexia or that all hyperlexic children are also autistic.

Global delay

Those pupils who have an all-round global developmental delay may be functioning at two years or more below the level of most of their peer group in all areas of the curriculum, whereas other pupils are academically above average but are held back by challenging behaviour or disturbed emotions. Still others will experience physical or sensory impairments that impact on their learning to a greater or lesser extent.

QUIZ

- What is the 'simple view of reading'?
- What is the difference between 'phonics' and 'phonology'?
- How do children become fluent readers?
- What difficulties might children with dyslexia experience in learning to read or write?

Strategies for supporting reading, writing, and speaking/talking and listening

The type of support you give to pupils will vary depending on their need, on their age and on their stage of development. For young pupils with dyslexia, for instance, emphasis may be placed on targeted programmes to develop their phonological skills, such as recognising syllables and being able to add or delete phonemes within words. As they get older and begin to develop strengths in comprehension and an understanding of grammar it may be better to shift the emphasis of support from seeking to build up weaknesses to using their strengths to compensate for reading deficits. In this case, your support may be more in the way of giving them strategies to use context to work out words rather than decoding skills.

Whatever actual support you give, some general principles apply:

- A range of skills will need to be developed rather than simply focusing on one.
- Teachers and teaching assistants will need to adapt the way they speak and teach to engage with the pupils on their wavelength, for instance, emphasising specific points of a lesson so that the pupils remember what is most needful: 'This bit you need to remember. . . .'
- Information presented to the children should be in manageable 'chunks' and, where possible, linked with what they know already or with something that interests them to maintain their motivation.
- Multisensory and imaginative teaching strategies should be employed to gain pupil interest, for instance the use of plastic or wooden letters to aid phonic development.
- For younger children, playing games can be a useful way of helping them learn. Games such as 'My granny went shopping' or 'pairs' can help develop memory skills; but these games need to be linked with lesson content. If they are experienced in isolation children are unlikely to gain much from them.

- As children grow older, teaching and thinking strategies should be made explicit to them – 'this is why we are learning that'; 'I am teaching you this in order that you might be able to. . . .' The aim is to give them the skills they need to develop their thinking skills and to learn for themselves. In short, they need to be shown how to become reflective learners.

The interactive use of listening, speaking, reading and writing to promote literacy development

The renewed Primary Framework stresses the interrelationship of listening, speaking, reading and writing. No one aspect of literacy is more important than any other and this should be reflected in the teaching provided for children of whatever age. Your role as a teaching assistant is part of the process of developing these interactive skills.

You can encourage timid or reticent pupils to share their ideas. You can help impetuous or impatient pupils to wait and listen before they leap into action. You can help pupils generalise their knowledge by saying something like, 'You remember what we talked about yesterday? Well, this passage is about the same thing.'

Listening, speaking, reading and writing interact throughout the whole of literacy development. One reinforces and progresses the others – the more words a child can say and understand, the more they are likely to read and to understand what they read; the more they read, the more vocabulary they will gain; the more vocabulary they have the more words they are likely to want to be able to spell and use in their writing.

How to spell and form grammatically accurate sentences

Spelling rules and conventions

'CUL8ter' may be all right for a text message, but it is not accurate spelling. English spelling is largely governed by rules and conventions, but the trouble is, there are so many rules and conventions. Another difficulty presented by English spelling is that our language has developed from so many others. Simple words tend to be Anglo-Saxon in origin, but English spelling has also been influenced by Latin, Norse, Norman French and French itself. Scientific and academic words tend to be Greek in their spelling (as evidenced in the use of /ch/ as in 'chemistry' or /ph/ as in 'phonology').

TEXTING MAY NOT HELP SPELLING		
Guess the word		
Addy	ne1	btdt
Bn	cu	wassup
Wkd	stycl	whrubn

Learning all the rules for spelling is not an easy task, but over 80 per cent of words are not complex. Numerous books and publications are available to schools that seek to outline the most essential spelling rules and conventions – such as 'no English word ends in /i/' or, probably something many of us remember from our own school days, '/i/ before /e/ except after /c/'.

Teach patterns

Teaching spelling patterns can be more effective than giving pupils endless lists of disconnected words. For instance, teaching the 'short-vowel pattern' (in words of more than one syllable there are usually two consonants between the vowels when the first vowel is short) can help pupils work out when letters need to be doubled, as in 'dinner', rather than kept single, as in 'dining'.

The example given on the box on the facing page is of a worksheet teaching the early aspects of the 'short-vowel pattern'. It is designed to give pupils practice in automatically recognising syllable divisions in phonetically regular words such as 'rabbit'. Having been taught the spelling pattern, they will be given experience in practising the pattern for themselves before being given spelling dictations to ensure they have understood the rule. They will then be given exercises to help them generalise this learning, and teachers and TAs will be monitoring the use of this pattern in pupils' independent writing.

Once pupils have grasped the short-vowel pattern in phonically regular words, they can then be introduced to exceptions (such as 'robin', where the first vowel is short but there is only one consonant in the middle of the word) and to the 'long-vowel pattern' (v/cv, e.g. 'robot').

Word processing

Word processing can be useful as ungrammatical sentences tend to end up with green squiggly lines under them. But take care that the pupils you support and you yourself do not become too dependent on spell check. An over-reliance on technology can diminish the skills of proof-reading and, sometimes, the spell-check grammar warnings may not be appropriate.

Physical and emotional factors that impact on pupils' abilities to engage in oral communication – ways of overcoming or minimising these effects

Most children learn the skills of speaking quite automatically and naturally, but many do not. Difficulties encountered in learning to speak are likely to have a major detrimental impact on all other aspects of literacy and learning. There can be a number of reasons why children experience barriers to developing the art of speech. Some of these are physical and others are emotional.

Physical factors

Physical issues such as brain damage or severe illness may mean that the child will never be able to develop the ability to speak. Other physical factors, such as a cleft

WORKSHEET EXAMPLE

SHORT VOWEL PATTERN

<u>vc/cv</u>

Read these words, then write v (vowel) or c (consonant) over the letters, putting in the vc/cv pattern.

Then divide the words into two syllables (vc/cv).

Lastly, write out the two syllables on the lines.

The first one is done for you.

	v c / c v	
pup/pet	pup	pet
rabbit		
magnet		
trumpet		
happen		
kitten		
button		

palate or mild cerebral palsy may mean that the child requires extensive operations or physiotherapy treatment in order to communicate orally. Physical factors are likely to be evidenced in the child finding it difficult to pronounce sounds or words properly. They may develop a stammer or a lisp that prevents them from either being able to express themselves orally or being understood by others.

Where physical factors are an issue, speech and language therapy programmes are likely to focus on training the child to make the correct mouth movements, to use their tongue appropriately, to develop facial muscles and so on. As a TA supporting pupils requiring this level and type of training, you yourself will need to be trained by a professional so that the support you provide is both appropriate and effective.

Monitoring and promoting pupil participation and progress in literacy

In order to ascertain what pupils are learning, effective monitoring processes need to be in place. This can take many forms – pupil observation, questioning pupils, discussing their work with them, **formative assessment** and **summative assessment**. Pupil participation is a crucial aspect of this – pupils need to be encouraged and enabled to take part in their own assessment and the monitoring of their progress.

'Assessment for learning' (AfL) is a national initiative that seeks to make such monitoring effective (see Chapter 11).

Checklist

✔ I am aware of the resources available in my school for supporting literacy.
✔ I understand the basics of how children develop literacy skills.
✔ I know where to find out about any special educational needs the children I work with may have.
✔ I understand the implications of these needs on their literacy development.
✔ I am familiar with ways of supporting children in literacy.

GATHERING EVIDENCE

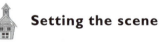 **Setting the scene**

Reading intervention programme with Year 5 pupils

Miranda is sitting at a table with six pupils within the class during guided-reading group work. The group is using a published special needs reading scheme. She will need to prepare further evidence to show how she meets the performance criteria for supporting writing skills and speaking/talking and listening skills.

Writing personal accounts: collecting evidence

PERSONAL ACCOUNT

Name: **Miranda Appleton**

Date: **4 October**

Support pupils to develop their reading skills

Activity: **Year 5 reading group in a literacy lesson**

Clarify and confirm with the teacher:

*   *Your role in supporting pupils to develop reading skills and how this relates to the teacher's role*

At the beginning of the term, Mrs Disraeli and I had agreed that during the guided reading part of literacy lessons I would be working with a group of six pupils within the classroom. Using 'Starstruck' reading scheme, which is part of a programme to develop their reading skills, I will lead a group discussion about what has just been read together. This is to be done twice a week for half an hour as part of the literacy lessons and will be reviewed at half term.

As I am doing this Mrs Disraeli circulates around the rest of the class sitting in on each group's discussions and helping pupils move on in their reading. The class is organised into five ability groups, each with six pupils. I am working with the group that finds reading the most difficult.

Clarify and confirm with the teacher:

*   *The learning needs of the pupils you will be working with*

When this group was set up at the beginning of term (a month ago) Mrs Disraeli told me that they all found reading difficult. They were all at least 18 months behind in their reading and spelling, with two pupils more than two years below age expectations. It may be useful to give each pupil a reading assessment as we come up to half-term to know what progress they have made. I will suggest this to the teacher.

Clarify and confirm with the teacher:

*   *The individual learning targets for the pupils you will be working with*

The class teacher had shown me her plans for the week and, at the beginning of the session, had discussed with me what she wanted the pupils to achieve in their reading during the session. Overall, this was to develop their sight vocabulary, phonic skills and comprehension skills so they can read with confidence, fluency and understanding.

I also read the pupils' SEN records. Four of them have a group education plan indicating they are all working on reading and spelling phonically regular words with common vowel digraphs (ai, ea, ee and ie). Two pupils are further behind. The targets for one are to read and spell initial consonant blends (st, sp, sl) and for the other to read cvc words with confidence.

Agree the support strategies you will use when working with individual and groups of pupils to develop their reading skills

During the half-hour session, the pupils will read aloud, discuss the story, answer questions on the book and discuss their answers. They will seek information from the text and will share their ideas. Some of the questions are closed to show that they can gain specific information; others are open questions showing that they can understand the text and make judgements from it. For instance, I will ask something like, 'What happened when Jimmy lost his football?' (closed question) and 'How do you think Jane felt when Lucy did not come home that evening?' (open question).

I will lead the group – deciding who is to read and what they are to read. I will instruct them in the written work. I will give them examples of how they can answer the questions. I will help them with spellings and with putting their answers into sentences. I will chair the discussion making sure that every one has a chance to say something.

Obtain the learning resources needed to implement the agreed support strategies

Before the lesson I gathered together seven copies of the book we are reading together – one for each of the group and one for me. The day before the lesson I had fetched the teacher's handbook from the SEN resource cupboard and photocopied the relevant worksheets (all perfectly legal!) so that each pupil had their own worksheet and did not need to share. I knew that all the pupils have their own pens and pencils so I did not need to provide them. Each pupil also has a ring binder where they keep the work they do with me.

Implement the agreed strategies correctly to support the pupils' reading development

I prompted reticent and shy pupils to read aloud. Where pupils became stuck on words I encouraged them to sound out the letters and blend the sounds. I made a point of giving 'pure' sounds myself and insisted that they did as well to make blending easier. I made sure each pupil took part in any discussion. I explained words used in the book that some found hard to understand – I did this by using questions and examples rather than just telling them what it meant. Thinking about this we could look at dictionary skills in another lesson so they can find out the meanings of words for themselves. I will add this to the planning. This will help pupils to use resources relevant to the learning activity. Overall, I provided a supportive audience both to the reading and to the discussion.

Monitor the pupils' progress towards the intended learning outcomes and provide feedback to the pupils in a manner appropriate to their age and achievements

I encouraged all the pupils to have a go at reading. There is one pupil who struggles a lot with reading. He doesn't like doing it and he certainly does not like to read out loud. I sat next to him, showing by my body language that I thought he could do it. I had talked with him before the lesson, as I do most weeks, and he was willing to read one page of the book out loud. I prompted him with words he did not know and he read most of them by himself.

When the pupils talked about the book or gave their answers I asked them questions to draw them out more, such as 'Why do you think that?' or 'What tells you that your answer is correct?'. I praised them when they were on the right track, which was most of the time. If they were uncertain I did not tell them they were wrong but encouraged them to look at specific sentences or words. Sometimes I told them what words meant.

Throughout the session I made a point of praising individual pupils when they had read or spelt words relating to their personal learning goals. Sometimes they were not aware they were doing this, so when I pointed it out to them they were very pleased.

Take appropriate action to resolve any problems in supporting pupils during learning activities

The greatest issue is the need to spend so much time with the pupil who is really struggling. In some ways he should not be in the group. He would be better off being taught one-to-one – but there is nobody to do it. Thinking about it though, I could support him more by choosing a page for him to read before the lesson and going over it with him before the group so that he can read it aloud without my help. I'll try this next time.

Provide the teacher with the information needed to maintain pupil records and reports

I keep a written record of what we do in the group (see pro forma). The teacher looks at this if she wants to. If there is something seriously wrong then I will speak with her. This needs to be tightened up. I need to know that the pupils are making the progress expected of them. We have read two books now, but I could not really say that they can read more words and that they understand more than they did three weeks ago.

ANYWHERE PRIMARY SCHOOL

FEEDBACK FORM TO TEACHERS

Name of Teaching Assistant:
Miranda Appleton

Date: 4 October

Lesson: Y5 literacy

Activity: Small group work in class – reading and comprehension

Names of pupils:
Billy; Jean; Serendha; Nicholas; John; Eric

Resources used:
Starstruck scheme level 4 reading books and comprehension pupil worksheets

Learning objective(s):

Overall levels of achievement (1–5 where 1 is not at all and 5 is totally achieved):
All group except Nicholas:

Develop sight vocabulary
Develop phonic skills
Develop comprehension skills

  Sight vocabulary: 3
  Phonic skills: 3
  Comprehension: 3
Nicholas: 2 or even 1 for each

Comments about any individual pupil or particular aspects of the activity:

The group work well together and enjoy the activity. They are growing in confidence in reading. It is hard to say exactly how much progress they make each lesson. Nicholas is really struggling.

Signature of TA: Miranda Appleton

Date: 4 October

TEACHER'S COMMENTS

Miranda worked well with the group. I have every confidence in her ability to lead the group and to teach them well. Before the session we discussed in detail the learning objective. During the session I observed Miranda modelling correct use of vocabulary (e.g. when commenting on the passage, one pupil said, 'He done well there, didn't he, Miss?' and Miranda replied, 'Yes, he did well didn't he?'). I heard her explaining words and phrases I had used in the initial input to the class with her group (e.g. 'When Mrs Disraeli said, "I want us all to think about inferential questions in our reading" she means she wants us to think about why things happen in the story we read and how it makes people feel.') She is right when she says that we need to 'tighten up' on how we record the progress of this group.

Teacher's signature	Name (printed and role)
Mrs Disraeli	**Emily Disraeli**, Y5 Class Teacher

ASSESSOR'S COMMENTS

This personal account clearly shows you have met the performance indicators. Your teacher's feedback is extremely valuable, especially as her comments are targeted at the specific performance indicators. It is always a good idea to discuss with your teacher what you are hoping to achieve. Well done on including your feedback forms. Again, this is good supporting evidence.

Signed: **Terrie Cole**, NVQ Assessor

Chapter 10

Support numeracy development

In this chapter we will look at two elements:

1   Support pupils to develop numeracy skills.
2   Support pupils to use and apply mathematics.

KNOWLEDGE AND UNDERSTANDING

The school's policy for mathematics

Schools' mathematics policies will state the principles behind the teaching of mathematics in the school. All primary school policies are likely to make reference to the renewed Primary Framework for Mathematics, which replaced the **National Numeracy Strategy (NNS)** in 2007. Secondary school policies will refer to the *Framework for Teaching Mathematics in Years 7, 8 and 9*, which aims to help secondary schools build on the Primary Framework.

Primary Framework for Mathematics

There are significant differences between the Framework for Mathematics and the NNS:

- it is electronic – allowing a much greater range and flexibility of resources to be accessed by teachers and TAs;
- the strands of learning are simplified to seven with learning objectives given for each strand to show how pupils should progress; these strands are:
  - using and applying mathematics;
  - counting and understanding number;
  - knowing and using number facts;
  - calculating;
  - understanding shape;
  - measuring;
  - handling data.

- there is clearer guidance regarding the use of calculators and how and when calculator skills should be taught;
- there is an emphasis on standard methods of writing calculations for the four operations of number (adding, subtracting, multiplying and dividing).

Age-related expectations of pupils with whom you work

To gain an indication of what is the expected 'norm' for development in all aspects of mathematics it is worth accessing the Learning Objectives in the Primary Framework for Mathematics or the *Framework for Teaching Mathematics* (for Key Stage 3), which set out what is expected of the majority of pupils in each year group.

How pupils develop mathematical skills

It is generally regarded that pupils move through stages of needing 'real' apparatus, such as small toys, beads, plastic or wooden blocks; then equipment such as number lines and number fans, before being able to think more abstractly. Pupils will move through these stages at different rates.

The factors that promote and hinder effective learning mathematics

Why is maths particularly difficult for some pupils?

Maths can present significant difficulties to children:

- The range of vocabulary and the number of alternative methods available to solve any one problem may cause confusion, for example 'add', 'total' and 'sum' are three different words, but all refer to essentially the same mathematical operation.
- Some pupils will find it hard to remember all the pieces of information and steps required to solve a problem or complete a calculation.
- The speed or pace of the lesson may be too fast for some children and they get left behind.
- Pupils may have to move onto a new topic before they have fully understood the current one.
- There may not be sufficient use of concrete, 'hands-on' materials to enable children to fully understand the concepts being taught.
- Some pupils are able to do the maths, but struggle because they cannot read the questions or write down their answers.
- Maths can provoke panic, causing the brain to 'shut down' or the pupil to react aggressively.

Confidence

Confidence is important in learning any subject, but perhaps especially so for maths. Many children, and adults, too, are simply scared of maths and freeze at the thought of doing it. To boost confidence in maths, pupils must be given tasks that they can do rather than activities that are always too difficult for them.

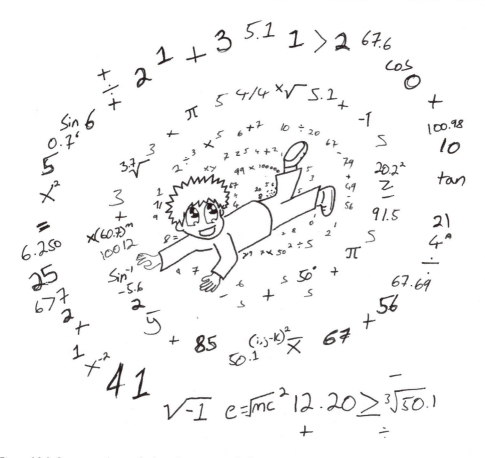

Figure 10.1 Some pupils can find maths an overwhelming experience

Obtaining and using information about pupils' current mathematical skills and abilities

Continuous monitoring, observation and assessment will enable teachers and TAs to establish the exact understanding of the pupils in their classes. Formal tests, including national testing, give some indication of the level of understanding. However, asking questions of the pupils individually or in small groups about what they are doing in maths will yield a depth of information not gained through testing alone.

Strategies for supporting mathematical development and how these relate to different learning needs

Your school's maths policy will outline the strategies used in the school to support the development of mathematical knowledge, understanding and skills. This may include the use of a published maths scheme. The policy is likely to refer to differentiation within lessons and possibly the setting into ability groups.

Case study

Miranda is working with Jez in maths. He is trying to work out the answer to:

$$\begin{array}{r} 28 \\ \times\ \underline{\ \ 3} \end{array}$$

He writes 84.

Miranda: Jez, that's a good answer. Can you tell me how you worked it out?
Jez: I added 28 and 28 and 28.

This shows he understand something about multiplication being continuous addition. However, if this is the only method he knows, it will not help him with more complex multiplication calculations.

All schools are likely to deploy TAs as part of their strategy for supporting mathematical development. There is also likely to be mention of the way maths resources are to be used throughout the school, including the use of ICT and calculators.

The nature of any special educational need or additional support needs of pupils with whom you work and the implications for helping them to develop mathematical knowledge, understanding and skills

The types of special need encountered by the pupils with whom you work will be outlined to you by the class teacher and/or the SENCO. You will need to read their IEPs to gain more information. Different types of special need will require different support approaches to gain maximum effectiveness. For instance, a pupil who is experiencing a specific learning difficulty in mathematics, known as '**dyscalculia**', is likely to benefit from an approach different to that provided for a pupil with all round global developmental delay.

However, some general principles apply to supporting pupils in mathematics who experience a range of barriers to their learning. You can:

*   Help pupils understand what is being said by repeating it in simplified language.
*   Help the pupil frame or formulate their own answers by asking questions such as, 'How could you explain that?' or 'Why do you think you got that answer?'.
*   Remind them of what they have learnt previously.
*   Use visual stimuli and concrete apparatus such as games, number lines, multi-link.
*   Keep a pupil who is easily distracted focused on the lesson.
*   Ensure that all pupils understand what is being asked of them and can read any materials that have been handed out.

- Go over the teaching points already made in the lesson, taking time to give more explanation if needed.
- Provide adapted resources, including work in large print.
- Work with pupils using ICT.
- Prepare pupils to participate in the plenary by going over their answers with them, asking them for their ideas and suggestions and encouraging them to speak up in the class discussion.

You are likely to use structured, cumulative (*i.e.* one fact or skill building upon another) and multi-sensory methods when seeking to develop numerical understanding.

Not too much at once

It is better to focus on a limited amount that can be understood, than try and teach everything and end up with the pupil confused. For instance, you may be supporting a pupil who finds it hard to process information quickly. During a mental maths session, therefore, where the class are required to answer ten or twenty questions within a certain time frame, you could encourage them to try to answer every other question. This will give them the opportunity to get at least half right, rather than seek to attempt all of them and, most probably, get most or all of them wrong.

'Can you explain how you did this?'

Asking pupils to talk about how they approached certain problems or arrived at particular conclusions is an important element of TA support. It may be that, by listening to what they say, you can see why pupils are making errors and can teach to that gap or misunderstanding.

Case study

Miranda is again working with Jez in maths. Now he has to work out:

$$16 + 23$$

He writes the answer as 48.

Miranda: That's an interesting answer, Jez. Can you tell me how you worked this one out?

Jez: I added 1 and 3, and that made 4, then I added 6 and 2 and this made 8. I put the 4 and the 8 together to make 48.

This shows that Jez is confusing the tens and units columns. He has not yet understood place value.

Ensure the basics are in place

As pupils get older and begin to experience difficulties in maths, it is tempting to try to tackle the immediate presenting problem. This, in itself, may well be insufficient. You need to check that the pupil has a grasp of fundamentals first.

Use concrete apparatus

Using concrete materials can effectively introduce or consolidate concepts. Number lines and number squares, while being useful, rely solely on visual skills. More tactile equipment such as plastic or wooden cubes and rods are readily available in primary schools and in special needs departments of secondary schools.

Constant review

'Use it or lose it' certainly applies to maths. You can support pupils by ensuring concepts and facts they have been taught are regularly and frequently reviewed.

Explain learning tasks clearly and allow pupils to ask questions and clarify their understanding

Often pupils struggling in maths find it hard to ask questions in front of the class as a whole – they fear they will appear stupid or ignorant. An important part of your role can be to get alongside such pupils in as private a way as possible so they can ask you what they want to know without other pupils knowing. Your role is therefore to create an environment of trust whereby pupils feel able to ask you questions about the tasks knowing that they will be treated seriously and not ridiculed.

Support pupils in pursuing their own lines of enquiry and finding their own solutions to problems

An important aspect of mathematical understanding is pupils taking what has been taught and developing it for themselves – using and applying it in new situations and exploring their own ways to solve problems presented to them. There will be times in maths lessons, therefore, when the class are asked to investigate problems for themselves. This can cause some pupils to panic – they feel they do not know what to do or how to proceed. You can support pupils in this pursuit by asking pertinent questions and offering suggestions. You are not there to provide answers for them nor to do the work on their behalf, but you could point the way forward allowing them to start the investigation.

Resources for developing mathematical skills and how they should be used

A large number of mathematical resources are available – you need to find out which ones are available in your school, how they are to be used and where they are stored. Popular resources include coloured plastic cubes (multilink), Dienes blocks, Cuisenaire rods and Numicon. All seek to teach the concept of number rather than simply support calculations and the manipulation of number.

To develop an understanding of space, shape and measure pupils will need to have access to a range of physical apparatus such as 2D and 3D shapes, protractors, rulers, pairs of compasses and set squares.

How to maintain pupils' interest, motivation and focus in pursuing lines of enquiry and solving problems

Pupils who struggle with maths often want to give up. Frustrations, despondency and a sense of failure are common experiences of many pupils in maths lessons. Part of your role is to seek to counter this almost sense of fatalism. You can do so in a number of ways:

- simply by offering verbal encouragement – 'yes, you can do this, I know you can';
- by pointing pupils in the direction of resources that may help their enquiry, e.g. 'Have you thought about using a number line to help you?';
- by showing them where they have already succeeded or by highlighting an area of the investigation that you know they can do but that they may have overlooked in the overall fog of misunderstanding;
- by pairing them with others who can help them through peer-support;
- by offering further teaching in aspects of maths that are hindering their progress;
- it often helps simply to be a listening and understanding ear for pupils to let out their frustration.

How to monitor and promote pupil participation

In order to ascertain what pupils are learning, effective monitoring processes need to be in place. This can take many forms – pupil observation, questioning pupils, discussing their work with them, formative assessment and summative assessment. Pupil participation is a crucial aspect of this – pupils need to be encouraged and enabled to take part in their own assessment and monitoring of their progress. This can be done from the first months of schooling right through to further and higher education.

'Assessment for Learning' is a national initiative that seeks to make such monitoring effective (see Chapter 11).

Self-assessment questions

I   Why do *you* think some pupils find mathematics hard to learn?

2   How do *you* feel you can best support such pupils?

3   What maths resources are available for you to use in your school?

4   How competent do you feel about using them?

The sorts of problems that might occur and how to deal with these

Learning resources

Prior to a lesson you will need to ensure that you have all the learning resources you need; that all equipment required is both available and in working order; and that you have access to the right quantity of written and curriculum materials. It is too late in the middle of the lesson to find out that half of the calculators you need have dead batteries. If some of the pupils you support require specialist equipment, you need to know it is available and in good working order.

Limited knowledge

The older the pupils you are supporting, the more knowledge of maths you yourself must know. One problem could be that they ask you questions to which you do not know the answer. You need to be honest with them, and tell them that you will find out to help them in a future lesson – but be sure that you do! This is one reason why it is important to be aware of the teacher's planning and objectives for the upcoming lessons. If you are aware of an area where you yourself have limited knowledge, you can brush up your own skills and understanding before the actual lessons are taught.

Working within the boundaries of your role

Some of the suggestions for support given above assume you as a TA have a large measure of independence within the class and can take a certain amount of initiative with pupils. This sort of thing must be agreed beforehand with the class or subject teacher. Your school may have established clear guidelines regarding what TAs can and cannot do within lessons. It is vital you keep to these and do not try to take matters into your hands that are beyond your responsibility. All sorts of tensions can arise if this happens.

There are two areas of possible tension regarding your role. One is that you feel you have a lot more to offer than is being asked of you – the issue of being 'underused'. The other is that you are asked to do more than you feel you have the competence to do – the issue of being overstretched. Both these scenarios are reasonably common and both need to be discussed with the teacher and/or the SENCO or the person in your school responsible for the deployment of TAs. You cannot let either of these situations continue for long without tensions arising within the class.

Checklist

✔ I am aware of my school's approach to mathematics teaching.
✔ I am familiar with the reasons why certain pupils find mathematics difficult.
✔ I am familiar with strategies for supporting mathematics.
✔ I know where to find out about any special educational needs the children with whom I work might have.
✔ I understand the implications of these needs for their mathematical development.

GATHERING EVIDENCE

 Setting the scene

Nicola is working in a Year 7 lower numeracy set where the students are continuing to struggle with concepts of multiplication. It is the first lesson in a new maths topic. The first part of the lesson is input from the teacher, Miss Salisbury, who uses an **interactive whiteboard** to explain how to use the grid method to solve multiplication questions. This is followed by whole class activity with pupils working independently practising the procedure being taught. The teacher puts ten questions on the board that the pupils are to try to calculate. There is a plenary towards the end of the lesson when pupils share their answers and the final activity is a card game played in groups to reinforce multiplication facts.

Writing personal accounts: collecting evidence

When writing up what she has done, Nicola does not cover all that is required to meet the standard for this unit and she will need to present a number of pieces of evidence to achieve this.

PERSONAL ACCOUNT

Name: **Nicola Wilson**
Date: **9 March**

Support pupils to develop numeracy skills

Clarify and confirm with the teacher your understanding of:

• *The learning activities you will be supporting*

Following discussion with Miss Salisbury (the teacher) and looking at her planning, I understood that this session dealt with understanding and applying mental calculations and written methods of calculation; recalling number facts; and being able to explain methods and reasoning using correct mathematical language in the context of multiplication.

• *The teaching and learning objectives of the activities*

As I had seen Miss Salisbury's planning beforehand, I knew what the learning objective was. We had talked about it before the lesson so I knew what she was expecting from the class. The learning objective was to use the grid method to multiply tens and units by units using facts from the 3, 7 and 8 multiplication tables.

- *Which pupils you will be working with*

Miss Salisbury and I had agreed that I would be working with the eight or nine pupils who struggled most in maths. They are not sat together in a group, but rather are scattered throughout the set so I will need to move around the whole class in order to work with each one individually as they need support from me.

- *How this support will be organised in relation to what the teacher and other pupils will be doing*

Miss Salisbury and I had discussed the type of support I was to give so that when it came to the actual lesson I did not need to be told what to do. It was agreed that I would make sure that all pupils had understood and were following the teacher's instructions and that they were using appropriate mathematical language and vocabulary. While I was moving around the class supporting particular individuals, Miss Salisbury would be doing the same, supporting the rest of the class. By me working with those who struggled most, she is able to provide more effective support for the rest.

- *Obtain accurate and up-to-date information about the pupils' current numeracy skills, including any specific learning targets or difficulties*

The previous week the class had been given a diagnostic numeracy test that Miss Salisbury had marked. She told me that this assessment showed that, although most pupils knew the multiplication tables 3, 7 and 8, they were uncertain about applying this knowledge when multiplying tens and units by units – hence this series of lessons. The pupils I will be working with scored the most poorly in the test.

- *Agree the support strategies you will use when working with individual and groups of pupils to develop their numeracy skills*

Miss Salisbury and I agreed that most of my support will be making sure that pupils have understood what to do and are able to complete the required tasks. I will do this by observing the pupils, asking them questions and making suggestions as to how they might approach their work differently. Much of my work will be encouraging them to continue to focus on the task as several of the pupils find it easy to avoid the work!

- *Obtain the learning resources needed to implement the agreed learning activities*

There were no specific resources for this activity beyond making sure there were enough individual whiteboards and dry marker pens for the pupils for the first part of the lesson and some laminated cards with multiplication facts on available for the plenary. Before the lesson started I checked that these were all in place so that pupils could get them when they needed to.

I certify that this is a true statement of what occurred.

Staff signature	Name (printed and role)
N. Salisbury	Miss N. Salisbury, Mathematics Teacher

What happened in the lesson itself could have been written up as a personal account. However, in this case, Nicola's assessor came to her school and sat in on the maths lesson making notes. Nicola said beforehand that she was anxious about having someone in the class observing her; but afterwards she commented that it wasn't that bad after all. In fact there were times when she forgot the assessor was there and when she saw all the performance indicators covered, she was thrilled. She even managed to provide evidence for her knowledge base by answering some questions from her assessor afterwards.

OBSERVATION NOTES

Candidate: **Nicola Wilson**
School: **Wherever Secondary School**   *Date:*   **9 March**

Support pupils to develop numeracy skills

- *Use the agreed strategies correctly to support development of the pupils' numeracy skills*

The class were sitting in their assigned places and Nicola moved to sit near specific pupils for short periods of time. Some of these pupils had special needs; others were learning English as an additional language. She ensured they were correctly setting out the tens and units on their personal whiteboards as directed by Miss Salisbury. She looked at what they were writing and listened to their answers to make sure that they were following the procedures and using multiplication facts correctly.

- *Monitor progress towards the intended learning outcomes and provide feedback to the pupils in a manner appropriate to their age and achievements*

When she saw some pupils struggling she quietly asked them questions or made suggestions about the task. She did not tell them what they should do. She repeated or simplified the teacher's instructions, using rephrasing techniques such as, '7 multiplied by 2, that's the same as 7 add 7, isn't it?'
Several of the pupils were getting correct answers but were reluctant to put their hands up in response to the teacher's questions. Nicola encouraged them to respond by saying things like, 'Go on, have a go' or 'I know you can do it.' She also encouraged them by her body language, such as giving them the 'thumbs up' sign.

- *Take appropriate action to resolve any problems in supporting pupils during learning activities*

Nicola made sure that all pupils could see the board with the learning objective and follow-up questions on. She wrote the learning objective on a personal whiteboard for one pupil to copy who could not easily see the board from where she was sitting. She then moved to another pupil and reinforced the procedure that Miss Salisbury had taught.

Then she went to a third pupil. Later Nicola told me that this pupil usually took a long time with her writing and she wrote the learning objective for her so the pupil could get on with the numeracy task immediately.

- *Deal with any difficulties in completing the learning tasks in ways that maintain the pupils' confidence and self-esteem*

As she went round the class, several pupils asked Nicola questions such as, 'Is this right, Miss?' or 'What do I do now?' In response to these she asked questions of her own, such as, 'What do you think?' or 'How can you check it?' She clearly wanted to build their independence and boost their ability to reflect on their own work.

- *Use the agreed strategies correctly to support development of the pupils' numeracy skills*

A good number of pupils were able to follow the procedure and use the grid method correctly, but they struggled because they did not know the relevant multiplication facts securely enough to give immediate recall. Nicola helped them by getting them to write down the appropriate multiplication tables so that they could use these in their calculations and practise them later.

When they were finding answers to calculations involving multiplying by 10, many pupils told Nicola, 'You add a nought.' She reminded them that they need to use correct mathematical language and that, 'Adding a nought does not change a number – three add nought is three.' She said they should rather be using vocabulary such as 'When multiplying by 10 the numbers move to the next higher column.'

- *Use praise, commentary and assistance to encourage pupils to stay on task and complete the learning tasks*

Throughout the lesson I noted that Nicola was careful to use appropriate mathematical language when she spoke with the pupils and with Miss Salisbury; for example, using the term 'multiplication' rather than 'times'. She made a point of saying 'well done' to all the pupils she supported, specifying what it was they had done well, e.g. 'Well done, you have remembered your multiplication tables of seven and are using this in your calculations.'

At the end of the plenary, along with Miss Salisbury, she praised all the class for their hard work and enthusiasm. Nicola specifically spoke with the pupils who were still struggling to understand the concepts being taught, praising them for their effort. She said that lots of people find it hard to learn about multiplication, but that there were lots of ways to help them remember what to do, which they would be looking at over the next few days.

- *Provide the teacher with the information needed to maintain pupil records and reports*

After the lesson I listened to Nicola's feedback to the teacher. She told Miss Salisbury that she thought most pupils had understood what they should be doing, but named five or six who were still struggling. She suggested that, in the next lesson, these pupils might be given grid templates upon which they could work directly rather than be asked to draw their own grids in their books as they had done today. She felt this might give them more structure.

She also noted that, despite what was indicated by the previous week's assessment; many pupils were not fully secure in their multiplication tables and had to work out each calculation from scratch. One or two pupils were even confused about what the multiplication sign (X) meant – they initially thought it meant addition. There was, she thought, therefore a need to revisit these basics.

She commented that, by and large, she thought the pupils had enjoyed the activity, even those who had struggled, because they could all see that they had learnt something. As it was only the first lesson in a series, she thought it went well and could easily be built upon.

ASSESSOR'S COMMENTS

A very effective session. I talked to Miss Salisbury afterwards and she stated that she was extremely appreciative of the help and support you offered.

Some questions that I would like to follow up with you:

- Do you have any SEN pupils with whom you work?
- If so, what allowances or support do you give to help them develop mathematical knowledge, understanding and skills?

Signed: **Terrie Cole**, NVQ Assessor

Chapter 11

Contribute to assessment for learning

In this chapter we will look at two elements:

1   Use assessment strategies to improve learning.
2   Support pupils in reviewing their own learning.

KNOWLEDGE AND UNDERSTANDING

The teacher's responsibility for assessing pupil achievement and your role in supporting this

Knowing where pupils are in their learning is an essential prerequisite to effective teaching. To pitch the lesson at an appropriate level, teachers need to assess their pupils. Assessment can either be formal, such as via tests, or informal, such as through observation.

The difference between formative and summative assessment

Essentially **formative assessment** is an ongoing process of finding out how well pupils are learning what is being taught while it is still in the process of being taught. This type of assessment is able to inform teacher's planning for future lessons. It also provides the opportunity for pupils themselves to see how they are doing and to agree targets for their next steps in learning. Formative assessment can be used to measure pupil progress against their past performance.

Summative assessment is a summation of what pupils have learnt. It usually takes the form of more formal testing at the end of a topic or unit of work. The most obvious summative assessments experienced by pupils in schools in England are the **Standard Attainment Tasks (SATs)** given at the end of each of Key Stages 1, 2 and 3 and the GCSEs sat at the end of Key Stage 4. These forms of assessment measure pupils against national standards rather than against their own past performance.

To put it succinctly, summative assessment is assessment *of* learning, whereas formative assessment is assessment *for* learning.

Assessment for Learning (AfL)

Background

An influential group of researchers and academics, the Assessment Reform Group (ARG), commissioned a number of investigative projects in the late 1990s and early 2000s. In 1998 *Inside the Black Box* was published (Black and Wiliam 1998), followed by *Assessment for Learning: Beyond the Black Box* (The Assessment Reform Group 1999) and *Assessment for Learning – Putting it into Practice* (Black *et al.* 2003). These publications, along with a growing number of articles and books published by other members of the educational establishment have shaped what is now called 'Assessment for Learning'.

Qualities of AfL

The whole purpose of AfL is to raise pupil achievement. The research noted above indicates that this sort of assessment, when applied properly, can have the effect of raising standards for all types of pupils, including those who are **gifted and talented** or those identified as having special needs. In order to be this effective a number of qualities of AfL need to be applied consistently in the classroom:

- Learning goals (for the individual pupils) and learning objectives (of the lesson) need to be shared with pupils.
- Pupils must know and understand what they are aiming for in any particular lesson and over a whole unit of work (the 'big picture').
- Feedback from the teacher (either oral or in written form) should relate to the learning objectives and help pupils identify how they can improve.
- Teachers (and TAs) must believe that all pupils can improve on past performance (i.e. intelligence is not a fixed entity).
- Both teacher and pupil must be involved in reviewing and reflecting on the learning that has taken place.
- Pupils need to learn self-assessment techniques enabling them to see areas for themselves in which they need to develop to make progress.
- There must be a recognition that motivation and self-esteem can be facilitated by effective assessment.

This is a far cry from a pupil's piece of work returned to him or her scribbled over with the teacher's red pen or with the ominous words 'Please see me' inscribed on the bottom!

The basic principles of how children and young people learn

Education has the task of developing children's cognition and learning. That is its explicit function. All members of staff should therefore give careful consideration to how children learn and to what factors are best suited to promote the development of their thinking and learning skills.

Many researchers and theorists have been influential in developing an understanding of cognition and learning; among these are:

- Jerome Bruner (born 1915)
- Jean Piaget (1896–1980) – see Chapter 2, pp. 42–7
- Lev Vygotsky (1896–1934) – see Chapter 2, pp. 47–8.

Bruner – 'scaffolding' and the 'spiral curriculum'

Bruner argues that whenever we learn something new, whatever our age, we go through similar stages in the process. This view is embodied in the concept of the 'spiral curriculum', which states that during their school career, students should visit on numerous occasions the same issues building upon previous knowledge. Children should initially be taught simple basic elements and subsequently be exposed regularly to ever more complex aspects of the same topics as they grow older.

What enables someone to learn a new concept, be they a child or an adult, is 'scaffolding' – that which is temporarily built around them in order for new thinking to take place. Scaffolding is any support mechanism that is put in place by others, teachers or teaching assistants in school, in order to help a child learn something new. This could be questions; ways of presenting information; or styles of teaching.

The interrelationship between motivation and self-esteem, effective learning and progress, and assessment for learning

AfL is designed to raise motivation and self-esteem; if it does not, it is not assessment that is for learning. The paper *Testing, Motivation and Learning*, commissioned by the Assessment Reform Group (Harlen and Deakin-Crick 2002) concluded that summative assessment is likely to reduce motivation and self-esteem for pupils who are 'failing' whereas AfL can be effective in stimulating the motivation and self-esteem of all pupils.

AfL focuses on what pupils *can* do, rather than what they cannot do. It highlights the next steps that can realistically be taken. It shows pupils how far they have travelled already rather than emphasising what they have failed to achieve. Appropriate feedback, rather than simply marking a piece of work, can be a great stimulus to pupil motivation, which is a key ingredient in promoting their learning.

QUIZ

1   Why is assessment important?

2   What are the essential differences between formative and summative assessment?

3   What distinguishes Assessment for Learning from other types of assessment?

Figure 11.1 TAs need to look for talent in all pupils

The importance of believing that every pupil can improve in comparison with previous achievements and the implications of this for how you support pupils' learning

'Could do better' is the archetypal banal teacher's comment in a school report. In itself it is meaningless. But there is a truth behind the comment that lies at the heart of AfL, and also is an important factor in developing inclusive education.

AfL challenges the understanding that intelligence is a fixed entity, something static you are born with and have a limited and measurable supply of. This has huge implications for teaching, some of which include:

- Pupils are able to improve and make progress on their previous experience, assuming there is not a medical or physical reason why this cannot be the case.

- Teacher and TA expectations of pupils shift from seeing them as being passive learners, in class to imbibe the received wisdom of the curriculum, to being **active learners,** participating in their own learning
- Teachers and TAs have the responsibility to ensure that their teaching methods and content, indeed the whole learning environment, promotes pupil learning and development.

The strategies and techniques for supporting assessment for learning that are within your role and sphere of competence

How AfL is being supported will vary from school to school. There is no 'one size fits all'. However, within schools, there should be a consistency of approach that should be made clear to you. Some of the most common strategies and techniques include:

- Setting out learning objectives for a lesson visually using acronyms such as 'WILF' (What I am Looking For is . . .) or 'RT's' (Remember To's).
- Pupils using 'traffic light' cards to let the teacher know how much they are taking in of what is being taught. A green card means 'It's fine, I understand', an orange card means 'I'm not sure, I could do with some more explanation', and red means 'I haven't got a clue!'.
- Learning boards – large display areas in the class presenting the 'big picture' of the topic being taught with key vocabulary and concepts written, illustrated and explained.
- Learning mats – where individual pupils have their personal targets written down with key ways explained to help them reach those targets.
- Questioning pupils using a range of styles to develop the understanding and reflection of all pupils (see pp. 119–22).
- Giving pupils 'thinking time' when all the class take one or two minutes to think of answers to questions before the teacher asks any one of them for a response – i.e. an end to 'hands up those who know the right answer'.
- Verbal feedback from the TA or the teacher to pupils individually as they look at their work.
- Written feedback in the agreed style of the school highlighting both where the learning objectives have been achieved and where improvements can be made.
- Giving pupils time to read and reflect on the marking of their work.

As a TA you can support pupils in any or all of these ways. For instance, if you are working with a group of pupils supporting them with a literacy task and the teacher asks for a 'traffic light' card response to the lesson so far, you can encourage your pupils to put up the cards that accurately express their understanding rather than the one that they think the teacher wants to see or the one they might like to exhibit.

How to communicate clearly and objectively with pupils about their learning goals and achievements

Ideally, learning goals will have been negotiated and agreed between pupil and teacher and, depending on the level and nature of support being given, the TA. Your role will be to reinforce those learning goals through discussion with the pupils. You may help them to write them down in the appropriate place – a learning mat or pasted into an exercise book. Where appropriate you could scribe for them, read the objectives to the pupils and make sure they understand what they mean.

In discussing learning goals with pupils you need to use language that fully describes the goal but is also something they can understand. For young children it may not be helpful to use over-technical language such as 'adjectival clauses' or 'conjunctions'. Instead you could talk about 'using description in sentences' or 'joining words'. The concept is the same, but the terminology makes more sense to the pupils. However, as the pupils get older the correct technical vocabulary will need to be used. Your role could be to ensure that pupils understand this terminology, know how to use it correctly and appreciate what they must do to put it into practice.

How to encourage pupils to keep in mind their learning goals and to assess their own progress in meeting these as they proceed

Much, if not all, of your support in this area will be through discussion with the pupils as you work with them during a lesson. They may ask you questions such as, 'What should I do now?' to which part of your response could be to ask them what their learning goals are.

Learning goals are not meant to be straightjackets whereby pupils can do nothing else but work towards these goals; rather they are designed to be used as signposts, as aids pointing the way forward in their learning. Most learning goals, at least in the primary sector, are likely to be related to literacy or numeracy. A pupil's literacy learning goals will be appropriate for every written task they undertake; for instance, remembering to leave 'finger spaces' between words. Each time you get alongside them, you can remind them of this. It is very easy for pupils to so focus on the immediate learning objective of the lesson that they forget these 'cross-curricular' goals that apply to all written work.

How to review and reflect on a pupil's performance and progress

When you yourself are reviewing and reflecting on a pupil's performance and progress you need to bear a number of things in mind:

* where they have come from – their previous ability in this particular task or subject;
* what they are actually doing now – the areas where they are doing well and also where they need to improve;
* what factors have helped them or hindered them in making progress.

How to provide constructive feedback to pupils

'Well done, that was good' or 'You really need to improve' are both feedback of sorts, but neither is constructive. The former begs the question, 'What was good about it? In what ways was it good? How can I tell in future what is going to be good as well?' Being told they need to improve tells the pupil absolutely nothing.

Constructive feedback, either verbally or in written form via marking, needs to state what has been achieved by the pupil and/or what needs to be done to improve. Being specific is the key.

Constructive feedback needs to relate to the learning objectives of the lesson and the learning goals of the pupils. You need to phrase your comments in such a way that the pupil understands to what extent they have achieved the targets, in what way they have achieved them and what has helped them achieve them. From what you say or write they should have a clear idea of where to proceed.

TRY IT FOR YOURSELF

Here is a piece of writing produced by a ten-year-old girl. How would you set about marking it and giving this pupil 'constructive feedback'? What information would you need in order for you to be able to do this effectively? *[The necessities of printing mean that the pupil's handwriting cannot be taken into account.]*

```
    Wot am I doing herer, the mna said.
    He lkd arund him and soer that he was nto alone, thee
was sumon round the corner. he wundred who it was.
    Is anyun ther? He calld out. Ther was no ansa.
    The man got scrd. He fout he must get out, but he did
not no were he wus.
    Suddenly a voiuc clad out – can I help you?
    It was a polcmen.
```

How to help pupils to review their learning strategies and achievements and plan future learning

AfL has not only to do with what pupils have achieved, but how they have achieved it. Part of the process of reviewing a lesson or a series of lessons is to analyse what has helped progress and what has hindered it. Within AfL the role of teachers and TAs is to support younger children in these areas so that, as they grow older, they can do this for themselves and review and reflect on their learning independently. In this way you are building skills for life and not just for school, and certainly not just to pass tests.

As in many aspects of AfL, the key to helping pupils reflect on this will be your questioning techniques. Children tend to learn without really thinking about why or how they are learning. They are likely to gravitate unconsciously towards those areas that best suit their learning – whether through hands-on experience, through listening, reading or whatever. You can ask them about this, helping them come to see for themselves how they best learn.

Figure 11.2 TAs need to encourage independence

Self-assessment techniques and how to support pupils in developing these

AfL is not an easy option for pupils. It demands that they become reflective learners who take responsibility for their own learning. In order to be fully effective, AfL necessitates a change in teaching strategies and in the overall philosophy of education. Pupils need to become participants in the learning process rather than simply recipients.

When pupils are asked to assess their work themselves, this can be very threatening if it is not something they are used to or have been trained to do. In order to train pupils to do this effectively, teachers and TAs need to change from being disseminators of knowledge to facilitators of process, and this can be threatening for them as well.

AfL, like inclusion, goes to the heart of what education is about and can never be merely a 'bolt-on' extra to what is being done already.

Pupil self-assessment is crucial to the process of AfL. In order to be able to effectively assess themselves, pupils need to be given specific training:

- They need to recognise and understand the learning objectives of lessons.
- They need to know and understand the success criteria for those lessons, i.e. how they will know when those learning objectives have been achieved.
- They need to know how to make use of the time given them for self-assessment, which can be daily and certainly should be at least weekly if it is going to be of any use.

It is important to recognise that self-assessment, along with peer assessment, is not a substitute for you or the teacher marking and assessing pupils' work, but it does add to it.

How to promote the skills of collaboration in peer assessment

Peer assessment – pupils working in groups to review and reflect on each other's work – is also a key aspect of AfL and something that needs to be taught. Pupils have not normally experienced this kind of assessment and they need to be trained and given experience in it before it becomes the natural thing to do.

For some pupils, this can be the most threatening aspect of AfL. It is one thing to have the teacher or TA look at your work, it is OK to be asked to review it yourself; but to expose your work to your friends (or otherwise) in the class is something else. Your support for such pupils can be crucial; but much will depend on the climate being established in the class and school as a whole. Peer assessment cannot be introduced in isolation from everything else to do with AfL.

There are several reasons why peer assessment can be effective and the pupils need to be made aware of these:

- Pupils can be more objective in assessing other pieces of work and, by doing this, can be helped to assess their own work – 'John wrote this which met the success criteria, but I did the same, so I met it as well.'
- Pupils can be motivated to work harder and to make improvements – 'If Claire is going to read this, it had better be good.'
- The whole group can come up with learning goals for themselves, which takes the pressure off individual pupils and can also aid the teacher in planning future lessons.
- Pupils can see that the mistakes they themselves make are made by others as well – 'Phew, Alistair and Jane did not understand what to do either, that makes me feel better.'
- When assessing each other's work pupils are likely to use language that all understand – it is not in 'teacher-speak'.
- Pupils often accept negative comments from their peers more readily than from teachers as there is not, or should not be, any implied threat in it – it is teachers and not pupils who give detentions or set extra work!

Teachers and TAs can be helped by peer assessment for, as it takes place, they have time to observe and monitor what is happening in the classroom. They can listen in on pupil discussions and assess the level of participation in the activity and its effectiveness.

How assessment for learning contributes to planning for future learning carried out by:

1   the teacher
2   the pupils
3   yourself.

Much of what has already been said in this chapter relates to planning. In order for AfL to be genuine, assessment must affect planning. If lessons continue just as if no assessment had been made, what was the point of the assessment?

Planning at all levels is affected by AfL.

Teachers will need to change their short-term, daily and weekly plans in response to what they have found out through AfL. If many pupils have not made progress towards the learning objectives, either the learning objectives need to be modified or the teaching strategies altered. If, on the other hand, all the class have easily achieved the objectives and it has become apparent that they already know a great deal about the topic, plans need to be altered accordingly to ensure new aspects are being learned and taught.

Pupils' plans for learning should be shaped by AfL in the ways already outlined. For this to be effective there needs to be a level of flexibility in the curriculum and shape of lessons that has not been the norm to date. Teaching needs to be learning-led rather than curriculum-led, and this presents obvious challenges at every level of education.

Your own plans for support need to be responsive to what is learnt via AfL. If you are allocated specific pupils to support in lessons, then what and how you work with them will be guided very much by what has been learnt through effective formative assessment. You may need to reinforce work or even go back to early stages and teach it again. This may necessitate changing the structure of the class or your support; so, here again, flexibility is required. As in all things to do with AfL, as with most aspects of your role, the whole-school approach is going to either facilitate or restrict what you can do.

Checklist

✔   I understand the principles of AfL.
✔   I am familiar with basic theories of how children learn.
✔   I know how to support AfL in my school.
✔   I can provide effective feedback to pupils, helping them reflect on their learning.
✔   I know how to support self- and peer-assessment.

GATHERING EVIDENCE

 ### Setting the scene

Sadie is working in a Year 3 class, providing general support in literacy. Her main focus is with a group of six pupils who are more than a year behind age expectations in reading and writing. The lesson she has chosen to base her personal account on is the third in a series of lessons on sentence construction and is focused on the pupils writing their own stories using time connectives. She will need to write a second account to show how she meets the performance criteria for STL30.2 Support pupils in reviewing their own learning.

Writing personal accounts: collecting evidence

PERSONAL ACCOUNT

Name: **Sadie Molapo**
Date: **4 December**

Use assessment strategies to improve learning

Clarify and confirm the following with the teacher

- *The learning objectives for the activity*

Through discussion with the teacher (Mrs Russell) and looking at her planning I knew that this lesson series fitted into the 'Sentence structure and punctuation' strand of the revised Primary National Literacy Framework, Core Learning in Literacy for Year 3, focusing on the learning objective, 'Show relationships of time connectives'.

- *The learning goals for individual pupils*

During this lesson it was agreed that I would focus my attention on the six pupils who were behind age-expectations in their writing. Their learning goals, identified on a group education plan and to be worked on for this term, are to write in complete sentences, to use capital letters at the beginning of sentences and to use full stops at the end.

- *The success criteria for the learning activity*

For these six pupils the success criteria for the learning activity were:

1　to join correctly formed sentences with 'then' and 'after';
2　to make sure that the sentences made sense;
3　to make sure the sentences were sequenced properly.

- *The assessment opportunities and strategies relevant to your role in the lesson/ activity*

The opportunities for assessment during this lesson are threefold:

1　listening to the pupils saying what they are going to write;
2　observing what the pupils write as they are in the process of doing this;
3　together, reading and revising their finished work.

- *Discuss and clarify the learning goals and criteria for assessing progress with the pupils using terms they can understand and providing examples of how the criteria can be met in practice*

Although all the six pupils are familiar with their learning goals, I make a point of discussing these with them before they start any writing activity. I try to make it fun and it has by now become something of a routine that they enjoy and respond to enthusiastically. As usual, then, as these pupils settled to their activity I sat with them at their table and said, 'Right then, what do we need to remember?' and they all chanted back 'We need to remember our capital letters, our full stops and that our sentences make sense!'

To remind them of their learning goals and give them examples of what they are aiming for, each pupil has a laminated A4 sheet of paper taped onto their desk called a Learning Mat. Every pupil in the class has one of these, each one with personalised learning goals on. The group I work with have examples of sentences with capital letters and full stops highlighted. There is one example of an incomplete sentence and there is one example of a complete sentence to reinforce the difference. As we began the activity I reminded them to look at their Learning Mats to see what they needed to be working towards.

Also at the start of this session I discussed with them how we would know that they had achieved the learning objective for the lesson. We agreed together that they would know this when they had written at least three sentences in time order and had joined two of them with the word 'then' or 'after'.

- *Encourage pupils to take responsibility for their own learning*

I encouraged them to take responsibility for their learning by:

1 moving away from the table as soon as we had gone over the learning goals and learning outcome;
2 working with other pupils in the class, indicating to this group that they needed to do the work themselves;
3 when pupils in the group put their hands up to ask me for help or to ask me whether what they had written was correct, I responded by saying something like, 'What do you think?' or 'How does this fit with what is on your Learning Mat?';
4 I always said to them that I wanted to see their own work and not my ideas.

- *Encourage pupils to keep in mind their learning goals and to assess their own progress towards meeting these as they proceed*

During the activity I sat with them occasionally, asking them to read through their work so far to look for the success criteria, highlighting where they had achieved these goals in their work. I suggested to them that they kept looking at their Learning Mats and at the Learning Board to remind them of what the activity was about. I asked each one to read through their work, looking for the words 'then' and 'after' and to see if they were being used properly.

- *Use the agreed assessment opportunities and strategies to gain information and make judgements about how well the pupils are participating in activities and the progress they are making*

Although they are all below what would be expected in literacy, there is a range of ability even within this group. This became most apparent in the first part of the session when they were talking about what they were going to write. I listened in on their discussion when I was near them in the class. All of them could speak in sentences, yet not all understood what they needed to do in order for them to make sense. One pupil, for instance, talked about 'him and his dog, and they went there to see her'. He clearly could picture in his mind what he wanted to say, but he was not aware that the sentences carried little meaning for anyone who did not know who 'he' or 'her' were nor where 'there' was.

As the pupils were writing their sentences I read over their shoulders as I was moving around the class, noting in my mind those who were achieving the objectives and those who were not. Although four of them were, two had difficulties framing sentences that would be understood by others. I was pleased to see that one pupil in particular was placing full stops in appropriate places. A few months ago she simply placed a full stop at the end of each line and hoped this would be good enough.

- *Provide feedback to pupils to help them understand what they have done well and what they need to develop*

During the writing activity I went up to each of the six pupils individually at least once, asking them to read me what they had written so far. As each did so I pointed out where they had correctly used capital letters and full stops, commending them for doing so. I especially focused on the time connectives. Where they had used 'then' or 'after' I commended them, telling them that they had achieved the learning objective. For those who were still working to achieve the objectives, I encouraged them to keep going, and to keep in mind what they were aiming for.

- *Be clear and constructive about any weaknesses and how they might be addressed*

One pupil in particular had not achieved the learning objective or her learning goals at all. She had written a great deal, but none of it made sense to the reader and, apart from the odd full stop there was no punctuation. Capital letters had been placed randomly within words and sentences. When I came to review her work with her, I asked her to show me the full stops. She pointed out two. I then asked her to read what she had written aloud to me, only taking a breath at these two full stops. She began to do this and soon ran out of breath. So I commented to her that that was what full stops were for – to let the reader know when to pause and take a breath. I read back her first two sentences, asking her to show me when full stops were needed as indicated by me stopping for breath. This she did, and put in the full stops. I encouraged her to read through the rest of her work, putting in full stops when she realised she needed to breathe. We will leave time-connectives for another time!

- *Encourage pupils to review and comment on their work before handing it in or discussing it with the teacher*

Towards the end of the activity I sat back down with the group and asked them to read out what they had written. As each one finished their reading I asked them how well they thought they had achieved the learning objective of using 'then' and 'after' to show time had passed. When they had given their opinion I asked the rest of the group what they thought – whether they agreed with the pupil or not and why they thought as they did.

- *Praise pupils when they focus their comments on the learning goals for the task*

During this last discussion I made a point of praising pupils who referred explicitly to the learning goals and objectives. For instance, 'Well done John, you have said that Jean has used the time-connective "then" to show what happened next.'

- *Provide opportunities and encouragement for pupils to improve upon their work*

I gave the group two minutes to look over their work again after our discussion and change anything they wanted to before handing it to Mrs Russell. Several of them had very specific things to do to improve their work and I told them that now was the time to do it while it was fresh in their minds.

TEACHER'S COMMENTS

Sadie understands a great deal about assessment for learning and how this can be applied in the classroom. Her work with pupils is both detailed and thorough and her feedback to me is invaluable.

I certify that this is a true statement of what occurred.

Staff signature	Name (printed and role)
K. Russell	Katie Russell, Class Teacher

ASSESSOR'S COMMENTS

I agree with your teacher's comments. You obviously know a good deal about assessment for learning and are putting it into practice in the lessons. Including examples of the way you speak with pupils and the terminology you use is helpful. Perhaps you could do this more often.

Signed: **Terrie Cole**, NVQ Assessor

Chapter 12

Support bilingual/multilingual pupils

In this chapter we will look at two elements:

1   Support development of the target language.
2   Support bilingual/multilingual pupils in accessing the curriculum.

KNOWLEDGE AND UNDERSTANDING

The process and stages of language acquisition and the factors that promote or hinder language development

Children of all languages learn to speak following similar stages. It is important to remember that when you are working with a pupil who is new to English, they have already gone through the process of learning at least one language, sometimes more.

Box 12.1	
Age of the child	*Language development*
0–6 months	Pre-linguistic stage – attract attention by making different sounds and gestures, which is reinforced by adults responding to them.
6–18 months	First words – begin to formulate words by repeating sounds and words made to them.
18 months to 3 years	Rapid vocabulary development – begin to formulate sentences; begin to respond to rhyme and simple song.
3–8 years	Increasingly complex language – most children fluent in their first language.

At each stage of language development children need to be listened to, responded to and helped to expand and correct their vocabulary. The language development of any child can be hindered or helped by the richness or otherwise of the language environment within which they are brought up. A home environment that uses a wide range of vocabulary and involves a high level of verbal interaction between family members will promote a greater level of language development than where there is very little verbal communication.

Obtaining and interpreting information about a pupil's language and educational background, capabilities and skills and language support needs

Schools will have records regarding the ethnic background of its pupils using the categories given by the government. As well as general information such as dates of birth, gender and any medical issues, these records should also include, where appropriate, the country or countries of origin of the pupil's family, the date of the pupil's entry into the UK, the language(s) spoken at home and any relevant cultural or religious information, such as dietary or clothing requirements.

More detailed information regarding a pupil's educational and cultural background will come through conversation with that pupil or with the pupil's parents or carers, with the support of a translator where appropriate. From such a conversation it is possible to find out about the pupil's previous educational experience, whether any particular abilities or difficulties have been evidenced and to what extent the pupil can read and write fluently in their first language. If they have learnt their first language without much difficulty, they are likely to learn English in the same way. Conversely, if they have experienced difficulties in their first language, they may well face learning difficulties when being taught English and extra support is likely to be needed.

Strategies suitable for supporting pupils in developing their speaking/talking, reading and writing skills in the target language and how these relate to specific learning activities across the curriculum

Visual cues

The use of picture cues is very important. It is hard for anyone to learn a language simply by listening to it. Linking words and phrases with pictures is a great help. You can make pictures up or you can select from the large number of resources available on the market.

Gestures

Use gestures to help your communication, but be careful, not all gestures mean the same in each culture. If in doubt, check it out. Having said this, smiles and 'thumbs up' usually mean the same to everyone.

Figure 12.1 'Thumbs up' is usually recognised by everyone

Begin with the most essential vocabulary

When seeking to build a pupil's vocabulary, begin with words and phrases that are going to help them communicate with those around them – hello, good-bye, yes, no, please and thank you are useful places to start. 'Can I go to the toilet?' is also a very useful piece of English!

Good peer role models

Where EAL pupils sit in class is important. It is tempting to place them with pupils of lower ability as there they are likely to have access to extra adult support. However, good practice suggests that this is not as helpful as placing such pupils next to those who can communicate effectively in spoken English. These act as good role models for the pupils new to the target language.

Encourage lots of talk between pupils so that the pupil learning English has plenty of opportunity both to listen and to speak in the target language in a non-threatening situation.

Dual language resources

For pupils who have some fluency in reading their first language, the use of dual language books or software can also be a help, particularly if the stories are familiar to the pupils. School libraries should have a stock of such books, both fiction and non-fiction, in the major languages that are likely to be encountered in the school. The local authority's ethnic minority advisory service is also likely to be able to loan such books to schools. All pupils should be encouraged to continue to learn to read in their first language.

Encourage the use of the pupil's first language

Provide as many opportunities as possible for pupils to work and converse in their first language. Pupils new to English make progress more rapidly if they also continue to make progress in their first language, so encourage them to keep using it.

Keep a positive attitude

Underlying all these strategies is your own demeanour and attitude. Whatever support you actually provide for pupils for whom English is an additional language, you can:

- encourage all children, including those from different cultures and ethnic groups, to have a sense of pride in who they are;
- encourage friendships between all children;
- challenge negative attitudes and low expectations.

Case study

Janet is a TA working in a Year 2 class in an infants school. Over a third of the pupils in the class have English as an additional language. Two pupils have just arrived in the country with no previous experience of English at all; one is from Poland and the other from Kerala, in southern India. He speaks Malayalam. The Polish pupil has never been to school before as children there do not start school until they are seven years old.

It is an art lesson – the pupils are preparing for Christmas and are drawing, colouring, painting or making decorations. This is an excellent opportunity for Janet to encourage the two new pupils to make relationships with other children and to introduce the two pupils to some English vocabulary.

The class teacher places the two pupils on a table where there are good English speakers and also where there are speakers of their first languages. During the activity Janet picks up various items, shows them to the two pupils and clearly says what they are, nodding to them to repeat what she says. In this way, they begin to learn vocabulary such as 'brush', 'paper', 'glue' and 'paint'. One pupil willingly tries to repeat the English words, the second pupil is far more quiet. Janet does not try to push this pupil into responding, knowing that it takes some pupils a long time to feel secure enough to attempt English words.

The other children talk easily to them, and having pupils who speak their own language helps them feel at home in the class.

Develop speaking and listening in a meaningful context

Generally speaking, supporting pupils new to English should take place within the classroom or ordinary lesson, whatever the subject or learning focus. Pupils need to learn to listen to the target language and to speak it in the context of real life. In this situation, your role could be to encourage them to 'have a go' at speaking in class or group discussions or to verbally answer questions. However, you need to make sure you do not put pressure on pupils to speak in the target language before they have the confidence to do so. You can also get alongside pupils and quietly explain and, where appropriate, simplify teacher instructions.

Specific focused teaching

All pupils learning English as an additional language will need to be taught the basic sound structure and phonic rules of the language. For younger pupils this is likely to take place within the class, but older pupils may well need to be withdrawn from class to teach these basic skills. However, not too much emphasis should be placed on learning phonics and the formal structure of the target language at first. Rather, pupils should be given books and texts to read that are both simple yet set in a context to which they can relate. It is important that pupils learn the meaning as well as the mechanics of what they read.

Bilingual support staff

Bilingual assistants may be available via the local authority's ethnic minority service. They can support pupils both in class and individually or in small groups outside of the class by explaining to pupils in their own language what is going on in the lesson. They will also be available to relay specific messages or instructions to pupils or to ask them questions that the teacher expressly wishes to communicate with the pupils.

Another important aspect of the role of bilingual support staff is to express to teachers and TAs any concerns and questions that the pupil may have. It can be a source of frustration and even distress for pupils if they are unable to communicate their needs to those who are trying to support them. Understanding where the pupils are coming from is a major factor in successfully meeting their needs.

Self-assessment questions

1   List as many ways as you can remember or think of to support pupils who are new to the English language.
2   Try and think of a particular situation where pupils learning English as an additional language may be at a disadvantage relative to those for whom English is their first language.
3   What strengths might a pupil learning English as an additional language bring to that process?
4   What differences do you think might be experienced by pupils who are learning English as an additional language between secondary schools and primary schools?

The interactive use of speaking/talking, listening, reading and writing to promote language development

Although pupils new to the language are likely to begin to understand more and more of what they hear before they have the confidence to start speaking, they should be given every opportunity and encouragement to speak out, without being pressurised to do so. Remember, they are not only learning a new language, they are learning to learn *in* that language as well.

They therefore need to be taught to read and write in the target language at the same time as learning to speak it. For pupils learning English as an additional language, the more they link what they hear and say with the written word the better. This will both reinforce their knowledge and give them the skills of communicating in a range of contexts and in a variety of ways.

How to plan and evaluate learning activities to support development of the target language

The extent to which you will be responsible for planning and evaluating activities to support development of the target language will be determined by the level and type of support you are asked to provide for pupils learning English as an additional language. There will be little planning involved if most of the support is to be provided within class, helping pupils to access the lesson. In this case, the planning may well be something like finding out what vocabulary the pupil is going to need to know in order to understand and participate in the lesson and organising ways to teach this vocabulary prior to the lesson. The evaluation will therefore be to what extent the pupil was able to access the lesson.

In order to evaluate learning activities you will need to keep records of the sessions showing how well the pupils have responded to what has been planned and how effective the resources you have used have been in promoting learning. Your plans will be altered by your evaluations – what has worked well can be continued and developed, what has not gone so well will need to be changed.

The principles of Assessment for Learning (AfL) apply just as much in this situation as they do in any other. See Chapter 11 for more details.

How aspects of culture, religion, upbringing, home and family circumstances and emotional health could affect the pupils' learning in the classroom and how to respond to these

The home background and culture for pupils new to English may be significantly different to the prevailing culture of the school. This can affect various aspects of the curriculum such as formal assessments. Pupils from cultures and backgrounds different from those assumed by the assessment may be placed at a significant disadvantage and so achieve lower scores than they would do otherwise.

Certain aspects of the curriculum, such as religious or sex education, may present difficulties for pupils from different cultures. Similarly, pupils from certain cultures may not feel comfortable participating in particular types of sport, such as swimming, which involve types of dress or undress contrary to their values. Whatever the specific issues, you as a TA need to be both aware of them and sensitive to them. Some issues, such as sex education, will be beyond your control, but others can be adapted to take account of cultural factors.

Valuing and promoting cultural diversity, pupils' home languages and the benefits of bilingualism/multilingualism and how to do this

One way to boost self-esteem is to take an interest in the pupil's own language and culture. As well as trying to teach the pupil English vocabulary, you could ask them to teach you some basic words in their language. When they see you struggling with words and sounds that come naturally to them but seem almost incomprehensible to you, they might not feel so bad about experimenting with the strange sounds and words of English. A word of warning may, however, be needed. Some pupils, for a whole range of reasons, may feel uncomfortable talking in their home language and wish to speak only English. If that is the case, do not push the issue.

Many teachers seek to promote a pupil's sense of identity and pride in their language and culture by having all the class learn some words in that language. This can be particularly effective when learning words of greeting. Where there are a number of languages spoken in the class, the teacher can ask that each pupil responds to the register in a language other than their own. In this way the sense that all languages are valuable is promoted and all pupils are placed in the same boat in having to learn unfamiliar words.

Class and school displays can also promote cultural and language diversity. Signs around the school in a range of languages, welcome displays showing a map of the world with flags pinned on to it of the countries from where pupils originate, or

Figure 12.2 TAs need to listen

photographs and pictures from different countries are all ways commonly used to show each pupil that they are valued.

Music and art are other ways in which cultural diversity can be reasonably easily celebrated. Musical instruments and art forms from different countries and cultures can be taught as part of the curriculum. When this happens, pupils from those countries and cultures can be placed at a significant advantage, which will make a change from them being mainly disadvantaged in an unfamiliar culture.

Curriculum plans and learning programmes

To adequately prepare your support for pupils learning the target language, you need to know what is going to be taught in the lesson. You need to see the teacher's plans for the lessons coming up and need to know the learning objectives for any particular lesson. If you get to see these a day or two before the actual lessons you can be thinking about how you can support the pupils and what resources you could draw upon or even make.

If you are asked to work with pupils learning to speak English, in small groups or individually outside of the class using specific programmes, you need to be familiar with those programmes before you start. You need to be given time to read through all relevant literature, such as teaching manuals, and to look through all the materials in the programme. You may need to alter some of it or to focus on particular aspects of it to best support pupils learning the target language.

How to provide appropriate support for bilingual/ multilingual pupils according to their age, emotional needs, abilities and learning needs

Boosting self-esteem

Your role is to help boost and maintain self-confidence so that, when they are ready, pupils can experiment with the language and not be held back by fear or apprehension. You should also make it clear that it is absolutely fine not to say anything but to enjoy a period of quiet, taking in what is happening around them.

You can promote self-esteem by praising their efforts in the language, by providing them with basic vocabulary and modelling its correct usage. Simply by getting alongside pupils and making them feel welcome goes a long way to overcoming their insecurities.

Uphold the culture and values of the pupils

Make sure you pronounce and spell their name properly. Some cultures place the family name or surname before the first name (note: not the 'Christian name'!), which can cause confusion. If you are unsure, ask the pupils and take advice from them.

As you work with pupils you need to ensure that both you and everyone else treats them with respect. Any form of racial harassment should be dealt with promptly according to the school's policy.

Be aware of background factors

Pupils may never have been exposed to English before; indeed, they may never have been to school before. Alternatively, the pupil you are supporting may have come to this country as a refugee or asylum seeker and their education has been severely disrupted. Even for those who have attended school before, their experience of education may be very different to that which is offered in England and Wales and they may find it difficult adjusting.

How to identify and develop culturally and linguistically appropriate teaching and learning materials

Unless you already know a great deal about this area it will probably be best to seek advice. Your local authority's library service or ethnic support service should be able to help you identify materials that are both culturally and linguistically relevant to the pupils you are supporting.

To be culturally relevant, materials will need to relate to the background of the pupil. Reading books, for instance, which include stories of people from a range of ethnic backgrounds, religions and cultures, are likely to be more accessible for pupils new to the language than ones purely about white middle-class English children. Traditional stories from a range of countries are often useful learning resources as the pupils you are supporting may know the stories in their own language and can therefore identify with the text even if they are unable to read all of it in English.

However, the texts chosen must be age-appropriate. Many of the stories available may be too young if you are supporting older pupils. In this case it may be better to choose non-fiction texts that transcend culture. It is therefore helpful to find out what the pupils are interested in and seek to find related reading matter. You may be asked to support a pupil who is new to English but really loves trains – a book on trains from many countries will therefore probably be an aid to his learning. He is likely to be familiar with the correct terminology in his own language and you can use the book on trains to develop both his English vocabulary and his ability to understand the English alphabetic system. Bilingual assistants can help you discover what interests the pupils have.

The sorts of problems that might occur in providing support for bilingual/multilingual pupils and how to respond to these

The problems of inadequate or irrelevant resources experienced in schools as a whole may be even more of an issue when seeking to support bilingual or mutlilingual pupils. This is likely to become more true the older the pupil. For the older years in Key Stage 2, and certainly into Key Stages 3 and 4, the pressure of the curriculum and upcoming national tests place restrictions on the type of support available for pupils new to the language. Where teachers are required to cover a certain amount of material each lesson, the pupil new to the language may well flounder as they struggle to make sense of what they are hearing.

Pupils learning English as an additional language may appear to be making more progress than they actually are. Many pupils learn to read accurately quite quickly, but they do not really understand much of what they read. Alternatively, some pupils appear to be making less progress than they actually are. Many pupils go through a period of silence, which can last for months. It may seem that they are not learning anything, but in actual fact they are taking in their surroundings, experimenting in their heads with the new language and making sure they have mastered much of it before they experiment with either speaking or writing it.

Checklist

✔ I know how to obtain information regarding pupils I support who are learning English as an additional language.

✔ I am familiar with the strategies for supporting such pupils.

✔ I know how to respond to cultural differences between pupils.

✔ I am able to promote cultural diversity within the school.

GATHERING EVIDENCE

 Setting the scene

Sadie is working with a Year 3 pupil who has newly arrived in the UK from Poland. It is February, part way through the school year. The boy, Lech, has been placed in a class where there is another Polish boy, Jaroslaw, who arrived in the UK in September and has therefore been learning English for five months. Sadie keeps a diary of her involvement with Lech. She submits extracts from this diary in order to show how she has met various performance indicators.

SUPPORT DEVELOPMENT OF THE TARGET LANGUAGE

Diary extracts of support given

(Performance Indicators in italics)

6 February

1.00 p.m. I met with the head teacher and the Inclusion Manager to *obtain accurate and up-to-date information about the pupil's first and target language development and use this knowledge in providing appropriate support for the pupil* – Lech. I read his parents' application form and the notes made by the Head Teacher at the time of an initial meeting with Lech's parents. We then discussed the best way to support him.

3.00 p.m. I met with Miss Hardcastle (Lech's class teacher) to *clarify and confirm the strategies to be used to support bilingual/multilingual pupils in developing language skills in the target language.* We also clarified my *role and responsibilities for supporting development of the target language* and agreed that I *will be working with this pupil.*

We agreed on the following:

- sit Lech with the other Polish speaker to provide mutual support;
- place the two of them at a table with pupils who are good English speakers and good workers to act as role models;
- I am to spend 10 minutes each day with the two Polish pupils to teach social vocabulary and basic school vocabulary;
- I will show him how to use ICT software held by the school to teach basic English vocabulary and phrases.

We agreed that *success is to be measured* by Lech being settled and feeling welcomed and secure in the class, then by him beginning to develop a basic English vocabulary.

9 February

8.40 a.m. I met with Lech and his parents at the Reception and took him into the class, introducing him to Miss Hardcastle. I showed him the seat next to Jaroslaw and gestured to him to sit down, smiling at him and giving him simple instructions, such as 'sit, please'. Jaroslaw was able to speak quietly to Lech, explaining what was happening in class. In this way we hoped to *respond to pupils' use of home language in a manner that values cultural diversity and reinforces positive self-images for the pupil.*

9.00–10.00 a.m. Literacy lesson – the focus of the week's lessons is to use the story of Red Riding Hood to identify main themes in traditional stories. Today, the focus for Lech is to make him feel at home; give him space to settle in and to help him learn social vocabulary. As agreed with Miss Hardcastle, my aim was to *provide opportunities for the pupil to interact with myself and others using their knowledge of the target language.* To this end, during group work, most of the time was spent with me chairing a discussion rather than asking the pupils to write anything. During the discussion I included Lech as much as possible, asking Jaroslaw to translate where appropriate. Lech was quite keen to make his views felt about good and evil in stories, and he found Jaroslaw translating for him to be most useful.

To *use language and vocabulary that is appropriate to the pupil's age, level of understanding and stage of target language development,* I placed a box of flash cards with pictures, photographs and signs in the middle of the table that all pupils, including Lech, with Jaroslaw translating, could choose from to help make their points. I asked Lech who he thought was good in the story and who he thought was bad. Lech himself chose appropriate picture cards and I modelled the words for him, which he repeated after me. Being aware of the need to *use praise and constructive feedback to maintain the pupils' interest in the learning activities,* I smiled at him, giving him the 'thumbs-up' sign and saying 'good' in response to his efforts.

11.00–12.00 Numeracy – Lech sat next to Jaroslaw on a table with four good English speakers. Resources for the lesson were placed in the middle of the table so that all pupils could use them – 2D plastic shapes of circles, triangles, squares, rectangles and pentagons. During the group work I *utilised opportunities to model the target language for the pupils and to scaffold their learning of the target language* by discussing the names of the 2D plastic shapes. Either I or the other pupils modelled the correct terminology for each shape and Lech copied us. He was then able to use this vocabulary to name the shapes himself.

1.00–1.15 p.m. I worked with Lech and Jaroslaw by themselves at a table just outside the classroom as agreed with Miss Hardcastle. The focus was to find out Lech's level of understanding of written English through observation and direct working with him. I laid out the alphabet with wooden letters, said the names of each letter then asked Lech to say the names of each letter as I pointed to them then asked him to name as many letters as he could, recording his responses. I repeated the exercise, focusing on letter sounds, which he found a lot harder.

3.00–3.15 p.m. At the end of the school day I met with Miss Hardcastle to *provide feedback to relevant people on the progress made by the pupil in developing language skills in the target language.*

10 February

8.40–9.00 a.m. Based on yesterday's findings regarding Lech's knowledge of the alphabet, I took him and Jaroslaw out for 20 minutes to teach/reinforce the sounds of the alphabet. I used wooden letters and alphabet picture cards to teach vocabulary as well. Through Jaroslaw, I asked Lech to write the letters down as we worked through the alphabet. He knew many of them as they are the same or similar to Polish letters. In this way I *used appropriate strategies for introducing the pupil to new words and language structures to help extend his vocabulary and structural command of the target language.*

1.00–1.20 p.m. The school has bought a box of resources aimed at teaching English social vocabulary and basic language structure to children new to the language. By choosing part of this resource box that teaches pupils the vocabulary of ordinary classroom objects I *used appropriate strategies for introducing the pupil to new words and language structures to help extend his vocabulary and structural command of the target language.* We began today by looking together at the large picture in the pack of the classroom, which has various items labelled, such as 'book', 'pencil', 'ruler'. I pointed to a particular item, then picked up the real thing and said the word. Lech repeated this after me. I used repetitive phrases: 'This is a pencil', 'this is a ruler' and so on. By the end of the session, Lech could say each of the items as I held up each one. In this way I *provided opportunities for the pupil to practise new language skills.*

TEACHER'S COMMENTS

Sadie has been a tremendous help in the class helping Lech settle in. She has a good manner with pupils who may be anxious about school and Lech warmed to her at once. Her diary extracts are an accurate account of what happened. Without her involvement, Lech would have found his first week in an English school much more difficult.

Teacher's signature	Name (printed and role)
Gillian Hardcastle	Gillian Hardcastle, Y3 Class Teacher

ASSESSOR'S COMMENTS

This is a very detailed and thorough account, Sadie. You have clearly grasped what is needed to support a pupil new to English. Almost all the performance indicators are covered explicitly in these diary extracts.

Signed: **Terrie Cole**, NVQ Assessor

Chapter 13

Support pupils with cognition and learning needs

In this chapter we will look at two elements:

1 Support pupils with cognition and learning needs during learning activities.
2 Support pupils with cognition and learning needs to develop effective learning strategies.

KNOWLEDGE AND UNDERSTANDING

The range of cognitive skills necessary for effective learning

Definitions

Cognition has to do with theories of how human beings 'know' and how they develop their knowledge.

From the time they are born until their death, humans typically have the ability to process information, make sense of information gained from their senses, reflect on that information, create new information, apply knowledge and, as a result, change the way they think, act or react. This 'cognitive ability' is, many would argue, what makes us human and differentiates us from every other type of living creature in the world. However, there is a great deal of debate as to the exact nature of that cognition and, especially, how it is formed and how it develops.

Nature or nurture?

At a fundamental level is the debate between 'nature and nurture'. All would agree that cognition is intimately linked to perception, the mind, the operation of the brain, to intelligence and to learning. But, is that learning capacity innate, something we are born with and that we can do little to alter; or is it rather something developed by our environment (both physical and social)? In other words, are our cognitive abilities fixed at birth by our genes or are they instead something flexible, able to grow and expand?

Range of processes needed

There is general agreement that a number of processes are necessary in cognition and learning, including:

- memory
- attention, concentration, focus
- motivation
- application
- making connections and linkages
- distinguishing between the relevant and the irrelevant
- organisational and sequencing skills.

Emotional literacy

Many educational theorists see emotion as being an essential aspect of cognitive development as well. 'Emotional literacy' is regarded as a vital part of the learning process – if you feel good about yourself and your abilities you are more likely to make progress than if you see yourself as a failure and out of step with what is happening in school.

Thought and language

Linked to cognition is language, but the relationship between language and thought is complex. Are children born with the ability to think, or do they need to be exposed to language in order to develop that capacity? If this is the case, does the richest language environment inevitably lead to the greatest thinkers?

Categories or types of cognition and learning need

Global development delay

Children who experience difficulties in every aspect of learning are said to have a 'global developmental delay'. This is subdivided into three areas – moderate learning difficulty (MLD), severe learning difficulty (SLD) and profound and multiple learning difficulty (PMLD).

- *Moderate learning difficulty* – pupils are only able to work at a level significantly below age expectations.
- *Severe learning difficulty* – pupils experience more serious difficulties in all aspects of the curriculum and require a high level of adult support in school and possibly also in life-skills.
- *Profound and multiple learning difficulty* – these pupils' needs are even more severe and complex. They also experience physical or sensory impairments and are likely to have significant communication needs as well. A high level of individual support and personal care will need to be provided for these pupils.

Specific learning difficulties

This term is used to indicate difficulties in learning that are limited in scope rather than general 'across the board' problems. Specific learning difficulties (SpLD) can relate to aspects of literacy, to numeracy or to issues of motor control; they include dyslexia, dyspraxia and dyscalculia. The common factor between them is that children experiencing them may be functioning at age-appropriate levels or even above age-appropriate levels in aspects of the curriculum not affected by these specific difficulties. However, some children with global delays may also experience specific learning difficulties as well.

The implications of needs for supporting different types of learning activities

The type of support provided for pupils with cognition and learning needs will not only be determined by the nature of their difficulty, but also by the learning activities in which they are engaged. In one way or another, all pupils with cognition and learning needs are likely to require support in lessons involving literacy and/or numeracy (see Chapters 9 and 10). However, pupils experiencing differing needs are likely to require different provision in other parts of the curriculum.

A pupil with dyspraxia, for instance, may need support and encouragement in aspects of the curriculum such as PE and games or where there is a high level of physical dexterity required such as ICT, art, music or food technology; whereas a pupil with a global developmental delay may actually shine in these subjects and require no support whatsoever. Conversely, the pupil with dyspraxia may be able to contribute extremely effectively in the more aesthetic aspects of the curriculum that focus on emotional literacy such as SEAL (Social and Emotional Aspects of Learning,

---

Case study

Richard is a Year 4 pupil at a large junior school. He is big for his age and can be quite clumsy – although he does not have an official diagnosis of dyspraxia, he shows many of the traits, such as finding it hard to write and to coordinate his movements. He cannot yet, for instance, tie shoelaces and he usually buttons his shirt up wrongly when changing back from PE.

In the playground he tries to join in other children's games, but does not really know how to play properly. He usually simply barges in and often knocks into other pupils. They, naturally, get annoyed with him and often tell him to go away. Richard does not really know how to respond to this. Sometimes he will get angry back, but usually he will go into a corner of the playground and simply wander about by himself. He rarely actually cries, but he is obviously unhappy. It is clear he does not understand how to make and maintain friendships or how to react when they go wrong.

How could you as a TA help him?

see pp. 12–14), RE (Religious Education) or PSHE (Personal, Social and Health Education with Citizenship). In these subjects a high proportion of lesson content could well be discussion and verbal interaction. In the same subjects, however, the pupil with global developmental delay may need a lot of support from a TA in order to understand what is being said in the lesson.

The 'informal curriculum'

Within school, however, pupils do not only learn through what is presented as the formal curriculum. What could be termed the 'informal curriculum' takes place on the playground, through clubs, social events and as friendships develop or break up, and what pupils experience here can have a profound effect on their learning. Many pupils with cognition and learning needs require support in these activities. Some need help learning to make and maintain friendships; others need to be taught how to play appropriately with their peers and how to develop an effective response when relationships falter. As a result of their needs, some may experience bullying and this needs to be responded to appropriately. Your role as a TA may therefore involve a lot more than helping pupils read and write in class lessons.

Responding to cognition and learning needs

Adapting and modifying materials

Materials used in the classroom can be adapted or modified in numerous ways to help support pupils with cognition and learning difficulties so that they are able to access the curriculum more effectively. The exact nature of the adaptation or modification will depend on the materials being used, the nature of the pupil's learning difficulties and the task in hand. For instance, pupils experiencing difficulties with fine motor control may benefit from using triangular pens or pencils, or pens and pencils with tripod grips in order to facilitate their writing; other pupils may find using scissors with long loops into which they can place all four fingers rather than just their forefinger gives them greater dexterity when cutting. Many pupils with dyslexia say that texts they are asked to read become more accessible when using coloured filters.

One method of adapting texts to help pupils with a range of cognition and learning difficulties access them is called DARTS (Directed Activities for Reading Texts). You can prepare a text for pupils in any of the following ways:

- Highlight key words, explaining their meaning where necessary.
- Put in captions or headings and subheadings.
- Change unknown words to new words.
- Simplify vocabulary.
- Simplify sentence structures.
- Break up the text with illustrations or diagrams and labels.
- Make the layout of the text easier to read by using underlining, colour, frames and indentation – but too much variation may actually make the text more complex.
- Insert signs and symbols linked to key words.
- Restructure sentences so that they begin with the object.

Adapting or modifying activities

Activities within the class can be adapted at two levels – the teacher can adapt what is being taught and pupils can be asked to undertake tasks that have been adapted or modified.

Adapting teaching requires using both vocabulary and means of communication that are understood by pupils. Sentence structures may be simplified and there may be use of illustrations or visual aids, including Internet access via an interactive whiteboard, which aid the understanding of pupils with learning needs. Teaching is likely to be in smaller chunks than would normally be the case and activities are likely to be simpler than the norm.

Adapting tasks is what differentiation is all about – the same learning intentions of a lesson are achieved in different ways and at different levels by pupils within the class.

Strategies for challenging and motivating pupils

Most pupils want to learn, at least in the first years of their schooling, and most who struggle with their learning know that they struggle. They do not need any one else to tell them that 'they must do better' or 'improve their spellings'. One obvious means of motivating pupils who find learning difficult is therefore to present such pupils with tasks in which they can succeed. It means setting them meaningful activities, linked to something they can identify with and in which they can achieve. It means that, when giving feedback to them about their work, teachers and TAs must be constructive – 'you have achieved this, well done'; and must also point the way forward – 'in order to reach the next step you need to do this . . .'.

Self-assessment questions

1   What factors do you feel are important in the development of cognition and learning?
2   How might pupils with cognition and learning needs experience difficulties in different areas of the curriculum?
3   What measures can you implement to support such pupils?
4   What factors might there be that make providing such support difficult?

The sorts of problem that might occur when supporting pupils with cognition and learning difficulties and how to deal with these

The sorts of problem you might encounter when seeking to support pupils with cognition and learning difficulties fall into two categories – physical problems and human problems.

Resources

Problems with resources occur when either the school does not have the resources your pupils require, or you cannot find the resources when you need them. To overcome these problems, preparation is needful.

If you know what sort of resources the pupils require, you need to check well in advance of the lesson with the teacher and/or the SENCO that they are available in the school. If they are not and the pupils really do need them you need to ask the SENCO to order them or to point you in the direction of alternatives that are in school.

Prior to a lesson you will need to ensure that you have all the learning resources you need; that all equipment required is both available and in working order; and that you have accessed the right quantity of written and curriculum materials. If some of the pupils you support require specialist equipment, you need to know it is available and in good working order.

The environment

You also need to ensure, so far as is possible, that the learning environment is suitable for the pupils you are supporting. There needs to be sufficient light and space to work and the area needs to be as free from distractions as possible. Problems can occur if the physical environment is not conducive to pupil learning.

Pressure

Within schools there are several types of pressure, all of which can cause problems when seeking to meet the needs of pupils with learning needs.

Peer pressure may make pupils resistant to receiving extra adult support. This is more likely to be the case with older pupils. Peer pressure may also contribute to pupils lacking motivation and considering themselves failures.

There can be pressure from parents, which can make it harder to support pupils. Some parents may not think there is a problem when school does, or, conversely, others feel their child experiences greater difficulties than they seem to do in school.

A further pressure can come from teachers who have too high an expectation of the level and effectiveness of the support TAs can provide for pupils in their classes. You are not the panacea of all ills and all you can do is your best. You can make a difference, but you cannot work miracles.

A final pressure is that of the education system itself. The pressure is on schools to achieve targets and this can result in teachers and TAs feeling they must teach at a faster pace than is appropriate for pupils experiencing learning difficulties or move on to new topics before these pupils have assimilated what has already been taught. The sense that the curriculum must be 'got through' runs counter to learning theory and good teaching practice.

GATHERING EVIDENCE

 Setting the scene

In the mornings Nazreen works in Year 4 supporting pupils who have cognition and learning needs. For the purposes of writing her personal accounts, she focuses on

---

Checklist

✔ I am aware of the cognitive skills necessary for effective learning.
✔ I know how the various types of learning need are identified in my school.
✔ I am familiar with the categories of learning need.
✔ I am able to adapt resources and lessons to meet the learning needs of pupils I support.
✔ I can promote active learning.
✔ I engage in active listening.

---

working with three pupils, each of whom has a specific learning difficulty. One has a diagnosis of dyspraxia (John) and two show aspects of dyslexia but do not have an official diagnosis. One of these pupils (Janet) can read at an age-appropriate level, but her writing is hindered by a difficulty organising thoughts and limitations in spelling. The other pupil (Peter) experiences difficulties in both reading and spelling. Nazreen's support is largely provided within the class.

Writing personal accounts: collecting evidence

PERSONAL ACCOUNT

Name: **Nazreen Begum**
Date: **14 November**

Support pupils with cognition and learning needs during learning activities

---

Obtain accurate and up-to-date information about:

•   *The pupil's cognition and learning needs*

I have obtained up-to-date and accurate information regarding these three pupils by:

•   talking with the class teacher and Inclusion Manager;
•   reading their IEPs;
•   reading the latest report on the pupil with dyspraxia (John) from the Occupational Therapist;
•   my own observations and knowledge of the pupils through working with them since the beginning of term.

- *The planned learning tasks and activities*

Through discussion with the class teacher, reading his planning and my own experience of being in the class for the past three weeks, I understand that the learning tasks and activities for this lesson are taken from the revised Primary Framework for Literacy Year 4 Narrative Unit 2 – stories set in imaginary worlds. The class are in the last phase of the unit, working collaboratively to plan and write a longer story about an adventure in an imagined world. Throughout this week they are to use language to create atmosphere or suspense and show how to use figurative or expressive language in short passages.

The learning objective of today's lesson is to write an opening paragraph, setting the scene for the rest of the story. Pupils need to 'show imagination through language used to create atmosphere or suspense' (part of Strand 9 from this unit).

- *Obtain and use equipment and materials as appropriate to the learning objectives*

As the learning activity is one of writing I made sure the following equipment was available for the three pupils to use:

- writing grids – an A4 sheet divided into four quadrants within which the pupils can write separate ideas to aid planning (one quadrant to describe the setting, one for the characters, one for the atmosphere or mood and the fourth for any other ideas);
- triangular pens – for John who finds writing laborious due to his poor fine motor control;
- lined paper (the rest of the class use blank paper) to aid presentation of the first draft.

- *Adapt and modify learning resources to suit the pupil's maturity levels and learning needs*

On each table in the class there are several dictionaries and a thesaurus, which pupils can readily access. The table I am working on has these, but I have also adapted this provision by making a wordbank on card using words that the pupils have come up with over the past three weeks as they have read or listened to stories about imaginary worlds and discussed their ideas together. We have also compiled a pack of images from the Internet and from the pupils' illustrations of possible worlds and settings.

- *Provide levels of individual attention, reassurance and help with learning tasks as appropriate to the pupil's needs*

So far, all three pupils have enjoyed the unit and have joined in class and group discussions very well. However, now it comes to the actual writing and they are all worried about this learning activity. They all have good ideas and they know what they want to write, but they are all three hampered by their specific learning difficulties.

I spoke to each of them, encouraging them with what they had learnt and come up with so far in this topic. I showed them the word banks I had prepared in response to their ideas and the words they themselves had used and said that this would help them with their spelling. I reassured them that they could help each other with spellings and sentence structure and that I would be around to support them if they needed.

- *Provide support as needed to enable pupils to follow instructions*

It was not that the pupils did not understand what to do; they had followed the teacher's instructions quite well. Their difficulty lay in actually carrying out those instructions – one because of the difficulties he has with writing, another because of her spelling and poor organisational skills and the third because of his limited reading and spelling skills. To overcome these barriers I showed them my idea of the quartered A4 sheet that provided some structure for their planning – the hardest thing for each of these pupils is to be presented with a blank sheet of paper and being told to write on it. Showing them the other resources, some of which they had used before, such as the triangular pens, helped them begin to follow the instructions.

- *Give positive encouragement, feedback and praise to reinforce and sustain the pupil's interest and efforts in the learning activities; and*

- *Monitor the pupil's response to the learning activities and, where necessary, modify or adapt the activities to achieve incremental and lateral progression towards the intended learning outcomes*

During the activity I walked around the class, giving these three pupils the opportunity to work independently without me constantly being there and giving me an opportunity to support other pupils. However, I came back to these three at frequent intervals to see how they were getting on. I praised them when they were working towards achieving the learning objectives, such as when they had chosen the illustration that best suited their imaginary world and had listed a number of adjectives in one of the quadrants of the writing frame which described that scene. They were all motivated to complete the task, but when they began to flag, finding it difficult to either write or spell, I sustained their interest by asking them to talk to me again about what they wanted to say and showing them useful words in the wordbank.

At the end of the activity we reviewed their progress. I asked each of the pupils to read what they had written and together we discussed how far they had achieved the learning outcomes. We then agreed what needed to be done in the next lesson to move this forward.

- *Take appropriate action to resolve any problems in supporting the pupil's participation and progress in learning activities*

During the activity, John found the physical act of writing tiring and his writing became increasingly illegible. I suggested times when he should take a rest break and do short hand-gym exercises to reinvigorate his hand and wrist muscles.

- *Provide feedback to relevant people on significant aspects of the pupil's participation levels and progress*

During each lesson I make brief notes on how the pupils participated and responded. These are kept in a ring binder that I give to the teacher at the end of the week for her to look through. If something important or unusual comes up I discuss it with her at the end of the lesson. At the end of this lesson I noted that each of the pupils were hindered by their respective needs in meeting the learning objectives, although each had worked hard and had made progress towards them. I also made suggestions as to what may help them in the future, such as access to word processing facilities or a tape recorder to speak rather than write their ideas.

TEACHER'S COMMENT

Nazreen is very knowledgeable about the needs of the pupils she works with and with the curriculum. She is very capable at both adapting the curriculum and in providing scaffolding, which maximizes their ability to access what is being taught.

I certify that this is a true statement of what occurred.

Staff signature	Name (printed and role)
E. Liverpool	Eric Liverpool, Class Teacher

ASSESSOR'S COMMENTS

An excellent piece of evidence. You show that you both understand the pupils' needs and are capable of supporting them appropriately. To give further evidence of this, could you provide me with annotated copies of the writing each of these pupils produced during this lesson? Be sure to note where you have supported them and what impact this had on their learning.

Signed: **Terrie Cole**, NVQ Assessor

Figure 13.1 Doing the victory dance

After much hard work, Miranda, Nicola, Sadie and Nazreen finally finish the course. As they look at each other's portfolios they realise that although there are similar features in their portfolios there are also differences.

As Terrie Cole, their assessor, comments, there is no one right way to put together the evidence for an NVQ 3.

When their certificates finally arrived, Miranda, Nicola, Sadie and Nazreen could be seen doing a victory dance.

Chapter 14

Legislation relating to SEN and inclusion in England and Wales

Major Education Acts

1981 Education Act

- 'Medical model' of need (i.e. there is something 'wrong' with the child) replaced by a more 'social model' (i.e. need is created by inappropriate environments).
- Enshrined the term *special educational need* within educational legislation – covers pupils who would previously have been in special schools and those who would have been in special or 'remedial' classes within mainstream schools.
- Defined 'special educational need' up to the present day. Children have a learning difficulty if they:
  - have a significantly greater difficulty in learning than the majority of children of the same age; or
  - have a disability that prevents or hinders them from making use of educational facilities of a kind generally provided for children of the same age in schools within the area of the local education authority.
- Parents given new rights.

Education policy from this Act has been to encourage schools to include those pupils who previously would have attended special schools. The implementation of this Act led to a rapid rise in the number of support staff being employed in schools.

1988 Education Reform Act

This Act introduced far-reaching and long-lasting changes for education:

- the National Curriculum – all pupils share the same statutory entitlement to a 'broad balanced curriculum'; and
- local management of schools (LMS) – schools rather than LEAs are responsible for managing funding and for the quality of education for all their pupils.

For the first time it was laid down in law that schools were to provide a common curriculum for all children.

1993 Education Act

Children with special educational needs should – where this is what the parents want – normally be educated at mainstream schools. The act enshrined this principle in law for the first time. However, pupils and their families had to satisfy a series of conditions. The act also set up the SEN tribunal system under which parents could appeal against certain decisions made by the LEA in the statementing process.

1996 Education Act

- consolidated the Education Act, 1993;
- LEAs have a general duty to educate children who have special educational needs in a mainstream school if that is what parents want;
- the board of governors of every maintained school must ensure that:

  - teachers are aware of children's SEN;
  - the necessary provision is made for any pupil who has SEN;
  - children with SEN join in the activities of the school with their peers as far as is 'reasonably practicable'.

- schools should appoint a SEN governor, however, the responsibility for SEN provision remains with the full board of governors as a 'whole-school issue';
- governors, with the head teacher, are required under the Act to:

  - develop a whole-school policy for SEN;
  - publish it in the school prospectus;
  - inform parents about the success of the policy in the governor's annual report.

2002 Education Act

Schools are required to offer extended services to their local communities. The aim is that, by 2010 all children should have access to a variety of extended services in or through their school in line with the *Every Child Matters* agenda. Children with disabilities and/or special educational needs must be able to access all extended services.

The Act also sets out the circumstances in which aspects of teaching roles can be performed by staff other than teachers in line with Workforce Remodelling. This relates to all staff other than teachers and not simply HLTAs.

Other legislation (in chronological order)

Health and Safety at Work Act (1974)

This is the overarching legislation covering health and safety policies, and all school polices must relate to it. Every school must produce a plan for Health and Safety to ensure that hazards are assessed and the necessary arrangements are made to avoid or control risks.

Under the Act, it is illegal for a member of staff to take no action if they spot a potential danger. All staff are required by law to ensure that their actions do not put others at risk. This includes tidying up materials and putting things away after use.

The Children Act (1989)

- Enshrines in law the principle that the interest of the child must always be put first.
- Children should be involved in all that happens to them – their views must be ascertained and taken into account by those working with them.
- All staff are required to protect children against risk and danger.
- Regulates child protection matters, particularly how disclosures should be responded to. Members of staff have a legal duty to report any concerns and suspicions.

The Disability Discrimination Act (1995)

- Duty *'not to discriminate against disabled pupils and prospective pupils in the provision of education and associated services in schools, and in respect of admissions and exclusions'*;
- Duty to plan for increased accessibility – *'wherever possible disabled people should have the same opportunities as non-disabled people in their access to education'*;
- Based upon a social model of disability:

  - recognises difference and diversity within the community;
  - sees the potential problems as within the environment *not* within the person;
  - need to identify *barriers* to be overcome;
  - a disability is only a handicap if the environment makes it so.

Data Protection Act (1998)

The aim of the Data Protection Act is to protect the rights of the individual by ensuring that any information kept is accurate and is protected. This legislation applies to records kept on pupils in schools. There are eight basic principles to the Act:

1 Information must be obtained and processed legally.
2 Data should only be held for specific purposes.
3 Personal data held for a purpose must not be disclosed in a manner incompatible with that purpose.
4 Personal data held should be accurate and not excessive.
5 Personal data should be accurate and up to date.
6 Personal data should not be kept longer than necessary.
7 An individual should have access to their records.
8 Appropriate security measures should protect the data.

Schools need to make individual records available to the appropriate parents as well as pupils; keep attendance and academic records only as long as they are relevant; and ensure that all records are stored securely, whether they be paper records or computerised.

Paper records must be stored in a secure cabinet or area; they must not be left lying around anywhere. Disposal of records must be undertaken with care – shredding is recommended. They must not simply be placed in waste paper baskets.

The Race Relations (Amendment) Act (2000)

Having its origins in the report following the murder of Stephen Lawrence, this Act built on the regulations laid down by the Race Relations Act, 1976. It made it incumbent upon all public bodies, including schools, not only to work against racial discrimination and address racial harassment, but also to actively promote racial equality and good race relations. This applies to staff, parents and pupils alike.

The Special Educational Needs and Disability Act (SENDA) (2001)

This Act states that public bodies (including schools) need to take account of the Disability Discrimination Act (DDA), 1995. In so doing it gave legal 'teeth' to some of the provisions in the revised SEN Code of Practice (2001):

- Schools have a legal obligation not to discriminate against pupils who have disabilities and to make all possible provision for their needs.
- The right to a mainstream education for children with special educational needs is strengthened both for pupils with statements and those without.
- Where parents want a mainstream education for their child everything possible should be done to provide it. Equally where the parents of pupils who have statements want a special school place their wishes should be listened to and taken into account.
- Mainstream education cannot be refused on the grounds that the child's needs cannot be provided for within the mainstream sector.

The Children Act (2004)

This Act provides the legal underpinning for the government's initiative 'Every Child Matters: Change for Children' with its 'five outcomes':

- Be healthy.
- Stay safe.
- Enjoy and achieve.
- Make a positive contribution.
- Achieve economic well-being.

Every school must be working towards these five outcomes.

Local authorities are required to ensure the delivery of extended services in or through schools. They are required to create children's services directorates, publish children and young people's plans and to identify a lead member for children's services. They must also take measures to ensure that 'swift and easy referral' to specialist services for those pupils who require such provision is available through all schools by 2010.

The Disability Discrimination Act (2005)

- Adds to DDA 1995 and SENDA 2001, does not supersede them.
- Duty to promote disability equality – the 'general duty' on public bodies.
- Duty on the 'responsible body' (for schools this is the governors) to *take such steps as it is reasonable to take to ensure that disabled pupils are not placed at a substantial disadvantage'*.
- Duty to prepare a Disability Equality Scheme – an action plan detailing the steps that the 'responsible body' will take to fulfil its obligations.

The Equality Act 2006

This Act established the Commission for Equality and Human Rights (CEHR), which replaced the Equal Opportunities Commission, the Commission for Racial Equality and the Disability Rights Commission. Any discrimination by public bodies, including schools, on the grounds of religion or belief or sexual orientation was made unlawful except for certain exemptions. All public authorities have a duty to actively promote equality of opportunity between men and women and to ensure sexual discrimination does not take place.

Chapter 15

National documents and strategies relating to SEN and inclusion

Government documents for England and Wales (in chronological order)

Special Educational Needs: Report of the Committee of Enquiry into the Education of Handicapped Children and Young People (The Warnock Report) (Department of Education and Science (DES) 1978)

The Warnock Report is the bedrock upon which all subsequent SEN strategy and legislation has been based. The Report coined the phrase *'special educational need'* (SEN) and established the understanding of a *'continuum of need'*, which required a corresponding *'continuum of provision'*.

At the heart of the Warnock Report was the belief that fundamental distinctions between children in the way they are educated are wrong: *'The purpose of education for all children is the same; the goals are the same'* (DES 1978: 5).

Code of Practice on the Identification and Assessment of Special Educational Needs (Department for Education (DfE) 1994)

This document set the tone for special educational needs provision throughout the country. It was based upon the findings of the Warnock Report and every school had to 'have regard' to it. However, it only related to identification and assessment, it did not say *how* pupils with learning difficulties should be taught or *what* they should be taught, neither did it detail what the learning difficulties might be.

Excellence for All Children: Meeting Special Educational Needs (Department for Education and Employment (DfEE) 1997)

This consultative document was produced by the newly elected Labour government to establish its commitment to inclusion: *'By inclusion we mean not only that pupils with SEN should wherever possible receive their education in mainstream school, but also that they should join fully with their peers in the curriculum and life of the school.'*

A Programme for Action: Meeting Special Educational Needs (Department for Education and Employment (DfEE) 1998)

This followed the consultation document *Excellence for All Children* and looked at ways of fostering inclusion by considering a range of issues in SEN practice. It led directly to the publication of the revised Code of Practice, which was first issued in draft form in July 2000 and was implemented in January 2001.

Social Inclusion: Pupil Support (DfEE, 1999, Circular 10/99)

This document identified groups of pupils at particular risk of disaffection and social exclusion. For pupils at risk of permanent exclusion, **pastoral support programmes** (**PSPs**) are to be set up by the school and relevant agencies, which could include social services, housing, careers services, community and voluntary groups. Educational psychologists and behavioural support teams are likely to be involved.

The National Curriculum (Curriculum 2000) Inclusion Statement (Qualifications and Curriculum Authority (QCA)/Department for Education and Employment (DfEE) 2000a)

Curriculum 2000 aimed to provide a more inclusive framework than previous versions of the National Curriculum. In planning and teaching the National Curriculum, teachers are required to have 'due regard' to the following principles:

1   setting appropriate challenges;
2   providing for the diversity of pupils' needs;
3   providing for pupils with SEN;
4   providing support for pupils for whom English is an additional language.

Working with Teaching Assistants: A Good Practice Guide (Department for Education and Employment (DfEE) 2000b)

This document was distributed to all schools in the form of a ring binder. Provided mainly for head teachers and managers, it was part of the government's strategy to improve the lot of teaching assistants in schools across the country. However, it also provides valuable information for teaching assistants as it looks at their role in school and gives guidance on how they may best be deployed and managed. It does not, however, deal with issues of pay and grading, explicitly stating that the government believes this is best left for negotiation at the local level. This document fixed the use of the term 'Teaching Assistant' to cover roles that had previously been described by a variety of terms.

Special Educational Needs Code of Practice (Department for Education and Employment (DfEE) 2001)

All schools 'must have regard to' this Code of Practice, which supersedes the Code of Practice of 1994. For more details see Chapter 7 – Common Themes.

Supporting The Target Setting Process (Qualifications and Curriculum Authority/Department for Education and Employment (QCA/DfEE) 2001)

This provides guidance on target-setting for pupils with special educational needs who are working towards Level 1 in the National Curriculum by setting out for English, maths and science finely graded attainments known as the 'P Scales' (Performance Scales).

Removing Barriers to Achievement: the Government's Strategy for SEN (Department for Education and Skills (DfES) 2004b)

This sets out the government's strategy for the education of children with special needs and disabilities. The key areas are early intervention, removing barriers to learning, raising expectations and achievements, and delivering improvements in partnerships.

This document identifies three levels of intervention in terms of 'waves':

- Wave One is normal high-quality teaching.
- Wave Two is additional adult support in small groups which could be in class or outside of class.
- Wave Three is more intensive, often individual, extra adult support to pupils, normally in a withdrawal situation outside of class.

Every Child Matters: Change for Children (Department for Education and Skills (DfES) 2004a)

The consultative Green Paper *Every Child Matters* was published by the government in 2003 alongside the report into the death of Victoria Climbie, seeking to strengthen services preventing the abuse of children. It focused on four themes:

- supporting families and carers;
- ensuring appropriate intervention takes place so that vulnerable children do not 'fall through the net';
- improving the accountability of all children's services and seeking to promote their inter-working;
- Ensuring that people working with children are valued, rewarded and trained.

Following the consultation, Parliament passed the Children Act, 2004 and published *Every Child Matters: Change for Children* in November 2004.

Every organisation involved with providing services for children is to work together, share information and develop networks so that every child, whatever their background or their circumstances benefits from the Government's stated 'five outcomes':

- Be healthy.
- Stay safe.
- Enjoy and achieve.
- Make a positive contribution.
- Achieve economic well-being.

As part of their strategy to meet these objectives, the government established a Children's Commissioner for England and created Children's Trusts throughout the country. Extended schools and the 'Common Assessment Framework' (CAF) also form part of this strategy. A further expression of ECM came in June 2007 when government reorganisation designed to integrate all services related to children led to the creation of the new Department for Children, Schools and Families (DCSF).

Workforce Reform/The National Agreement (2003)

In order to reduce teacher workload (and thereby improve 'work–life balance') and to raise standards in schools a 'National Agreement' was signed by government, employers and trades unions in January 2003. Under this, routine administration tasks have been removed from teachers and given to support staff, and guaranteed professional time for planning, preparation and assessment (PPA) has been introduced.

The National Agreement recognises that support staff have a crucial role to play in Workforce Remodelling and led directly to the establishment of 'Higher Level Teaching Assistants' (HLTA). The government also developed nationwide strategies to improve training and career possibilities for all support staff. The Teacher Training Agency (TTA) became the Training and Development Agency for Schools (TDA) and for the first time included training for support staff as well as teachers. This body oversees the work previously undertaken by the National Remodelling Team.

See www.remodelling.org/remodelling/nationalagreement.aspx.

Appendices

ESTABLISHING ROLES AND RESPONSIBILITIES: TA AND TEACHER AGREEMENT

(Please discuss the following points and note down any agreed points before signing the agreement. See notes at bottom of form for clarification)

Contribution to class work/discussion

(**Notes:** Can the TA join in a class discussion spontaneously? Can the TA contribute to asking and/or answering questions?)

Seeking clarification

(**Notes:** Can the TA seek clarification from the teacher in front of the class if they don't understand something or feel that certain students need clarification?)

Marking work

(**Notes:** Can the TA give a verbal comment on the quality of the work? Can the TA mark written work where immediate feedback might be useful and/or where answers are easily marked? Can the TA provide formative comments when assessing work?)

Changing tasks set

(**Notes:** Can the TA alter the task set to enable students to complete it? For example: altering the wording of a question or simplifying the instructions for a task. If 'yes', does the TA need to check with the teacher first or can they do this independently?)

Suggesting appropriate learning activities

(**Notes:** Can the TA suggest strategies that may suit the preferred learning styles of students? Can the TA suggest strategies that may suit students with particular learning difficulties?)

Giving permission

(**Notes:** Giving pupils permission to: go to the toilet, get out of their seats for a legitimate reason, move places for a legitimate reason or anything else?)

Managing pupils' behaviour

(**Notes:** Which pupils can the TA be responsible for? Allocated pupils? Other pupils? Whole class?)

Sanction imposition

(**Notes:** What sanctions is the TA able to give? For example, who is responsible for issuing detention slips?)

```

```

Removing pupils from the class

(**Notes:** Under what circumstances can the TA remove pupils from the class? Which pupils will the TA be responsible for if they are removed from class?)

```

```

Intervening in pupil/teacher conflict

(**Notes:** Are you comfortable with the TA intervening under any circumstances, or specific circumstances, or not at all?)

```

```

Signed: _____ – Teacher

Signed: _____ – Teaching Assistant

Template courtesy of Jason Illingworth (2005)

PROBLEMS THAT MIGHT OCCUR IN SUPPORTING LEARNING

Problems that might occur in supporting learning	Possible explanations	Ways forward – how to adapt or modify activities to achieve learning outcomes	When to report difficulties
Pupils may find the task too difficult			
Pupils may not understand the task			
Pupils may say they are bored and they don't want to do the task			
One pupil may not want to join in with the group			
Pupils may not be paying attention			
A pupil may say that they are stupid and that they cannot do a task			
Pupils may be distracted by other activities			

ROLES AND RESPONSIBILITIES RELATING TO BEHAVIOUR

Routine	School and class rules: Pupils are expected to	Role and responsibility of yourself and others		
		I (the TA) will intervene when	I (the TA) can use these strategies	I (the TA) will inform the teacher if	The teacher will
In the playground					
Standing outside in the corridor waiting to come into class					
Beginning of the day					
Where to sit					
When wishing to participate in class					

ROLES AND RESPONSIBILITIES RELATING TO BEHAVIOUR *continued*

Routine	School and class rules: Pupils are expected to	Role and responsibility of yourself and others		
		I (the TA) will intervene when	I (the TA) can use these strategies	I (the TA) will inform the teacher if	The teacher will
When requesting help					
Going into assembly					
Walking in corridors					
Using ICT equipment					

ANYWHERE PRIMARY SCHOOL INDIVIDUAL EDUCATION PLAN

Name:	Date of birth:	Class/year:	IEP no:
Male/Female:	Stage:	EAL: Y/N	First drawn up:

Summary of concern:			
Medical condition:		External agencies:	
Review dates:	Present:	Comments:	Actions:

Start date: Targets	Success criteria	Possible resources	Possible strategies	Date: Outcomes
1.				
2.				
3.				

ANYWHERE PRIMARY SCHOOL INDIVIDUAL EDUCATION PLAN
continued

ASSESSMENT RESULTS, PROVISION AND EXTERNAL AGENCY COMMENTS	NOTES/PARENTAL CONTACT
Screening tests (name of assessment):	
Reading (name and date of test):	
Spelling (name and date of test):	
Maths (name and date of test):	
Provision	
External agencies	

EXAMPLE OF IEP TARGETS

Start date: Targets	Success criteria	Possible resources	Possible strategies	Date: Outcomes
1. To read and spell words with the long vowel phonemes ai/ ee/ ea/ oo	Pupil reads and spells a selection of these word accurately on five occasions	Plastic letters, worksheets, phonic books and CDs, phonic cards	Play games such as pairs, complete worksheets, listen to pupil read and focus on these phonic patterns	
2. To use the above spelling rules in own writing	Pupil uses spelling rules being worked on in five pieces of independent writing	Spelling banks, prompt cards	Make sure pupil understands the spelling rules, talk through written work with pupil focusing on the rule	
3. To listen to and follow instructions that have been given by an adult to the whole class	Over a period of one week 75 per cent of instructions are followed within one minute of them being given	Target sheet, behaviour star chart, reward stickers	Make sure expectations of this behaviour are clearly understood and that pupil is aware of this target. Praise when achieved. Remind when missed.	

ANYWHERE PRIMARY SCHOOL INDIVIDUAL BEHAVIOUR PLAN

SECTION ONE

Name of pupil:_____   DOB: _____

Class teacher: _____   NC Year: _____

Name of Parent(s)/Carer(s): _____

Nominated person responsible for operating the plan: _____

Start date of plan, as agreed with parents and pupil: _____

Review dates:

- mid point: _____

- end: _____

External agencies (where applicable): _____

Persons contributing to the plan:

Name	Contact no./address

SECTION 2
Approaches/Behaviour causing concern 1.   2.   3.
Pupil's strengths
Desirable alternative behaviours (long-term goals) 1.   2.   3.

Short-term targets	Success criteria
1.	1.
2.	2.
3.	3.

SECTION 3
Strategies to support pupil • • •
Special arrangements to be made • • •
Support to be offered to help the pupil Home: Other agencies:
Rewards: Home: School:
Agreed consequences • •

SECTION 4

Review arrangements

Distribution list

_____

Form completed by

Name: _____

Designation: _____

Signature . . . .

CONFIDENTIAL: _for monitoring purposes only_

Number of fixed term exclusions this academic year and total days:

Is the child on the Child Protection Register?   YES/NO

Is the child in public care?   YES/NO

If YES

Accommodated by Local Authority?   YES/NO

Subject of an interim or full care order?   YES/NO

Subject of a supervision order?   YES/NO

Ethnic origin: _____

First language: _____

ANYWHERE PRIMARY SCHOOL INDIVIDUAL BEHAVIOUR PLAN REVIEW MEETING

Name of pupil:_____   DOB: _____

Class teacher: _____   NC Year: _____

Name of Parent(s)/Carer(s): _____

Date of initial behaviour plan: _____ Review No: _____

Date of review meeting: _____ Time: _____

Venue:

Attended by:

Apologies from:

Summary of progress since the last meeting:

Agreed action:

1.

2.

3.

Arrangements for next review meeting: _____ at _____ in school

Agreed circulation for this review form: _____

TEMPLATE FOR SELF-APPRAISAL FOR TEACHING ASSISTANTS

Name:	
Position:	
What I feel have been the key tasks/ responsibilities of my job in relation to: • Supporting the school • Supporting the pupils • Supporting my colleagues • Supporting the curriculum	
Aspects of my work I'm most pleased with and why	
Aspects of my work I would like to improve and why	
Things preventing me working as effectively as I would like	
Changes I feel would improve my effectiveness	
My key aims for next year	
Training I would like to have	
How I would like my career to develop	
Signed	Date

TEMPLATE FOR APPRAISAL WITH TEACHING ASSISTANTS

Name of TA: _____

Name of appraiser: _____

Date of current appraisal: _____

Date of previous appraisal (where applicable): _____

Targets set at last appraisal (where applicable)	Outcomes
1.	1.
2.	2.
3.	3.

Achievements over the past year with regard to:
(i.e. what has gone well, what the TA is most pleased with)

Support for pupils

Support for the teacher(s)

Support for the school

Training received by the TA over the past year	
Type of training received (with dates)	Summary of what was learnt
Impact on what the TA does	Further considerations

Areas for development
(i.e. what may not have gone so well or what needs to be learnt/taken on board)

Support for pupils

Support for the teacher(s)

Support for the school

Career aspirations and possibilities

Targets for the next year

1.

2.

3.

Action to be taken

What action?	By whom?	By when?
1.		
2.		
3.		

Date for next appraisal:

Signed:

TA _____

Appraiser _____

MATCHING EXERCISE

Promoting positive behaviour

As we have seen throughout this book there is a real art to writing personal accounts.

What follows are three different versions of the *same event*.

Account 1

Description

While I was walking down the corridor, five minutes after the start of the last lesson of the day, I met Jocelyn S. walking in the opposite direction crying. As Jocelyn is one of the students I support, I asked her what the problem was and she reported that she was looking for the Head of Year. I told her that the Head of Year was in a meeting and asked if I could help. She started to cry even more and said that one of the girls in her English Class had called her a slag and now all the girls were joining in. She said this had been going on for several weeks and that she could just not face going into a classroom with them again. I took Jocelyn to the classroom where she should have been and went inside to explain to the teacher why she was not there, leaving Jocelyn outside. I tactfully suggested to the teacher that as Jocelyn was so upset I take Jocelyn to the Learning Support Unit for the rest of the lesson. The teacher thought that was a good idea and gave me some work for Jocelyn to do. I took Jocelyn to the Learning Support Unit and told her that the school had an Anti-Bullying Policy and that the girls would be spoken to. Jocelyn was a much happier girl when she left the school at the end of the day. I then informed her head of year and her tutor. They both agreed to deal with it.

Account 2

Description

I met J.S. walking in the opposite direction crying. J.S. said that she had a problem with other girls bullying her. I stepped in and sorted the problem and talked to the relevant people involved, in doing this I recognised when pupil behaviour conflicts with school policy and I responded promptly in line with my role and responsibility.

Account 3

Description

While I was walking down the corridor, five minutes after the start of the last lesson of the day, I met J.S. walking in the opposite direction crying. J.S. said that one of the girls in her English Class had called her a slag and now all the girls were joining in. She said this had been going on for several weeks and that she could just not face going into a classroom with them again. As J.S. was so upset the English teacher (Miss L) gave me some work for J.S. and I went to the Learning Support Unit with her. At the Learning Support Unit the Anti-Bullying Policy was discussed with J.S.

Questions

1   In the various accounts: make a note of what performance indicators are covered. (Hint – underline the key phrases that prove that a performance indicator has been met.)
2   How well do you think the personal accounts meet the performance indicators?
3   Would you include any other details in the accounts?
4   If you were the teaching assistant who would you get to witness the event?
5   Are there any issues regarding confidentiality?

References

Assessment Reform Group (1999) *Assessment for Learning – Beyond the Black Box*, Cambridge: University of Cambridge School of Education.

Bandura, A. (1977) *Social Learning Theory*, Morristown, NJ: General Learning Press.

Bandura, A. (1986) *Social Foundations of Thought and Action: a Social Cognitive Theory*, Englewood Cliffs, NJ: Prentice-Hall.

Berndt, T.J. (1983) 'Social cognition, social behaviour, and children's friendships', in E.T. Higgins, D.N. Ruble and W.W. Hartup (eds), *Social Cognition and Social Development, A Sociocultural Perspective*, Cambridge: Cambridge University Press.

Berne, E. (1991) *Transactional Analysis in Psychotherapy*, London: Souvenir Press.

Black, P. and Wiliam, D. (1998) *Inside the Black Box – Raising Standards Through Classroom Assessment*, London: School of Education, King's College London.

Black, P., Harrison, C., Lee, C., Marshall, B. and Wiliam, D. (2003) *Assessment for Learning – Putting it into Practice*, Maidenhead: Open University Press.

Booth, T., Ainscow, M., Black-Hawkins, K., Vaughan, M. and Shaw, L. (2000) *Index for Inclusion*, Bristol: University of West of England.

Breakwell, G.M. (1997) *Coping with Aggressive Behaviour*, Chichester: Wiley Blackwell.

Brown, G. and Wragg, E.C. (1993) *Questioning*, London: Routledge.

Chivers, J. (1995) *Team-building with Teachers*, London: Kogan Page.

Coie, J. D., Dodge, K. A. and Coppotelli, H. (1982) 'Dimensions and types of social status: a cross-age perspective', *Developmental Psychology*, 18: 557–70.

Collins, J. and Simcoe, N. (2004) 'The emergence of the teaching assistant as reflective practitioner: a well-established norm, a new reality or a future aspiration?' Paper presented at BERA, University of Manchester, 16–18 September, 2004.

Conners C.K., Sitarenios G., Parker J.D. and Epstein J.N. (1998) 'Revision and restandardization of the Connors' teacher rating scale (CTRS-R): factor structure, reliability, and criterion validity', *Journal of Abnormal Child Psychology*, 26 (4): 279–91.

Damon, W. (1983) 'The nature of social-cognitive change in the developing child', in W.F. Overton (ed.), *The Relationship Between Social and Cognitive Development*, Hillsdale, NJ: Erlbaum.

Daniels, H., Visser, J., Cole, T. and Reybekill, N. de (1999) *Emotional and Behavioural Difficulties in Mainstream schools*, School of Education, University of Birmingham, DfEE, RR90.

Dennison, B. and Kirk, R. (1990) *Do, Review, Learn, Apply – A Simple Guide to Experiential Learning*, London: Blackwell Publishers.

Department for Education (DfE) (1994) *Code of Practice on the Identification and Assessment of Special Educational Needs*, London: HMSO.

Department for Education and Employment (DfEE) (1997) *Excellence for All Children: Meeting Special Educational Needs*, London: HMSO.

Department for Education and Employment (DfEE) (1998) *A Programme for Action: Meeting Special Educational Needs*, London: HMSO.

Department for Education and Employment (DfEE) (1999) (Circular 10/99) *Social Inclusion: Pupil Support,* London: HMSO.

Department for Education and Employment (DfEE) (2000a) *The National Curriculum,* London: HMSO.

Department for Education and Employment (DfEE) (2000b) *Working with Teaching Assistants: A Good Practice Guide* London, DfEE Publications.

Department for Education and Employment (DfEE) (2001) *Special Educational Needs Code of Practice,* London: HMSO.

Department for Education and Science (DES) (1978) *Special Educational Needs: Report of the Committee of Enquiry into the Education of Handicapped Children and Young People (The Warnock Report)* London: HMSO.

Department for Education and Skills (DfES) (2001) Standards and Effectiveness Unit, *Literacy across the Curriculum: The Management of Group Talk,* London: HMSO.

Department for Education and Skills (DfES) (2004a) *Every Child Matters: Change for Children,* Nottingham: DfES Publications www.everychildmatters.gov.uk.

Department for Education and Skills (DfES) (2004b) *Removing Barriers to Achievement: the Government's Strategy for SEN,* Nottingham: DfES Publications.

Department for Education and Skills (DfES) (2005) *Excellence and Enjoyment: Social and Emotional Aspects of Learning (SEAL),* London: HMSO.

Department for Education and Skills (DfES) (2006a) *Effective Provision for Gifted and Talented Children in Primary Education,* London: HMSO.

Department for Education and Skills (DfES) (2006b) *Ethnicity and Education: the Evidence on Minority Ethnic Pupils Aged 5–16,* Research Topic Paper, Nottingham: DfES.

Department for Education and Skills (DfES) (2006c) *Independent Review of the Teaching of Early Reading (The Rose Report),* London: HMSO.

Department for Education and Skills (DfES) (2006d) *What To Do if You Are Worried a Child is Being Abused,* London: HMSO.

Disability Discrimination Act (2005) Available at www.opsi.gov.uk/acts/acts2005/ukpga_20030013_en_1, London: HMSO.

Erikson, E.H. (1982) *The Life Cycle Completed. A Review,* New York: Norton.

Flanders, C. (2008) 'How pupils communicate online: implications for pupils, parents and schools', unpublished MA (Ed) Dissertation, University of Chichester.

Glasser, W. (1998) *Choice Therapy: a New Psychology of Personal Freedom,* New York: Harper Collins.

Harlen, W. and Deakin-Crick, R. (2002) *Testing, Motivation and Learning,* Cambridge: University of Cambridge Faculty of Education.

Illingworth, J. (2005) 'From reaction to pro-action: an action research project to develop the effectiveness of teaching assistants through improving aspects of teamwork with teachers', unpublished MA (Ed) Dissertation, University College Chichester.

Jolivette, K., Stichter, J., Sibilsky, S., Scott, T.M. and Ridgley, R. (2002) 'Naturally occurring opportunities for preschool children with or without disabilities to make choices', *Education and Treatment of Children,* 25 (4): 396–414.

Lane, P.S. and McWhirter, J.J. (1992) 'A peer mediation model: conflict resolution for elementary and middle school children', *Elementary School Guidance & Counselling,* Oct., 27 (1): 15–24.

Lorenz, S. (2002) *First Steps in Inclusion,* London: David Fulton.

McCormick, S. (1999) *Instructing Students Who Have Literacy Problems,* (3rd edn) Englewood Cliffs, NJ: Merrill.

Margolis, H. and McCabe, P. (2006) 'Improving self-efficacy and motivation: what to do, what to say', *Intervention in School and Clinic,* March, 41 (4): 218–27.

National Curriculum (2008) online available from: www.nc.uk.net (accessed 29 January 2008).

National Curriculum in Action (2008) online available from: www.ncaction.or.uk/subjects/science/levels.htm (accessed 22 Janurary 2008).

National Joint Council for Local Government Services (2003) *School Support Staff – The Way Forward*, London: The Employers Organisation www.lge.gov.uk.

National Remodelling Team (2003) *Raising Standards and Tackling Workload: A National Agreement*. Available at www.remodelling.org.

Piaget, J. (1970) *The Science Of Education and the Psychology of the Child*, New York: Viking Press.

Pilkington, M. (2007) 'Disciplinary and grievance procedures', *Report*, February, p. 20.

Qualifications and Curriculum Authority/Department for Education and Employment (QCA/DfEE) (2000) *The National Curriculum (Curriculum 2000) Inclusion Statement*, London: HMSO.

Qualifications and Curriculum Authority/Department for Education and Employment (QCA/DfEE) (2001) *Supporting The Target Setting Process*, London: HMSO.

Rogers, B. (1995) *Behaviour Management: a Whole-school Approach*, London: Paul Chapman.

Rogers, B. (1998) *You Know the Fair Rule and Much More: Strategies for Making the Hard Job of Discipline and Behaviour Management in School Easier*, London: Pittman Press.

Sanacore, J. (1999) 'Encouraging children to make choices about their literacy learning', *Intervention in School & Clinic*, 35 (1): 38–43.

Schön, D. (1983) The *Reflective Practitioner: How Professionals Think in Action*, London: Temple Smith.

School Standards and Framework Act (SSFA) (1998) London: HMSO.

Selman, R.L. (1980) *The Growth of Interpersonal Understanding*, New York: Academic Press.

Sigelman, C.K. and Shaffer, D.F. (1991) *Life-span Human Development*, Belmont, CA: Brooks/Cole.

Smith, R. (1996) *The Management of Conflict in Schools*, Oxford: Framework Press.

Smith, R. (2002) *Creating the Effective Primary School*, London: Kogan Page Limited.

Training and Development Agency for Schools (2006) *Primary Induction for Teaching Assistant Trainers: Inclusion*, London: TDA.

Training Development Agency (TDA) (2006) *Developing People to Support Learning: a Skills Strategy for the Wider School Workforce 2006–2009'* www.tda.gov.uk.

Training and Development Agency for Schools (2007) *National Occupational Standards in Supporting Teaching and Learning in Schools*, London: TDA.

Tuckman, B. and Jensen, N. (1977) 'Stages of small group development revisited', *Group and Organizational Studies*, 2: 419–27.

Vygotsky, L.S. (1986) *Thought and Language*, new edn (ed. A Kozulin), Cambridge, MA: MIT Press.

Zimmerman, B.J. (2000) 'Self-efficacy: an essential motive to learn', *Contemporary Educational Psychology*, 25: 82–91.

Index